Rough Magic

Rough Magic

Making Theatre at the Royal Shakespeare Company

Steven Adler

With a Foreword by Chris Parry

Southern Illinois University Press
Carbondale and Edwardsville

Copyright © 2001 by the Board of Trustees,
Southern Illinois University
All rights reserved
Printed in the United States of America
04 03 02 01 4 3 2 1

Library of Congress Cataloging-in-Publication Data
Adler, Steven, 1953–
    Rough magic : making theatre at the Royal Shakespeare Company / Steven
Adler ; with a foreword by Chris Parry.
        p. cm.
Includes bibliographical references and index.
    1. Royal Shakespeare Company. I. Title.

PN2596.S82 R682 2001
792'.06'041—dc21
ISBN 0-8093-2376-1 (cloth : alk. paper)
ISBN 0-8093-2377-X (paper : alk. paper)   00-068020

The paper used in this publication meets the minimum requirements of American National Standard for Information Sciences—Permanence of Paper for Printed
Library Materials, ANSI Z39.48-1992. ∞

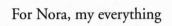

For Nora, my everything

Contents

Illustrations

Foreword

The Royal Shakespeare Company is a chameleon—it changes its character and mode of operation quietly from year to year. I should know—I worked there from 1976 to 1989. I started out as a lighting technician, literally and figuratively climbed the ladder, and ended my tenure as a lighting designer. I continue to design productions for the company from time to time and now find myself in the position to evaluate its work as both an insider and a free-lancer. People on the outside of the RSC see *only* a long history of seemingly concerted and accomplished work from what is arguably one of the world's most famous theatre companies. They are aware, perhaps, of the pantheon of excellent artists who have worked there and praise the RSC's efforts to imbue the classics with a contemporary urgency. But exactly how *does* the show go on? What are the artistic and pragmatic challenges faced by the people who make it happen on a daily basis? And why has the RSC found it necessary to make radical adjustments in its production process, just when the company seemed to have established a successful operating mode?

The RSC is a major landmark in British theatre, having carved a significant niche for itself as a presenter of works of theatrical excellence that have been heralded at home and abroad. It has offered many celebrated productions of works by Shakespeare and other classical playwrights as well as bold and innovative new works. It has launched or enhanced the careers of generations of British theatre artists. The RSC has also received its share of plaudits over the years, but there have been detractors as well, who have criticized the company alternately for its ambitious production schedule or for resting on its laurels. There is some veracity in this criticism—an institutional theatre, especially one the size and scope of the RSC, will at times find its artistic vision blurred. When this happens, the company's willingness to perform some serious introspection and adaptation is critical to its continued survival. The RSC has had to make some difficult decisions in the last few years to remain artistically viable, and the RSC today is in some significant ways a very different organization from the one I first encountered twenty-four years ago—as well it should be.

It's an extraordinary place to work, and I felt it was my "family" for many years. My first year there, I was in awe of the work we were able to produce in repertoire—in the main house in Stratford alone. Subsequently, I was to learn just how complex the life of the RSC is. It is no mean feat to mount a few dozen productions in five theatres in two cities one hundred miles apart as well as on tour, performing in repertoire throughout the year. I remember clearly how impressed I was by the ferocious dedication of my colleagues, this company of artists, technicians, craftspeople, and administrators who are able to produce such a volume of work, year after year, much of it of extraordinary quality. It was a truly wonderful training ground for me, both artistically and professionally, and during my tenure there, I naturally experienced a full spectrum of emotions ranging from great pride in the work we produced to frustration at the occasional petty squabbles that seem to accompany working in a high-pressure theatrical environment. However, everyone in the organization was aware of why we there. We always attempted to produce the most vital and immediate theatre we could, and we offered our audiences a vast range of theatrical experiences. This balance of Shakespeare, the classics, and new work defined the company and gave us our identity and artistic suppleness. I have seen some pure theatrical magic at the RSC—I would like to think I contributed to some of it—and believe that the company's significance in the world of theatre stems from its ability to offer such luminous productions as *Marat/Sade, Les Misérables, Les Liaisons Dangereuses,* and other creative works.

Steven Adler, greatly experienced in the American theatre as a Broadway stage manager, director, and teacher, has written a very important book. He affords us an objective American take on a very British institution. There have been other fine works that have examined specific aspects of the RSC—its history or the building of one of its theatres—but now we have a detailed, well-constructed, and intimate chronicle of the life and workings of this internationally renowned theatre company. However, Adler is not sycophantic or ironic—he offers us a clear and in-depth examination of the theatrical processes of the RSC and of some of the complex and often contradictory forces that have shaped it over the years. Perhaps because he *is* an American, and thus an outsider, he has been able to persuade dozens of RSC artists and staff to talk candidly and fervently about a raft of topics—their personal process within the company, the arduous task of selecting and marketing a season, the production process, the RSC's stature within the world of British theatre, and the success of the company's recent efforts to redefine itself, to name a few.

Adler has an enviable eye for detail—he even alludes to the menu of the Box Tree Restaurant!—and frames it all within the context of why and how the RSC makes the choices it does. The book provides an excellent profile of a very public, institutional, and highly subsidized theatre company. Perhaps even more important, it provides a profile of the life, the people, the challenges, the compromises, and the constant evolution that keep the organization viable and alive—both artistically and financially.

Adler paints a portrait of the RSC from many perspectives—the artistic, the technical, the administrative, and the fiscal—with the assured brushstrokes of an accomplished theatre professional and educator, all in an accessible and intriguing format that will be of great import for scholars as well as for general theatre enthusiasts. Enjoy it!

—Chris Parry

Preface

But this rough magic I here abjure—
—Prospero, *The Tempest*

*I*t is perhaps fitting that as a child of the 1950s, my first exposure to the Royal Shakespeare Company was on television. I remember quite distinctly that evening in the early 1970s when, as an undergraduate at State University of New York at Buffalo, I watched, mesmerized, a public television broadcast of Peter Brook's astonishing film version of his stage production of Peter Weiss's *Marat/Sade.* I realize now, after more than twenty years as a theatre practitioner and educator, that a seventeen-inch, black-and-white image of Glenda Jackson stabbing Ian Richardson in Marat's bathtub pales by comparison to the explosive theatricality of the event performed in the flesh. But as a theatre student enthusiastically seeking theatrical experiences that would transcend the Broadway musicals and comedies with which I grew up, I was enthralled by the extravagant, superbly crafted performances and dynamic staging. This was, I realized, as finely wrought an embodiment of ensemble production as I was likely to see, television or no. The Royal Shakespeare Company had created not a fusty restaging of a work from the Shakespearean canon but a gripping production of a provocative play by a modern German playwright.

I was sufficiently intrigued that I wrote a paper that semester on Brook's highly experimental staging at the RSC of *A Midsummer Night's Dream.* I discovered that with its prodigious schedule of productions, the company embraced a variety of styles and methodologies as it produced both classics and new plays in theatres in Stratford, in London, and on tour. I was determined to see a production live, but circumstances prevented me from doing so until 1984. By that time, I was a stage manager working in New York and was invited to the Broadway openings of Terry Hands's productions of *Much Ado About Nothing* and *Cyrano de Bergerac*. This duo of vividly staged productions, starring Derek Jacobi and Sinead Cusack, proved immensely satisfying. I was thrilled by the buoyant theatricality of the productions—the opulence of design, mastery of language, sharply etched characterizations, exuberance of spectacle, and coherence of performance style. Subsequent trips to Stratford and London confirmed my belief that the company was capable of frequent displays of theatrical alchemy.

In 1987, I joined the faculty of the University of California, San Diego, to create a graduate program in stage management. My new colleague Chris Parry—a lighting designer and RSC member—hosted a steady stream of English theatre colleagues on holiday searching for surf and sun in San Diego. I met several of them, and our informal chats led me to formulate the idea for an article that would compare English and American styles of theatrical management. A UCSD research grant allowed me to spend several weeks in England in 1992, visiting the RSC, the Royal National Theatre, and the Royal Court Theatre, and interviewing a cross section of theatre artists and administrators. When I returned to San Diego and put fingers to keyboard, I realized that the RSC offered the most intriguing and complex theatrical paradigm and eclipsed the other institutions in the sheer scope and size of its operations. It presented more than two dozen productions annually, maintained five theatres in two cities, toured extensively, employed several hundred artists, administrators, artisans, and managers, and maintained a commitment to stage both the classics and new work. Beyond that, however, lay the fact that for more than a century the RSC, in its various incarnations, had provided the theatre world an extravagant legacy of stellar productions featuring the most accomplished artists of the British stage. I began to focus my energies on a book that would investigate why and how the RSC made theatre.

During the next six years, I returned to England on several occasions and saw more than forty RSC productions in England and the United States. Through the exceptional graces of the artistic director, Adrian Noble, and the general manager, David Brierley, I was allowed the opportunity to observe activities from both sides of the curtain as well as in rehearsal rooms and administrative offices. I interviewed more than sixty RSC members—actors, directors, designers, producers, stage managers, craftspeople, stagehands, and administrators—and received permission from all to print their observations in this book.

Rough Magic: Making Theatre at the Royal Shakespeare Company is the culmination of those efforts. I have attempted to fashion a book that allows the reader to explore the RSC from several vantages—theatre facilities, the season, budgeting, producing, directing, designing, and acting—with the hope that this style of presentation will convey the complex challenges faced by a large institutional theatre as it responds to constantly shifting aesthetic and economic parameters. The success of such a theatre depends on the union of a well-articulated artistic mission and a wise administration, and over the last decade, the RSC has had to make considerable adaptations to its established methodology to maintain its viability as a leading, innovative theatre company. In the book, I examine many of the factors that necessitated these changes and the ways in which the RSC has responded. An institutional theatre is a work in progress, and it is inevitable that some aspects of life at the RSC will have changed by the time this book is in print.

In May 2001, for example, just prior to this book's publication, artistic director Adrian Noble announced a new operating model for the RSC. This broad revision to company policy will entail more attractive contractual terms for actors and directors, the development of a classical actor training academy in Stratford, a more flexible approach to the company's performance season, and a stronger presence in London's West End. A greater number of distinguished actors will also appear in a wider variety of venues throughout the United Kingdom and on tour. These innovations should be viewed as part of the continuing evolution of the RSC.

Whenever possible, I have allowed company members to speak in their own words, as they offer insightful, eloquent, and frequently passionate observations about their work at the RSC and the challenges inherent in working in subsidized, not-for-profit institutional theatre.

The 1990s was a period of great flux at the RSC. The decade marked the change of artistic and administrative leadership, the opening of a remodeled theatre and new workshop facilities in Stratford, the abbreviation of the company's annual presence in London, a long freeze on the company's government subsidy that eroded its financial footing, policy changes that affected the production season, and some barbed criticism by the press and the artistic community. But the Royal Shakespeare Company seems to have survived it all. In writing this book, I have tried to portray, as fully as possible, the complicated and painstaking process of theatrical production at one of the most prolific and innovative institutional theatres in the world.

The title of the book is taken from a speech by Prospero in the last act of *The Tempest*. Scholars have long posited that Prospero's magic, capable of unleashing storms and uniting lovers, is the theatrical embodiment of Shakespeare's own art of playwriting. It struck me as a remarkably apt title because it suggests the difficult, inexact, imperfect, marvelously textured, and mysterious nature of making theatre.

Acknowledgments

I spent a number of years visiting the Royal Shakespeare Company as well as researching the process of making theatre there, and this book would not have been possible without the generous contributions of the company, whose members conceivably had more important things to do than chat with an American poking his nose into every nook and cranny of their theatres. Their gracious cooperation and willingness to talk frankly about their work was critical to the success of this project.

I wish to thank my friend and colleague Chris Parry, who first introduced me to the backstage world of the company and made those crucial, initial connections for me. Absent his support, this book would never have progressed beyond the conceptual phase.

Adrian Noble and David Brierley, the artistic and administrative leaders of the RSC during much of my research, graciously allowed me free rein to explore the world of their theatre. They provided, as well, invaluable insight into the workings of the company. Without their endorsement of the project, I could not have proceeded.

Sonja Dosanjh, Geoff Locker, Tim Smith, and Anne Tippett arranged countless interviews and indoctrinated me thoroughly into the ways of the RSC. They responded time and again to my ceaseless queries with good humor and patience, and their ongoing support and encouragement were essential. I am extremely grateful to them.

Michael Attenborough and Lynda Farran are key figures in the artistic and administrative sectors of the RSC. They were wonderfully candid, and their many wise observations were of immeasurable value.

Katie Mitchell, an extraordinary director, revealed much about her own process and the challenges of working in the RSC. Her perspective on directing at the company helped me see the work through a different lens.

The company members who so willingly gave of their time and contributed so generously to my process of research deserve profound thanks. They allowed me to observe them at work and revealed vulnerabilities to which I hope I have been sensitive. This book is in many ways theirs. The following people granted me interviews and allowed themselves to be quoted, and without their generosity of time and wisdom, this book would not exist: Simon Ash, Michael Attenborough, Sally Barling, John Bluck, Simon Bowler, Robert Bowman, David Brierley, Stephen Browning, Peter Cadley, the late Andrew Canham, Alison Chard, Michael Dembowicz, Terry Diamond, Sonja Dosanjh, Wayne Dowdeswell, Kate Duchêne, Lynda Farran, Rick Fisher, Stuart Gibbons, Jasper Gilbert, Brian Glover, Mark Graham, Wendy Greenhill, Tony Hill, Roger Howells, Robert Jones, James Langley, Geoff Locker, William Lockwood, Nigel Love, Frank McGuire, Katie Mitchell, Alan Morris, Adrian Noble, Nick Paladina, Chris Parry, Bronwyn Robertson, Maggie Roy, Simon Russell Beale, Graham Sawyer, Martyn Sergent, Kevin Sivyer, Tim Smith, Graham Sykes, Anne Tippett, David Troughton, Kate Vinnicombe, Andrew Wade, and Chris de Wilde.

Other RSC members arranged interviews and meetings, contributed background information, sent me invaluable material, or allowed me to observe their work. They took time out from busy schedules, and I am grateful for their assistance. They include Lisa Bayliss, Sheonagh Darby, Gregory Doran, Charles Evans, Jude Gray, Sir Peter Hall, Sheila Haswell, Kate Horton, Chick Hughes-Webb, Piers Ibbotson, Sue Lefton, Maggie Mackay, Alison Owen, Nigel Pentland, Peter Rowell, Ian Rowley, Chris Savage, Bill Stoyle, Jane Tassell, Jane Taylor, and Anthony Ward.

Gathering photographs proved a formidable task, and were it not for the contributions of the following people, the book would lose much of its vitality: Dean Asker of the RSC Press Office, who pointed me in the right direction and generously accommodated my requests; Gareth Richman of the Electronic Press Office; Karin Brown and Sylvia Morris of the Shakespeare Centre Library; Allison Sommers; and Alena Kyncl.

The artistic contributions of photographers Ivan Kyncl, Theodore Shank, and most especially, the indefatigable Zuleika Henry, were

vitally important. Theodore Shank graciously offered to shoot photographs of the Barbican Centre during his summer research trip to
London. Zuleika Henry provided the majority of the photographs in
the book, and without her superb artistry and exemplary commitment to this project, I would still be searching for photographs.
Thanks, too, to Chris Parry, David Brierley, Robert Jones, and Lynda
Farran for the generous use of their personal photographs.

My colleagues at UCSD—all of whom I gratefully count as
friends—were always supportive of my work and forgiving of my
occasional absences. Some of them deserve special thanks. Current
department chair and dear friend Walt Jones, whose unflagging support has meant so much to me over many years, was always willing to
assist and offer generous advice. I owe considerable gratitude to
Jonathan Saville, who first read the manuscript in its most primitive
incarnation and offered me the encouragement I needed to proceed
to the next draft. Allan Havis is a constant and wise friend and adviser. He unraveled many mysteries of writing and publishing, always with humor and compassion. Adele Shank, John Rouse, Jim
Carmody, Frantisek Deak, and Jorge Huerta offered valuable advice
and sage counsel. Jim Winker, my touchstone for all knowledge
Shakespearean, provided many excellent research materials. Thanks,
too, to Michelle Null of the UCSD Committee on Research, who
helped me refine my grant proposals. I must also humbly thank all
my students in the MFA program in stage management at UCSD
who, over the years, indulged my frequent tangents on the RSC.

Good friend Rick Gale offered good advice about how to approach
publishers. Dave Hirshey of HarperCollins and Kris Dahl of International Creative Management also offered guidance in the publishing process. My old college roommate, Harry Zaltzberg, helped me
with many of my Internet research questions.

My former professors and constant mentors, Saul Elkin and Bob
Leonard, were always available for encouragement and support.

If the extraordinary Julia Fulton had not lovingly chided me for
setting aside the project midstream, I would not have had the gumption to resume my work on the book.

My wonderful friends Robyn Hunt, Therese O'Connor, William
Parry, Steve Pearson, Paul Pinegar, Burt Rashbaum, Amy Scholl, Keith

Shandalow, Tiger, Danny Trigoboff, Eileen Trigoboff, Emily Weiss, and Jonathan Weiss all either read portions of the manuscript or offered much-needed moral support along the way.

Danielle Amato, Ella Gudis, and D. J. Hopkins provided critical technical support as I gathered photographs.

As a neophyte in the world of publishing, I earnestly wish to thank James Simmons, Barbara Martin, and Carol Burns at Southern Illinois University Press, who hand-held me through the process of getting this book into print. Their good humor and ability to answer so many questions with grace and cheer were invaluable. My editor, John Wilson, supplied clarity, precision, and gracious assistance aplenty.

Thanks to all those generous family members who assisted me. Nora Stein, Paul Neuberg, and Sophie Neuberg opened their wonderful home to me and provided a comfortable base in London. The very patient Steve Cohen is my constant and wise computer guru. Stanley Cohen, Fimi Zolas Cohen, Amara Willey, Mary Lee, and Tom Cohen were all steadfast and generous with their extraordinary support—moral and otherwise. Beth Lebowitz, Max Adler, and Ben Adler are always there for me in every way.

My dear brother Jerry Adler, a senior editor at *Newsweek* and an extraordinary author, has always served as my personal exemplar of excellent writing, and his ironic perspective of the world always provides me with great pleasure and sustenance.

My adored parents, Hilda and Harry Adler, provided unconditional love and the encouragement to pursue a career that was initially alien to them but which they came to respect.

And last, but first always in my heart, I offer all possible gratitude to my darling wife and eternal traveling companion, Nora Cohen, whose years of experience in publishing afforded me consistently wise counsel. She read, edited, prodded, suggested, listened, reassured, and soothed throughout the process of writing and researching this book. Her love and wonderful sense of whimsy are a constant beacon in my life.

Rough Magic

Introduction

Say what the play treats on, then read
the names of the actors, and so grow to a point.
—Bottom, *A Midsummer Night's Dream*

*T*he Royal Shakespeare Company is a name to conjure with. From its inception in 1879 in Stratford-upon-Avon as the Shakespeare Memorial Theatre, the company has matured into one of the dominant theatre institutions in the world, widely recognized for its instrumental role in revitalizing the production of Shakespeare's plays in the last century. Bound by the artistic dictates of its founders and subsequently by its royal charter to present the plays of Shakespeare, the company later expanded its purview to embrace theatrical experimentation and new writing. Today, the RSC has established its reputation for artistic excellence by producing a provocative mixture of classical and contemporary works. Presenting plays in the midlands town of Stratford and in the heart of corporate London as well as on domestic and international tours, the RSC has maintained its dedication to theatrical innovation. Begun as a week-long theatrical tribute to

Shakespeare in his home town, the theatre in Stratford has grown over the decades from an annual seasonal festival to a company of more than seven hundred employees producing theatre year-round through-out the United Kingdom and the world.

The RSC has survived the vagaries of theatrical taste, financial cri-ses, occasional artistic blunders, and physical catastrophe to retain its position as one of the world's preeminent classical theatres. Like any institution its age, the RSC has experienced evolution and growth that have often been painful, but no other major theatre has produced so large and so historically significant a body of work with such contin-ued excellence. Perhaps because the RSC has never been in thrall to one guiding aesthetic principle or ideology, other than its initial charge to produce the work of Shakespeare, it has been able to adapt and respond to the visions of its artists and the needs of its audiences.

At the RSC, past and present coexist in productive symbiosis. The center of its artistic soul is found at the intersection of Shakespeare's continued vitality and the immediacy and vigor of contemporary writers, directors, designers, and actors. Experimentation and tradi-tion are inextricably bound together in the theatre's history, its archi-tecture, and its aesthetics. The intrinsic friction between new and old sometimes generates internal conflict as the company continues to redefine its artistic mission, but it can also yield theatrical magic: Peter Brook's productions of *King Lear* with Paul Scofield, *Marat/Sade,* and *A Midsummer Night's Dream;* Peter Hall's staging of Pinter's *The Home-coming* and *The Wars of the Roses* trilogy; Trevor Nunn and John Caird's epic *Nicholas Nickleby* and *Les Misérables;* Howard Davies's produc-tion of Christopher Hampton's *Les Liaisons Dangereuses;* Adrian Noble's staging of *The Plantagenets;* Ian McKellen and Judi Dench in *Macbeth;* Alan Howard in *Good;* Antony Sher in *Richard III;* Derek Jacobi in *Cyrano de Bergerac;* and Kenneth Branagh in *Henry V* were some of the RSC's more influential offerings of the last four decades.

Is the RSC still capable of stunning the theatre world with such audacious and groundbreaking work? In recent years, the company faced a rising deficit, an onslaught of criticism for radical changes in its production life cycle, and some biting accusations of artistic com-placency. But periodic rough patches are part of a theatre's natural evolution. If a theatre is to remain artistically vital and to flourish, it must continually refresh itself by interrogating its guiding aesthetic principles and production methodologies. The RSC has done so, albeit with some inevitable criticism from within and without, and is currently enjoying a period of renewed vitality. Undoubtedly, the company will experience such cycles in the future. A brief examination of its origins and evolution demonstrates that on more than one occasion the RSC has had to reinvent itself.

It is beyond the purview of this book to thoroughly examine the complex history of the RSC. Sally Beauman has done so in richly rewarding and enlightening fashion in her book *The Royal Shakespeare Company: A History of Ten Decades.* However, a basic understanding of the RSC's genesis and growth is essential for appreciating its current workings.

In 1769, David Garrick, the greatest Shakespearean actor of his time, produced a Shakespeare Jubilee in Stratford-upon-Avon to raise funds for a bust of the Bard for the newly renovated Town Hall. While this expensive venture—one that eventually lost some £2,000—included every festivity and entertainment imaginable *except* the production of a Shakespeare play, the undertaking seemed an augury for the sleepy little Warwickshire market town. In 1864, local brewing magnate and Stratford mayor Edward Flower and his son Charles decided to celebrate the playwright's three-hundredth birthday with appropriate pomp by hosting a Shakespeare Tercentenary, including six productions staged in a temporarily erected wooden pavilion. Fifteen years later, after tireless fund-raising efforts by the Flower family, the Shakespeare Memorial Theatre opened, and plays have been performed in Stratford ever since. The dogged determination of the Flower family and their steadfast dedication and guidance have been critical to the growth and stability of the RSC from its beginnings to the present.

The Shakespeare Memorial Theatre, entirely self-supporting and independent of government subsidy until the 1960s, was considered— at least by the supercilious London press—a provincial theatre for much of its lifetime. Over the years, its production season grew from a short spring festival celebrating Shakespeare's birthday to one that lasted several months. A succession of directors oversaw its fortunes as it continued to present the works of Shakespeare to local and vis-

iting audiences. Although some of the biggest names in the theatrical world were lured to Stratford for one show or sometimes a full
season, the Memorial Theatre remained an artistic outpost. Aside from
sporadic presentations in London and occasional tours, Stratford was
its home and the center of activity. The nearly one-hundred-mile separation between London and Stratford was more than geographic.

By the late 1950s, however, mainly because of the fortitude and
innovations of the artistic triumvirate of Anthony Quayle, Glen Byam
Shaw, and George Devine, Stratford was on the verge of realizing
Charles Flower's dream of more than seventy years earlier—a permanent, resident acting company. Peter Hall, whose artistic directorship
in the 1960s marked a critical juncture in the theatre's life, initiated
the changes that would set the RSC inexorably on its course to its
current position in British theatre. In 1961, Hall changed the name
of the theatre building to the Royal Shakespeare Theatre and the name
of the organization to the Royal Shakespeare Company.

Although the Shakespeare Memorial Theatre had previously assembled large casts of actors for entire seasons in Stratford, a true
company attitude and spirit had never been created. The theatre had
worked primarily on the principle of casting stars in leading roles and
surrounding these luminaries with a corps of lesser-known actors.
Since the average salary in this not-for-profit theatre was fairly low
when compared with West End standards, to say nothing of film and
television salaries, most prominent actors could not afford to remain
in Stratford, far from production studios and film sets, for any substantial length of time. Hall was determined, however, to create a
theatrical center that was so dynamic and artistically rewarding that
actors would be willing to commit themselves for up to three years.
The name change to the Royal Shakespeare Company sounded a
clarion call for his intention to create a nationally prominent company of artists committed to serious theatrical investigation of both
classical and contemporary works. Many actors—Peggy Ashcroft was
the first to sign on—were so intrigued by the prospect of such work
conducted in a relatively stable and secure environment that Hall had
no trouble attracting a strong group. The idea of a *company*, an ensemble of artists anchored by the works of Shakespeare, performing
in repertoire, continues as the polestar that guides the RSC.

Hall recognized the necessity of expanding the new company's artistic mandate. The 1950s had seen a tremendous spurt of adventurous work by English playwrights, and Hall recognized that his company needed to flex its muscles and work beyond the scope of the Shakespearean canon. He believed that the company's efforts on the classics would benefit immeasurably from the opportunity to tackle the plays of living writers. He aggressively sought out a theatre in London in which the RSC could develop a permanent presence and began to commission new plays. The Aldwych, on the fringes of London's West End, became both the RSC's base for presenting the occasional transfer of Shakespearean work from Stratford as well as a platform for new works. However, this expansion did not come cheaply and resulted in the RSC's transition from financial independence to reliance on government subsidy, which Hall believed the company would need to continue to grow. The repercussions of Hall's audacious expansionism are still being felt by the RSC forty years later.

For decades, the RSC's affairs have been inextricably linked with the difficult birth and growth of another major institutional theatre in the United Kingdom, the Royal National Theatre. It was founded in 1962 after more than eighty years of fierce internecine battles by partisan factions within the government and the theatre elite. In 1960, a committee of politicians and prominent figures in the arts—most notably Laurence Olivier, who was to be the first artistic director of the National—proposed the foundation of a tripartite national theatre consisting of the new National Theatre (to be built on the South Bank), the Old Vic, and the newly constituted Royal Shakespeare Company in Stratford. No mention was made of the RSC's continuing at the Aldwych.

Hall had added luster to the RSC's venerable reputation by establishing a vigorous presence at the Aldwych. He hoped that this would be sufficient to cement the RSC's claim to the title *national theatre,* making it unnecessary to unite with the other two theatres to create what he viewed as an unwieldy colossus. Any new national theatre would compete for artists, audiences, and funds with the RSC, and Hall feared that it would sound the death knell for his company. He toiled publicly and privately to drum up support for the RSC's claims. But Olivier's backing in the arts, the press, and the government for a new national theatre was strong as well. In a case study in competing artistic egos, this battle royal to establish the identity and leadership of the national theatre was waged between Olivier, Hall, and their supporters during the early 1960s. Olivier and Hall, who had worked together at Stratford, had great respect for each other's talents and equally high regard for the tenacious machinations of which the other was capable. Olivier and his party continued to manipulate their highly placed government contacts, and in 1962, thanks largely to the efforts of Oliver Lyttleton, chair of the Joint Council of the National Theatre, the government's funding and commitment for the National Theatre on the South Bank were in place. Subsequently, National Theatre partisans attempted to undermine the new government subsidy recently earmarked for the RSC, but the public response to such a gambit was strong enough to ensure that the RSC would receive its funding.[1] However, the money that was needed to create the new National Theatre facility was much greater than that apportioned to the RSC, and to this day the National's subsidy outstrips the RSC's.

In the early 1960s, Hall and his associates apparently took to heart both the letter and the spirit of the royal charter that the theatre had received in 1925. The words of that charter proved to be emblematic of the company's new growth, as Hall breathed new life into a classical theatre company: "To conserve, advance, and disseminate the dramatic heritage of Shakespeare and to keep alive his memory by the production and presentation of his works to the highest artistic standards at the Royal Shakespeare Theatre . . . To conserve, advance, and disseminate Shakespearean drama, literature and knowledge both in our United Kingdom and throughout the world . . . To advance and improve the dramatic art . . . by developing, extending, and refreshing the skills and experience of dramatic performances of all kinds and by teaching and training and other educational activities."[2]

During this period, the RSC expanded its activities beyond Britain's borders, establishing an international presence with tours to other countries. In the period 1968–1970, the RSC toured twice to the United States, twice throughout Europe, and once to Australia and Japan.[3] The importance of ongoing training as a component of the life of the RSC was defined, and company members began to work with some of the nation's leading voice, fencing, and verse coaches.

This process of learning and honing skills was one of the company's tenets that set it apart from so many other theatres, and it continues as a vital feature of the RSC's work. Rigorous outreach programs to develop and educate new and future audiences were also undertaken.

Hall was also responsible for establishing an environment in which serious theatrical investigation could flourish outside of the constraints of the main production season. He encouraged two innovative directors, Michel St. Denis and Peter Brook, to develop workshops that would explore theatrical styles and genres not immediately applicable to the company's current productions. These workshops would prove invaluable in the 1960s. St. Denis, a respected directing and acting teacher, founded the RSC Actors' Studio, where company members—actors, designers, directors, and technicians—could continue to review and revitalize their skills and talents through a variety of classes and workshop productions. Brook, whose reputation for innovation had been established with his 1955 production of *Titus Andronicus* with Laurence Olivier, formed a workshop in 1963 with RSC actors that explored the "Theatre of Cruelty" theories of French director and theorist Antonin Artaud. This workshop would eventually lead to one of the company's most triumphant and controversial works, Brook's production of Peter Weiss's *Marat/Sade*. In expanding the scope and nature of the RSC's theatrical investigation by developing these laboratories, Hall was following in the footsteps of Konstantin Stanislavsky. It was in the studios of the Moscow Art Theatre that much of the important work of Stanislavsky, Meyerhold, and Vakhtangov was accomplished.

Peter Hall resigned from the RSC at the end of 1967 to pursue an independent directing career; by 1972, he would replace Olivier as head of the National Theatre. The RSC's new artistic director, Trevor Nunn, continued to diversify the company's work. The internationally heralded eight-hour adaptation of Charles Dickens's *Nicholas Nickleby* was Nunn's handiwork. So, too, was the decision to point the RSC in the direction of musicals, both original productions and revivals. Nunn, who during his tenure with the RSC enjoyed terrific success as a free-lance director with the heralded production of *Cats,* recognized that the drawing power of successful musicals could do much to offset RSC losses on less commercially viable productions.

This insight led, in the mid-1980s, to his and John Caird's epic production of *Les Misérables,* and more than a decade later, the RSC continues to enjoy the financial rewards from that venture. Not all RSC musicals have turned out successfully, however. Terry Hands's 1988 production of the musical *Carrie,* based on the Brian De Palma film and the Stephen King novel, was gleefully derided by reviewers as one of the great disasters on Broadway.

In 1978, Hands was appointed joint artistic director with Nunn, in part because Nunn's increasing activity as a free-lance director necessitated another set of eyes and ears in running the company. Nunn was initially criticized by the press for his extracurricular work, but the assault eventually abated when it was made known that RSC artistic directors' contracts were drawn for nine-month periods, thus allowing and encouraging them to augment their income with outside projects. This new joint directorship of Nunn and Hands would prove a viable solution to the growing administrative workload, but it also diluted the strength of a single leader's vision.

Nunn made significant changes to the RSC infrastructure. The 1974 opening of The Other Place in a tin shed across the road from the Royal Shakespeare Theatre would mark a critical turning point in the RSC's direction. This quirky space, not originally intended for use as a theatre, would serve as a venue for the more experimental work that the company hungered to do.[4] Three years later, the Warehouse in Covent Garden was chosen—largely for its proximity to the Aldwych—as a London theatre to house Other Place transfers and its own small, new works. Nunn also implemented the policy of transferring most of the Stratford shows to the Aldwych—this had been done only occasionally under Hall—to increase the revenues from London.

Hall had successfully engineered the RSC's simultaneous seasons in London and Stratford, but the Aldwych was a rented facility, with all the attendant problems that tenancy implies. Hall thus initiated plans in 1965 to secure a permanent home for the RSC in London, one that would have its own identity and the requisite ancillary services that were lacking at the Aldwych. The RSC had been invited by the City of London to be the resident theatre company in the new Barbican Centre, part of a larger urban planning scheme to renovate the East End. But because of the glacial pace at which plans were developed by the city government, Hall had long since departed the RSC when the company finally opened two theatres, the Barbican and the Pit, in the Barbican Centre in 1982. In 1986, as the result of the unprecedented generosity of American philanthropist Frederick Koch, the fifth jewel in the RSC's crown was unveiled. The Swan, a modern version of a Jacobean theatre, opened on its site adjacent to the Royal Shakespeare Theatre in Stratford and presented new possibilities for dynamic staging.

Each new artistic director of the RSC has implemented significant changes in company direction, in part to leave an imprimatur and in part to respond to the changing needs of the company. Adrian Noble replaced Terry Hands in 1991 and has been responsible for radical revisions in company policy. In 1997, Noble articulated his position about the changes he had undertaken: "I want to accomplish what I'm in the middle of doing, changing our season around. It's a period of massive change. The first few years of my time were characterized, I think, by getting the company back onto the stable artistic and structural financial footing. It then seemed to me we were faced with a choice, which was whether we wanted to carry on doing what we did, which was fine, or whether we needed to respond to a shifting world and a shifting artistic agenda by a process of diversifying around the company but refocusing back at home."[5]

Noble was referring to his 1995 decision to transform the RSC into a theatre that was truly "a theatre for the nation." To accomplish this end, he completely restructured the company's season, altering the parameters of its Stratford schedule, reduced its presence in London from eleven months to six, undertook greater touring, and targeted Plymouth as a second resident city in addition to Newcastle (a northern industrial city that, since 1977, had received shows from the Stratford repertoire for one month each winter). These changes caused seismic repercussions in the company and in the British theatre community. The causes and effects of Noble's decision will be explored in subsequent chapters.

The very fact that the RSC's artistic center is also Shakespeare's birthplace offers another challenge to the company. Many tourists attending Shakespearean plays in Stratford expect to see them rendered in an "authentic" way. They anticipate a rousing Elizabethan costume

drama, but what they envision is a nineteenth-century-style production of Shakespeare—which is no more historically accurate or appropriate than one set in a contemporary milieu. According to Brian
Glover, the recently retired curator of the Shakespeare collection at
the RSC—an impressive gallery of theatrical artifacts and memorabilia housed above the Swan—the company continuously wages a
battle against the traditionalist mind-set.

> The nineteenth century must have had an amazing PR team to in-
> fluence the world, because everybody *knows* what historical figures
> look like, and they're all based on nineteenth-century interpretations,
> the pre-Raphaelite image. The dressing up has become greater than
> the text of the actual plays. There are a lot of people who come here
> with a preconceived notion of what they'll see. "It's very good, but I
> do wish it had been done properly," as if what they saw onstage was
> a mistake. What they're *really* looking for is a traveling museum. Is
> the RSC going to sit still or look for new ways to produce? In the
> more than twenty years since I've been here, it's kept looking for new
> ways of working, and what keeps the ingredients going is by being
> able to work with contemporary dramatists at the same time, so it's
> bringing a contemporary vision to the company to ensure that Shake-
> speare isn't in danger of becoming a theme-park presentation here.[6]

Balancing the works of Shakespeare with those of his contempo-
raries, later playwrights, and modern authors has also prevented the
RSC from getting stuck in amber. Principal associate director Michael
Attenborough articulated the company's challenge in 1995.

> I think there have developed over the years a number of things that
> you could argue have become central to our lives here and probably
> for the foreseeable future won't be reinventing themselves. Probably
> most obvious is the way in which we focus on the work of one dra-
> matist. Secondly, that we work now unlike anybody else in this coun-
> try, with a semipermanent company that works in repertoire. The
> National doesn't do that; they cast for every play.[7] This is central to
> what we do. Working in repertoire with a company is essential to who
> we are. When Adrian Noble and I arrived in 1990, what we wanted
> to do was reestablish the center of our work, which was essentially
> classical. How do you make plays written anywhere from two hun-
> dred to four hundred years ago or more still live for a modern audi-
> ence? How do the modern actor and director confront that central
> question of how to make formalized poetic language work for the ear

of a person at the end of the twentieth century on the stage? We continue to shift our focus from time to time, but certain tenets are absolutely immovable: the classical work, the repertoire, and the company. The company and repertoire issues are difficult; they are not cost-effective but are *cost-ineffective,* if you will. You would not put the most eloquent and ardent supporter of arts funding in front of the Houses of Parliament to explain how important it was for the RSC to remain in repertoire. An opponent would immediately stand up and inform the House of the cost. Now, we would say it's worth it, but whether the MPs would think it's worth it is questionable.[8]

The particulars of the seasonal calendar may change from year to year, but there is a basic framework, as Attenborough referred to, on which the RSC rests. Much of the work originates in the three Stratford theatres, plays in repertoire throughout the season, and then transfers to London and other designated cities (currently, Newcastle and Plymouth). Occasionally, shows originate in London and then play in Stratford. Others—chosen from the slate of seasonal offerings as well as specially produced works—take to the road in the United Kingdom. In some years, the work is taken to international audiences; in 1998 and 2000, the RSC toured much of its repertoire to both New York and Washington, DC, and many other productions have played abroad for months at a time, from Mexico City to Delhi. According to Sir Geoffrey Cass, chair of the Council of the Royal Shakespeare Company, in a 1993 report: "It is hard to understand from within the United Kingdom just how highly British theatre in general and the RSC in particular are regarded abroad. That national reputation rests not only on the success of particular touring productions, but on an appreciation of the collective artistic strength of British theatre at home. It is recognised that this is a strength which is founded in the uniquely collective characteristics of British theatre, with an interdependent economy which embraces the smallest touring company, the grant-aided repertory theatres, the 'national companies' and the commercial theatre both in the regions and in London."[9]

Sir Geoffrey's assertions about the RSC's stature abroad still appear current, using as a yardstick the company's continued popularity on the international touring circuit. Its standing at home, however, was tarnished in the press in the mid-1990s. The decision to curtail the London season as well as charges of lackluster repertoire choices and

the failure to lure star names to its casts—especially in light of the renewed vigor seen at its main competitor, the Royal National Theatre—
contributed to a diminution of its reputation. But the RSC regrouped
and refocused its efforts. It continues to produce prodigiously, and
lately it has generated several productions that have garnered significant critical acclaim.

As will be shown in subsequent chapters, it is the company ethic
that continues to define the RSC. According to an Arts Council of Great
Britain appraisal some years ago, "The RSC perceives its strength as
lying in the collaboration and creative conflict of talents working together, rather than in the talents of single individuals. . . . The concept of a company is crucial to the very nature of the RSC."[10] The
following pages explore the process of making theatre at this distinguished company of passionate and committed artists.

Royal Shakespeare Theatre, Stratford-upon-Avon. © Copyright Zuleika Henry.

Swan Theatre, Stratford-upon-Avon. © Copyright Zuleika Henry.

The Other Place, Stratford-upon-Avon. © Copyright Zuleika Henry.

Stage and auditorium of the Swan Theatre. Photo by Simon McBride, courtesy of the Royal Shakespeare Company.

Forestage and auditorium of the Royal Shakespeare Theatre. Courtesy of the Royal Shakespeare Company.

Silk Street entrance to the Barbican Centre, London. Photo by Theodore Shank.

Lobby of the Barbican Centre. Photo by Theodore Shank.

Interior of the Barbican Theatre. Courtesy of the Royal Shakespeare Company.

Interior of the Pit. Courtesy of the Royal Shakespeare Company.

Regional touring production of *Henry VI: The Battle for the Throne,* 1994, directed by Katie Mitchell. Photo by Ivan Kyncl.

Regional touring production of *The Comedy of Errors,* 1996, directed by Tim Supple; Robert Bowman as Antipholus of Syracuse *(second from right).*
© Copyright Zuleika Henry.

Antigones Project, 1992;
Mike Shepherd directing
young actors in Cornwall.
© Copyright Zuleika Henry.

Robert Jones's sets and costumes for *Henry VIII*, 1998, directed by Gregory
Doran; Paul Jesson as Henry *(on horse)* and Jane Lapotaire as Catherine of
Aragon. © Copyright Zuleika Henry.

Robert Jones's sets and costumes for *The Winter's Tale* (act 1, scene 2), 1998, directed by Gregory Doran; Ken Bones as Polixenes, Alexandra Gilbreath as Hermione, and Antony Sher as Leontes. © Copyright Zuleika Henry.

Robert Jones's sets and costumes for *The Winter's Tale* (act 3, scene 3), 1998, directed by Gregory Doran; Jeffry Wickham as Antigonus. © Copyright Zuleika Henry.

Chris Parry's lighting for Christopher Hampton's *Les Liaisons Dangereuses,* 1985, directed by Howard Davies; sets and costumes by Bob Crowley. Photo by Chris Parry.

Chris Parry's lighting for *The Plantagenets,* 1988, directed by Adrian Noble; sets and costumes by Bob Crowley. Photo by Chris Parry.

Stratford-upon-Avon

And here's a marvellous convenient place for our rehearsal.
—Quince, *A Midsummer Night's Dream*

*T*he RSC began life in an ornate Victorian temple to the arts on the banks of the river Avon in 1879. Today, a complement of three architecturally and dynamically distinct theatres in Stratford affords the company the luxury, enjoyed by few others in the United Kingdom, of selecting the most appropriate theatrical environment for each of its productions. With the addition of two theatres in London, the RSC enjoys an embarrassment of theatrical riches.[1]

The theatres reflect the aesthetics and conventions of the times in which they were built. Each, with its unique ambiance, configuration, and audience capacity, extends the RSC's options for staging and enables the company, within certain guidelines, to consider a play's box office potential as well as its theatrical dynamic as factors in a theatre's selection. It is unusual for an institutional theatre to occupy so many spaces and frequently places extraordinary demands on the patience and skills of the staff. Touring several productions annually in the United Kingdom and abroad adds another layer of complexity to the challenges faced by the administration and the artists. Exceptional planning and adaptability are critically important in averting a host of potential disasters that could arise amid so much theatrical activity.

The Royal Shakespeare Theatre—the RST, or "main house"—is the flagship theatre in Stratford by virtue of its history and size, if nothing else; it has serious flaws in its front-of-house facilities and even more problematic theatre dynamics in the auditorium. Still, it was on this stage that some of the signal performances of the company were produced. It opened in 1932 on the site of the original Shakespeare Memorial Theatre, which had been destroyed by fire six years earlier, and was rechristened the Royal Shakespeare Theatre in 1961, when Peter Hall decided to jettison the backward-looking "Memorial" from its name. Although it has always been a popular theatrical destination for audiences and artists, it has been drastically remodeled several times over the years in attempts to render the auditorium more hospitable to audiences and actors alike. As the largest of the Stratford theatres both onstage and backstage and in the audience, it is the premiere venue for the works of Shakespeare. These large-cast plays, with their potential for spectacle, are most at home in this space, although the works have also been staged effectively in the other theatres. In the past, the RST presented only the works of Shakespeare during the RSC's regular repertory season; it would occasionally house a touring production or the transfer of a non-Shakespearean work at the end of the season or during the Winter Visitors' Season. It seemed a sacrosanct space, given its history and the company's original mandate to produce Shakespeare. The current artistic director, Adrian Noble, however, broke with tradition in 1998, offering Richard Brinsley Sheridan's acerbic eighteenth-century comedy of character assassination, *The School for Scandal*, and *The Lion, the Witch and the Wardrobe*, an adaptation of the C. S. Lewis children's fantasy.

The Other Place, originally much beloved for the threadbare, intimate atmosphere that engendered many experimental works in the 1970s, was redesigned and rebuilt on a new site in 1991 to compensate for the deterioration of the original structure as well as to accommodate an expansion of the company's rehearsal space. The Other

Place is most often the home to new plays and more experimental, alternative works that seem most comfortable in a black box environment, but Ibsen, Shakespeare, and Euripides, among other playwrights, have all been performed there.

The Swan, opened in 1986 and the favorite of many audiences and artists, was fashioned to re-create the dynamics of a Jacobean playhouse, allowing directors and designers the chance to produce theatre in a uniquely styled, hospitable, yet challenging environment. The Swan was initially intended to house the works of those playwrights who either influenced, or were directly influenced by, Shakespeare—mainly Elizabethan, Jacobean, and Restoration writers—but gradually and inevitably, the lure of working in this theatre was so great that directors could not resist staging Chekhov, T. S. Eliot, Goethe, and Shakespeare himself in the Swan. The artistic directorate has acknowledged that rigid programmatic guidelines often prevent the flexibility necessary for accommodating a large number of artists producing works in a variety of genres, so the Swan's initial mission has evolved to embrace a broader range of plays.

Currently, the RSC presents two separate production seasons in Stratford—the seven-month Summer Festival and the five-month Winter Season, which overlap briefly in March—as well as one seven-month season in London. Stratford Summer Festival productions usually premiere in Stratford and then move on to Newcastle, London, and Plymouth. The Stratford Winter Season is relatively new, having been created in 1998, and its six or seven productions are generally presented first in Stratford and then play in London or on regional tour; occasionally, they may be shown only in Stratford. From time to time, however, shows originate in the fall at the start of the London season and then move north to perform in Stratford's Winter Season, as with the 1999–2000 productions of Yukio Ninagawa's *King Lear,* featuring Nigel Hawthorne, or Lindsay Posner's *The Taming of the Shrew.*

Despite the RSC's presence in London and throughout the United Kingdom, it is Stratford-upon-Avon that is most closely associated with the Royal Shakespeare Company. The town of twenty thousand is located about one hundred miles northwest of London in Warwickshire. A motorway links Stratford and London, but those who cannot or will not drive from the capital usually take a coach. Rail travel is less convenient because it requires at least one transfer; the most convenient rail link from London deposits passengers in Coventry, and then a taxi or bus trip of almost thirty minutes is needed to reach Stratford.

Stratford is situated in gently rolling hills in the northern limits of the Cotswolds, famous for its jewel-like villages of honey-colored, thatched-roof cottages and pristine gardens and farms. Just minutes away is the magnificently maintained Warwick Castle, one of the finest examples of medieval fortress architecture extant in England. It was in Stratford that Shakespeare was born, and it was to Stratford that he retired after his successes in London.

Stratford's town center is visually grounded in Elizabethan times but decidedly in tune with the present. It is viewed at its romantic best on a stroll along the tree-lined banks of the Avon opposite the theatres. The bold outlines of the RST and the Swan, the graceful Avonbank gardens, the weeping willows, and the lonely spire of Holy Trinity Church provide a soothing contrast to the constant stream of tour buses whose passengers scour the souvenir shops for Shakespearean trinkets with the fervor of medieval pilgrims vying for a splinter from the cross.

Stratford attracts about two and a half million tourists annually, and to a visitor, the town can appear to have only one purpose: the marketing of Shakespeare. The town center is a tourist trap, but despite the pervasive hucksterism, it has its charms and displays its impressive array of historical landmarks with relative restraint. In the narrow streets of the old section of town, half-timbered Tudor houses and contemporary shops and restaurants commingle comfortably. Plaques on the sides of buildings provide information for the historically inquisitive. A bust of Shakespeare, presented by David Garrick during the great festival of 1764, graces the front of the old Town Hall on Sheep Street. In the town center, most hotels, tea rooms, restaurants, and souvenir shops flaunt an Elizabethan theme. Shakespeare's likeness can be found on everything from cocktail napkins to CD-ROM disks.

The lovely Avon, hardly more than a wide stream at this juncture, splits the town in two. Manicured gardens and grassy swales grace both banks, ducks and swans glide peacefully, and colorful canal boats, sculls, and other small craft ply the gentle waters. Small footbridges, a boat basin, and rudimentary canal locks form a town nucleus adjacent to the stone span of the fifteenth-century Clopton Bridge, from which several streets of the old town radiate. Anglers try their luck in the Avon's waters, although as one resident noted in a Stratford website bulletin board posting, "The canal has bugger all fish in it. I should know, I fished it for five years as a nipper and never caught a thing!" Sitting and gazing imperturbably at the Tourist Information Centre and Moat House Hotel, his back to the picturesque Bancroft gardens and the theatre bearing his name, is the likeness of Shakespeare himself captured in an imposing statue by Lord Ronald Gower, dedicated in 1888. The Bard is surrounded by smaller statues of his creations: Lady Macbeth, Hamlet, Falstaff, and Prince Hal.

Holy Trinity Church—the transepts of which date to the early thirteenth century and a fine example of Gothic architecture on a modest, human scale—perches precariously on the riverbank several hundred yards down river. In the chapel crypt, behind burgundy velvet ropes and a brass rail, are the "Grave of the poet William Shakespeare, 1564–1616," and those of his wife, Anne Hathaway, and their family. Shakespeare was entitled to burial within the church walls after he became a lay rector in 1605. Adjacent to the church is a picture postcard-perfect country cemetery and the serene Avonbank gardens and its Brass Rubbing Centre.

The town maintains several exceptionally well-restored Tudor properties, all linked to some period in Shakespeare's life in Stratford, which provide an entertaining and insightful glimpse into the life of Elizabethan country gentry. The five Shakespearean homes—Shakespeare's Birthplace, Nash's House/New Place, Hall's Croft, Mary Arden's House, and Anne Hathaway's Cottage—are located in either the center or the outskirts of town, and ubiquitous double-decker buses provide a frequent and convenient link for the thousands of tourists who visit them. The Shakespeare Birthplace Trust, the supervising authority for these sites, also runs—in conjunction with the RSC—an excellent library and Shakespeare research facility in the town.

But theatre is the main attraction for visitors in Stratford. During the 1998–1999 season, the three Stratford theatres played to audiences totaling 498,257. According to the 1990 Arts Council appraisal report, "in the words of the Leader of Stratford District Council, the RSC keeps the town alive."[2] Graham Sawyer, who as theatre manager oversees the physical plant of all RSC properties in Stratford, said that the RSC "is the major attraction in town—we're the reason the town is there." However, Stratford had recently seen about a 20 percent drop in tourist trade, occasioned in part by the 1998 economic crisis in Asia, which had a significant adverse impact on the RSC's box office. Some RSC members attribute this decrease to the opening of the new Globe Theatre in London, offering tourists "the entire Shakespearean experience without having to travel up to Stratford," according to one company member.

The Royal Shakespeare Theatre and the adjoining Swan are situated on the banks of the Avon, set back only a few feet from the water and just a brief walk upstream from Shakespeare's burial place inside Holy Trinity Church. The RST and the Swan are fronted on the north by the Bancroft gardens, bordered by the Avon to the east, and by a bustling, narrow street, Waterside, to the west.

The RST and the Swan are physically joined at the hip, as their backstage areas are connected by a series of hallways and a common stage door. The rather squat and boxy outline of the RST and the ornate, soaring roof of the egg-shaped Swan form an arresting architectural complement when viewed at a distance. They are built of similar red brick and harmonize on an aesthetically pleasing note. Although they share a canteen, dressing rooms, and access to offices, each is a fully functional theatre with its own production staff, stage crew, musicians, box office, bar, rest rooms, and gift shop. Above the Swan theatre, perched under the building's impressively arched roof, is a wonderfully airy and well-appointed rehearsal hall, named after actress Dame Peggy Ashcroft. The Swan's upper lobby, built on the site of the Shakespeare Memorial Theatre's original Picture Gallery, houses the impressively mounted collection of RSC set models, costumes, photos, and other memorabilia.

Heading left—or south—from the two theatres, a few hundred yards down the Waterside road and across the street, one comes upon The Other Place. The new theatre, which opened in 1991 after the demolition of its predecessor a few hundred feet away, is a tidy, inviting red brick building that houses a small, flexible, black box theatre as well as dressing rooms, offices, a box office, a concession stand, a small technical workshop, and two superb rehearsal halls. Down towards the Swan, the west side of Waterside is lined by charming brick cottages, the half-timbered Arden Hotel, and the RSC's unofficial pub—and, as it often seems after a performance, satellite greenroom—the Dirty Duck.

Directly across Waterside from the RST and the Swan is a row of Georgian townhouses. The RSC owns many of them—over the years, it has amassed a large holding of properties throughout the town, utilizing some and leasing others—and uses them for actor housing as well as for its armory, millinery, boot, and costume shops. In 1992, the company opened a new workshop facility on Timothy's Bridge Road, about two miles away in an industrial estate, where the scenic, paint, properties, rental wardrobe, and storage facilities are maintained.

The Royal Shakespeare Theatre

The Shakespeare Memorial Theatre opened in 1879. It was built on marshy land on the riverbank bought by Charles Flower, the son of Edward Flower, the founder of the eponymous brewing company. It was Flower who devoted himself to the establishment of a Shakespeare theatre in Stratford and slavishly oversaw the birth of the theatre and its annual festivals. Brian Glover, the recently retired curator of the RSC Collection, provided insight into Flower's theatrical vision.

> What was fascinating about Flower's concept, not being a theatre director but a brewer, was that he wanted a kind of Shakespeare experience, a kind of nineteenth-century Pompidou Center. So, on the site of a bed where reeds were grown for thatching roofs in the area, next to a coal yard and sheepskin sheds, he found land to build the theatre. The tourist today certainly gets the Elizabethan touch in town, combined with the shopping mall. The flower gardens around the theatre provide a cozy, middle-class, nineteenth-century respectability, which is very different from what Elizabethan theatre would have been like, especially on the South Bank of the Thames, where you'd be lucky to leave without getting your throat cut. In a sense, what Flower was trying to do was to bring into the countryside— when theatre was really only associated with major cities—a theatre that was a memorial to Shakespeare in his home town. And that was outrageous. Where on earth would the audiences come from? Yes,

Stratford is Shakespeare's birthplace, but this wasn't a university town
with a populace passionate about seeing Shakespeare. It was a working market town, with a canal and a river. He buys a piece of land,
has the reed bed filled in to stabilize it, and has about £20,000 to build
the theatre, which was most likely not going to perform all year
round. He built the art gallery and library the next year to provide
the general public an access to Shakespeare.[3]

The original theatre, designed by the London firm of Messrs.
Dodgshun and Unsworth of Westminster, incorporated a number of
features that did not necessarily coalesce gracefully, according to RSC
historian Sally Beauman.

> The inside of the theatre . . . had an oddly ecclesiastical appearance,
> emphasized by a high pointed roof, and Gothic arches which flanked
> the gallery.
>   The outside of the building was frankly fantastical. Clearly a strug-
> gle had gone on in the architect's heart between the fashionable style
> of his day, and the Elizabethan half-timbering he felt evocative of Shake-
> speare. The result, built of red brick with dressings of stone, was a
> weird and unsuccessful mixture of architectural styles, incorporating
> Tudor gabling, Elizabethan chimneys, gothic turrets, and minarets.[4]

The theatre burned to the ground in March 1926; the cause of the
blaze was never discovered. All that remained was the Picture Gallery
and the library. Perhaps it was a blessing in disguise. By all accounts,
the theatre's artistic and aesthetic obstacles were so great that, despite
the overwhelming challenge of funding and erecting another building, the leadership of the theatre was grateful that a new start could
be attempted. Artistic director William Bridges-Adams and theatre
council chair Archibald Flower were concerned that if another, albeit
temporary, home for the theatre was not found immediately, the festival would wither and die before a new theatre could be built, so performances were transferred to a local cinema. A national competition
was held to select an architect, and it came as something of a shock at
the time when the winning design was submitted by a woman, Elizabeth Scott. But fund-raising proved difficult in England, and about
half of the £192,000 it took to rebuild the theatre came from American contributions, including a substantial gift from John D. Rocke-
feller. Finally, in 1932, the new Shakespeare Memorial Theatre opened.

The new red brick theatre, squat and prosaic by today's standards, was at the time considered a modern and thoroughly no-nonsense approach to playhouse design that, according to Swan architect Michael Reardon, "earned it the nickname of 'The Jam Factory.'"[5] It was built adjacent to the burnt-out remains of the original theatre, which was reconstructed as a conference hall, later converted to a rehearsal room, and finally served as the site of the Swan. The backstage area of the new theatre was equipped with the most modern technology culled from contemporary European models. Scott's theatre, although plain and austere on the outside, was full of lovely interior details, according to Sally Beauman: "The entrance foyer was a great empty hall, the floor of Hornton stone with sections of Ashburton marble and Derbyshire fossil; the walls were lined with fawn-coloured brick. Great ebony doors with exquisitely worked finger-plates in aluminum, representing the twin masks of Comedy and Tragedy, and surrounded by pilasters of stainless steel and green Swedish marble, led into the theatre itself. . . . At one end of this hall was a long couch of ebonized wood, upholstered in green horsehair. . . . All was icily elegant."[6]

If the design of the foyer was pleasant for the audience, the auditorium itself was problematic for both the audience and the company. As the proscenium was too far from the first row of the stalls (orchestra section), there was no intimacy possible between performer and audience. Sight lines were disastrous from parts of the house, especially the balcony, and the backstage mechanics, so carefully designed, proved fraught with unforeseen problems, to the dismay of those who had hoped that the theatre's innovative technical facilities would place it in the vanguard of modern theatrical architecture. It is ironic that a theatre built in 1879 and rebuilt in 1932 to stage the works of an Elizabethan playwright never utilized any of the architectural hallmarks of an Elizabethan theatre.

In 1950, considerable renovations were made under Anthony Quayle's direction. The dress circle was remodeled so that it curved gently towards the stage, in an attempt to create some sense of intimacy and connection between performer and audience. Side boxes were added along both walls, and 135 seats were added to the front of the stalls, increasing the seating capacity to 1,377 and shortening the gap between stage and audience. Additional dressing rooms and a new greenroom were added on the river side of the building, and the light board was moved from backstage to a booth in the back of the house.[7]

In 1960, Peter Hall undertook another extensive renovation, as the stage was extended into the audience—creating a thrust from the proscenium—and a rake was added to the stage.[8] The use of a flexible rake built on top of the actual stage floor has become a mainstay of the RST. Hall wanted to create a two-thousand-seat auditorium with a fly system above the forestage and to tear down the problematic proscenium arch to expose the larger space behind it, but fears that it would cause the collapse of the stage house prevented his doing so.[9] In 1972–1973, the balcony was extended above the dress circle boxes on the sides of the auditorium. Subsequent alterations have included the installation of air-conditioning, the repainting, recarpeting, and refurbishing of the auditorium, lobby, and restaurants, and various reconfigurations of the stage facilities themselves.

When viewed across the Bancroft gardens from Gower's statue of Shakespeare, the RST appears as a solid, square, humorless building. With its car park in front, glass-enclosed foyer, and row of flagpoles adorning upper-level windows, it looks like a modest, 1930s-era corporate headquarters. The large aluminum letters spelling out "Royal Shakespeare Theatre" to the right of the copper-roofed entrance provide the only immediate indications that this is a theatre. Inside, however, it is more visually inviting. Leather banquettes and skylights provide a generous waiting area and a natural transition to the main front-of-house facilities. The long, narrow main lobby can become uncomfortably crowded before curtain time and during intermissions, but the flagstone floors, the resplendent deco-style box office in marble with aluminum and copper piping, and the burgundy, green, and blue patterned doorways to the auditorium provide a welcoming environment, especially during poor weather. The walls are adorned with production photos, and the right corner of the lobby houses a bookstall and shop. A stone plaque commemorates Archibald Flower, the son of the founder, Charles, and the guiding light of the theatre's fortunes for many decades. It reads: "To the memory of Archibald Flower, 1865–1950. He made this theatre his life's purpose, that others might enjoy the genius of Shakespeare."

To the left of the lobby, a brick rotunda is adorned with a small fountain, a bust of Shakespeare by Clemence Dane, CBE, and production photos and mementos.[10] From there, a circular staircase leads patrons to the theatre's upper levels; alternatively, handsome wooden doors lead into a lounge area that adjoins the River Terrace restaurant, a self-service cafe with large windows that overlook the river. On the floor above is the Box Tree, a quite respectable, not inexpensive restaurant, serving such delicacies as carrot and coriander soup, wild mushroom and truffle cappelletti, filet of red snapper, and passion fruit bavarois. Above the restaurant is the dress circle lounge. White walls, worn green and blue striped carpet, wicker furniture, and a bar at the far end provide a welcome relief to those who have made the climb. The stairs then continue on to the balcony above.

Modern technology has replaced the theatre's rolling stages, cyclorama, and lighting equipment of the 1930s, but the look and feel of the house still firmly reflect the aesthetics of the period in which it was built. Polished wood doors and stainless steel wall sconces, plum velvet seats, purple and violet auditorium walls, and clean, graceful curves all lend an elegance and style to the proceedings. The decor of the auditorium calls to mind that of a 1930s luxury ocean liner.

The handsome, inviting interior can only go so far, though, in mitigating the effects of the theatre's size and the unfortunate distance from the stage to the farther reaches of the auditorium. There are three discrete audience areas—the stalls, seating 656; the dress circle, seating 347; and the balcony, seating 499. Two main aisles trisect the stalls and dress circle, and three aisles divide the balcony. Many theatregoers consider the dress circle the best vantage point in the house, as the front section of the stalls is too close to the stage to allow for a comfortable full-stage view, and the seats towards the back of the stalls feel weighted down by the dress circle above. The balcony, which is even farther back and overhangs the dress circle's last rows, is severely raked, and from the rear, the stage appears small and insignificant. From the balcony's last rows, the upstage areas are cut off from view by the top of the proscenium arch.

The dress circle and the balcony wrap around the sides of the house, with dress boxes extending down towards the stage. The balcony and its boxes wrap around as well on the level above. At the back of the

dress circle, three booths accommodate the sound and lighting operators and their control boards as well as the director or assistant,
should either wish to take notes during a production.

The facade of the proscenium arch, although constructed of red
brick, is often masked in black cloth. A house curtain is not generally used, as it would allow the downstage portion of the thrust to spill
out unceremoniously beneath it. Instead, the stage is usually left open,
although British fire regulations require that each proscenium theatre
be equipped with a fire retardant curtain that must be tested and displayed to the audience at each performance by being lowered and
raised during intermission. The RST's fire curtain is chocolate colored, with the words "Safety Curtain" emblazoned in white.

The stage itself is amply equipped and of sufficient size to produce
large-cast Shakespearean shows. Still, according to the production
manager of the RST, Geoff Locker, there is never enough storage
space. The three Stratford theatres are all plagued with insufficient
storage, because several shows in the repertoire may be performing
in each theatre in the same week, and each show needs to store its sets
and props completely within allotted areas. To alleviate the problem,
a corrugated steel storage container is sometimes parked outside the
stage-left loading doors to house the overflow of scenery and props
from four or five productions.

The RST's proscenium opening is twenty-eight feet across, smaller
than that in most Broadway theatres. Although it provides those in
the front of the stalls with a stage view that does not uncomfortably
stretch the limits of peripheral vision, its small opening relative to the
length of the auditorium creates a sense of tunnel vision from the back
of the house. The height of the proscenium arch is twenty-six feet, but
venting ducts at the front of the proscenium reduce the effective height
by a few feet. The distance from the upstage edge of the proscenium
arch (sometimes called the plaster line) to the back wall measures forty-
five feet, and as the last fifteen feet are used for storage and not available for staging purposes, about thirty feet of stage depth is available
to the plaster line. The wings are large, as the theatre measures about
one hundred twenty feet from wall to wall backstage.

A stage thrust has been built downstage of the proscenium arch.
The real stage floor—known as "the teak," in reference to the type of

wood used for the deck—extends about three feet beyond the proscenium arch. The thrust, when it is used, is installed for all shows in that season, but it can be modified annually if the directorate chooses. A distance of sixteen feet from the plaster line is typical for an RST thrust. Similarly, the stage floor is almost always raked for an entire season. RSC directors and designers tilt the action towards the audience on an angled stage, largely to compensate for problematic sight lines in the balconies and the rear stalls. A rake of 1:15 (one inch of rise for every fifteen inches of distance upstage) is a common ratio employed. If a designer so chooses, an "anti-rake" can be constructed so that the stage floor is effectively leveled for a given show. The rake extends beyond the proscenium arch to the edge of the thrust, so that the downstage edge of the thrust is actually a foot lower than the stage floor. The rake and thrust are sometimes removed during the off-season when the RSC productions move on to other venues and a variety of local and touring companies perform in the theatre.

Prior to each season, decisions are made concerning the dimensions of the thrust and the rake. The thrust is usually built to extend straight downstage from the proscenium arch. Concrete slabs called "assemblies" flank both sides of the thrust to a height of three feet and extend to the side wall of the house. Generally, they are covered in black carpet. Sometimes the rake is built out over the assemblies so that they are raked as well. This decision, however, is left to each show's designer, and these assembly rake units can be set or struck for each show. Although the assemblies add to the sweep of the thrust and create a wider stage, they are not often used for scenery or primary staging, as they are visually weaker areas than more central parts of the thrust. A door at each side of the proscenium arch leads from backstage to the assemblies, although sometimes they are blocked for a play or for an entire season. At the offstage ends of the assemblies, black masking covers the brick walls at the sides of the auditorium closest to the stage. The deputy stage manager, the DSM, "calls," or cues, the show from the curtained-off house right dress circle box.

The stage floor is not fully equipped with traps leading to the basement. When the theatre was redesigned after the fire, it was decided that rather than install traps, it would be better to equip the theatre with the latest stage mechanics—lifts and rolling stages—that were then being employed in German opera houses. This technology was designed to facilitate rapid scene changes involving a large amount of scenery. Two elevators, or lifts, were built into the teak stage floor, one immediately upstage of the other. Slightly wider than the proscenium opening itself and about fifteen feet deep, these lifts, braced heavily with steel, could be lowered by motors to the first basement below the stage where scenery was loaded on. In either wing on stage level, two sections of a substitute teak floor, or rolling stages, were stored on tracks that extended to the side walls of the theatre. The onstage section normally functioned as the actual stage floor in the wing; due to a lack of foresight in planning the width of the theatre, the offstage section had to be stored perpendicular to the deck on tracks that curved up the side wall of the theatre. When the front stage lift was lowered, the first rolling section of flooring in either wing would be moved into place onstage, carrying new scenery to replace that which had just been lowered into the mezzanine below. This new section covered the hole created by the lift's descent, and the second, or offstage section of rolling stage, would follow to take the first section's place in the wing. After the scenery was shifted in the basement, the replacement floor sections would be rolled back into the wings, and the lift would rise up to stage level—or higher, since it could rise some ten feet above stage height.

This technology initially appeared to be a creative solution to the problem of slow and clumsy scene transitions and was intended to provided a degree of scenic fluidity not seen in other theatres. It was all very sensible, except that the machinery was never properly installed, and it eventually proved more cumbersome and problematic than anticipated. It was thus rarely used. In 1971, Trevor Nunn directed and Christopher Morley designed a slate of Shakespeare's four Roman plays—*Coriolanus, Julius Caesar, Antony and Cleopatra,* and *Titus Andronicus*—for which a new hydraulic stage floor was installed. It, too, proved problematic and was not used again. The rolling stage sections were eventually removed, and the offstage decks were filled in. The old tracks can still be seen, however, on the side walls. Newer, more efficient means of scene shifting are now employed, including computer-controlled winches and hydraulic lifts.

Simon Bowler is the head of technical services at the RSC. All the stage machinery used by the company in its Stratford and London theatres falls under his purview, as does the maintenance of the physical plant. He described the original devices and their use.

> Lots of masking had to be used to keep sight lines working and prevent the scenery in the wings from being seen by the audience. In the 1930s, there was no use of the stage downstage of the proscenium arch, no thrust, so the stage could be masked to allow for this. And upstage of the lifts was a big curved cyclorama, made of plaster on a metal frame, that was motorized and could be driven up and down the stage. There were star clusters built into it, eight or nine constellations that could be lit. The cyclorama was removed in the 1970s. The last time the lifts were used was when Robert Stephens played Falstaff in *Henry IV* back in 1992. The back lift has an electrical fault that we can't locate, and it's been out of service since. There are no drawings around, and we can't find the short. We're trying to find the money to buy a new control system, and then we'll overhaul it, because if we try to fix it we'll undoubtedly ruin it.[11]

Bowler's oversight of all the RSC stage machinery is a considerable challenge. Since the European Community (EC, now called the European Union, or EU) began to develop and enforce safety rules for all industry, including theatre, Bowler found his job an even greater challenge. "Now, every piece of equipment must be certified and documented, with a design trail we can trace. It's going to cause horrendous problems. There's a horrible amount of red tape, and it's all to keep faulty goods out of the market. Everything sold under EC rules has to have a design trail, and we're caught in this. It could be a nightmare."

Upstage left in the RST is the loading dock. Built for street level access, these twenty-two-foot-high double doors provide a means to load scenery from the street and allow direct access to the outdoor storage containers. Behind the upstage brick wall is the "back dock." This slightly asymmetrical corridor forms a natural boundary between the back of the RST and the Swan and is used as a crossover space by actors from both theatres. Beyond the stage left doorway to the back dock is a small corridor to the stage door and the Swan lobby. The upstage right door leads to the Green Room—a company canteen overlooking the Avon—and a staircase leading up to the two floors of dressing rooms.

On a loft ten feet above the deck of the back dock is the "band box," a thirty-by-twelve-foot partitioned space that houses the musicians who play at almost every RST performance. Live music is a critical component of the RSC experience, and a full staff of musicians is employed in each of the five theatres. In some productions, they play offstage, and in others, they are costumed and incorporated into the action.

There are two lower levels in the RST. The first, the mezzanine, provides a walkway around the framework of the lifts. The available space is used for storage. The actual basement, about twenty-five feet below the stage, houses the original lift mechanism and is also used for storage. The crew members have a room in a subbasement of the back dock, where they keep personal lockers and often play cards or relax between scene shifts.

The grid of the RST is sixty-five feet above the stage floor. Flying scenery is accomplished by use of a double purchase counterweight system, operated from a fly rail twenty-eight feet above the deck stage right. This double purchase system, working on a 2:1 ratio of counterweight to scenic weight, allows for shorter line sets that terminate at the fly rail, saving valuable space on the deck below. Designers often employ motorized computer-controlled winches in order to achieve greater synchronization of flying scenic pieces. There is a second gallery above the fly rail floor, used for access to stage lighting bridges as well as for the placement of the fly's winches. Two similar galleries are located at the same levels stage left. The grid comprises sixty working battens—or pipes—but the production manager, Geoff Locker, tries to save about eight to ten battens for scenery storage each season.

There are two levels for the fourteen dressing rooms located above the stage, of which four on the top floor are used for actors in Swan productions. Actors, many of whom perform in three or four shows a season, shuttle between the dressing rooms, depending on which theatre they're appearing in (The Other Place has its own dressing rooms). Stage managers ensure that makeup and other necessities are in the proper rooms for a given performance. There are wardrobe maintenance and wig rooms as well on these floors; both are usually shared by the two theatres, although the Swan has its own, smaller wardrobe room as well.

The RST was the first theatre in the United Kingdom to use a computer-controlled lighting board and utilizes an inventory of more than three hundred fifty lighting units in a season. Most of these are "point and shoot" units that take little time to adjust for each performance. Of the total number of instruments hung each season—and all RSC theatres hang repertory lighting plots, or "rep plots," designed by each theatre's master electrician—perhaps fifty units are available for designers to focus for individual shows. The rest are permanently focused and cannot be rehung or refocused by individual lighting designers during the season, although the colored gels and patterned gobo inserts used are changeable. Although instruments can be hung on pipes along the front of the dress circle and balcony, these positions are rarely used. Lighting designers don't favor the flat angles they offer and prefer to use the steeper-angled steel grids dropped from the ceiling of the auditorium. Horizontal steel structures attached to the proscenium arch and the balcony boxes afford reasonable "box boom," or sidefront, lighting positions. Over the stage, four lighting pipes are reached from one of three motorized bridges that span the width of the stage.

Geoff Locker, in addition to his post as production manager of the RST, is also the head of production and stage operations in Stratford, essentially a production supervisor for the technical workshops. Locker joined the RSC in 1976, and after ten years in a variety of technical positions at the RST and The Other Place became the Swan's first production manager, overseeing the design and installation of the technical facilities there. In 1991, he assumed the job of production manager at the RST. All five production managers at the RSC work under the direct supervision of the production controller, James Langley, who oversees production budgeting and planning for all company productions.

Aside from the complex job of planning any given production, Locker also must ensure that the RST continues as a viable, functioning theatre, a considerable task. As the RSC has grown since the 1970s, adding new theatres and new facilities, the need is more pressing than ever for greater coordination among administrators, artists, production and workshop staff, stage managers, and financial officers. A critical aspect of Locker's job is guaranteeing that each show in the repertoire has adequate space and facilities in the RST. Locker has to apportion space to designers well in advance of the submission of each design so that equity among the productions can be assured. "It's difficult to plan ahead for a design you've never seen, but you have to do it. That makes it important to not give away the farm with the first show in. It's an easy pitfall; after all, at that point, the theatre is in its pristine state and a designer sees all that empty space and doesn't envision the theatre six months later with four or five productions' scenery, props, and special effects stored up. You have to make sure that everyone is responsible from the outset."[12]

To safeguard the fair disbursement of space and facilities, Locker offers concrete advice to designers as they plan their sets. The production department has drafted a directive that each designer receives, outlining how much space is available, which line sets are to be used, and other factors. According to Locker, "One of our biggest concerns is storage. There is only so much space available in this theatre, and it is part of my job to ensure sufficient room for the functioning of the set that's up at the moment, as well as the four other sets in storage by the end of the season, when all the shows in the repertoire are up and running. Designers never want to hear about storage; their only concern, and rightly so, perhaps, is the needs of their show. But I have to juggle those needs, vital as they may be at the moment to that designer, with the needs of all the other shows and designers coming in later in the season. It's always a nightmare."

Despite the stress of overseeing the largest of the Stratford theatres and all the workshops, Locker enjoys running the obstacle course of a rotating repertory. "I like having my back up against the wall, being constantly challenged. It would be boring to do a straight, open-ended commercial run."

Locker may find his back up against a very different wall in years to come. In an RSC press release dated August 24, 1998, the company announced plans to modernize the RST. The decision, said Locker, was based on several factors. Actors frequently criticize its cavernous feel, lack of intimacy, the gap between stage and back of the house, and the difficulties in projecting to the far reaches of the auditorium (for more on this subject, see chapter 10). The amenities for audiences are deemed insufficient; there is always a long line waiting to use the bathrooms, and there is no proper place for audiences to have a drink or a quick sandwich during intermission. "Backstage, it's all outdated," said Locker. "The equipment is old, there is a problem with the pro- scenium arch, there is no adequate storage space, you can't light it properly, the get-in doors are too small for the sets. And in the audi- torium, the people in the balcony are too far away, and the sight lines are atrocious."[13]

The company recently received a grant of £755,000 from the gov- ernment's lottery, established in the early 1990s to subsidize capital improvements to cultural organizations, to fund a feasibility study to develop plans for a new theatre and/or to renovate the RST. Accord- ing to Locker, "I don't know yet what it would entail, although there's plenty of gossip. The Swan would stay where it is, but beyond that we don't know whether we'll leave the shell of the RST and remodel the inside or knock the whole thing down. We want to keep perform- ing, so we're speculating about everything, from tents to another building in town." One possible plan calls for the complete refurbish- ment of the RST and the building of another theatre closer to Clopton Bridge. In this scenario, The Other Place would be converted into an education center.

In 1999, artistic director Adrian Noble undertook steps to address some of the problems in the RST by implementing several modifica- tions to the stage configuration for the summer season. The rake was extended several feet, requiring the removal of the first three rows of seats in the stalls. The thrust was modified from its usual 1:15 ratio to a gentler 1:24 ratio, resulting in the downstage edge of the rake posi- tioned higher off the floor of the auditorium, at about eye level with people sitting in the new first row. Locker said, "We hope this will make a better connection between actor and audience." Michael Attenborough observed that the extension of the rake did much to mitigate the sense of audience remove from the action. "By the subtle shift of nine or ten feet, it's moved from being a two-room space to being a one-room space."[14] Locker remarked that one strong moti- vation for a new theatre with better sight lines is that the need for a rake might then be eliminated. Rakes, while often desirable for both sight lines and aesthetics, wreak havoc on the actors' and stagehands' legs and backs and have come under fire by performing arts unions around the world in the last decade. "We currently have to play on a rake, with the sight lines we have. However, Health and Safety is putting pressure on us to use a flat floor, but you can't use a flat floor and a thrust in the RST because it screws up the sight lines. I think sooner or later it will be illegal to play on a rake," said Locker.[15]

The side boxes in the dress circle and first balcony levels were extended to wrap around the front of the theatre to the proscenium arch. These new boxes, accessible by steps from the stage or by doors in the proscenium wall, were to be used for actors, musicians, and technical equipment, but not for audiences. The black masking that covered the proscenium arch and side walls was removed and the brick exposed. "The directors wanted to make a statement about a common look or feel for all of the plays in the summer season," noted Locker.

As the RSC attempted to produce two separate, shorter seasons for the first time in 1998–1999, they decided to employ the traditional rake, thrust, and configuration for the Winter Season. During the one week layover between the Winter Season and the Summer Festival in March, the considerable task of installing the new configuration and loading in the first show's sets was undertaken.

The Swan

The RST provides a traditional proscenium stage on which large-scale productions readily can be mounted, but its size and structure inhibit designers and directors who want to stage productions in a more dynamic and intimate actor-audience relationship. In 1949, Anthony Quayle recognized the need for a second Stratford theatre and drew up plans for a building that would emulate an Elizabethan stage. But the projected costs were so high that the plans were abandoned.[16] In the 1970s, The Other Place was created as a flexible black box for experimental work, but this jury-rigged theatre could not fulfill the company's needs for a midsized auditorium in which to present the works of Shakespeare's contemporaries. Box office figures factor heavily in deciding which venue best serves each production, and the clear indications were that the overwhelming majority of tourists who visit Stratford to see only one show flock to a production of Shakespeare. In order to accommodate those numbers, it was obvious that the RST needed to continue as a space primarily dedicated to those works. A third theatre was the solution.

Trevor Nunn, who became artistic director in 1968, had a great affinity for the old Conference Hall. The handsomely decorated rehearsal room adjacent to the RST had been built within the burnt-out hulk of the original Memorial Theatre, as the blaze had spared the theatre's outer walls as well as the Picture Gallery and the library. As part of the reconstruction after the fire, a grand public hall was built on the old theatre's site, which abutted the back wall of the new Memorial Theatre. Although the room was popular with local groups for meetings and civic dances, by the late 1940s it had been taken over by the theatre as a rehearsal space. It seemed logical to Nunn, as the RSC grappled with its needs to expand in the 1970s, that if money could be found and adequate designs developed, the Conference Hall would be an ideal location for a third theatre. The RST and the new theatre could share dressing rooms, administrative offices, and ancillary services.

Nunn asked RSC associate designer John Napier to develop plans for a new theatre; Napier was joined by Michael Reardon's architectural firm on the project. Since the new theatre was to be built within the egg-shaped shell of the old and had to conform to those spatial limitations, they decided it would be both sensible and desirable to utilize some of the features of similarly shaped Elizabethan or Jacobean theatres. The RSC designers and directors wanted a single space that could contain both actors and audience without the artificial separation of the proscenium arch, a feature absent in Elizabethan and Jacobean playhouses.[17] A model was produced of a brick-walled theatre with a long, slightly elevated wooden thrust stage, stall seating on the floor, and galleries of exposed pine stacked above the stalls. It was an inviting, warm, vital space, full of possibilities for dynamic staging. The process, however, stalled there.

The funding for such a theatre was outside the purview of the Arts Council's subsidy and would have to be generated entirely by the RSC. The company, however, was unable to raise the money, either at home or in America, where Nunn visited with the hope that the pockets of the American Friends of the RSC might prove deep enough to provide what the British patrons would not. The oil company Amoco had originally promised to fund the construction, but the huge expense of cleaning up the oil spill of its tanker *Amoco Cadiz* off the Brittany coast forced it to withdraw its commitment to the RSC. No other money could be found.

It appeared that the Swan would spend eternity as a cardboard model relegated to a display case in the RSC Picture Gallery. But in true storybook fashion, a knight in shining armor rescued the project. According to what is now legend in the RSC, American philanthropist and oil millionaire Frederick Koch was visiting Stratford in 1983, sought shelter from the rain within the Picture Gallery, and noticed the model. He inquired as to its purpose and was told of the now defunct plans to build a new theatre. Intrigued, he made some inquiries and a few days later met with Trevor Nunn to discuss the feasibility of funding the theatre in its entirety, at a cost of more than £1.5 million. RSC Collection curator Brian Glover, who participated in the events, elaborated on the story, filling in some of the gaps in the legend.

> I wanted £150 for some special glazing material for an ultraviolet filter I was working with. I was in general manager David Brierley's office, and he said to me, "you won't believe this, but I have a check here for £1,000 from a Frederick Koch, who is one of our Friends of the Theatre." I made some inquiries about him and found out he was in oil. I wrote him thanking him for his contribution and told him to ring me up if he came into town, and I'd show him what we'd done with it.
>
> Maybe six months later, I got a call from him, in a very quiet voice, telling me he was coming to visit in a week, and perhaps we could get together. He came, saw the exhibit, and was very knowledgeable about art and theatre. After that, we would meet on his annual trips. After three years or so, I got a call telling me he was coming, at a time that I was trying to put together an exhibition about staging the plays of Shakespeare. I was going to use Michael Reardon's model for the now-defunct new theatre. When Koch came to visit, he saw the model and inquired about it. I told him it had been planned for the site of the Conference Hall. He asked how much it would cost, and I told him about £1.5–2 million. He said, "Right, well, could we have tea after the show?" He asked during tea if it would be possible to get him a revised costing. I called the architects on Monday, and we began talking about it, about putting a new rehearsal room on top so we wouldn't lose that valuable space, and I kept Mr. Koch informed. By Wednesday, one third of the money had been deposited by Koch into an English bank to get the ball rolling. I think Trevor was so surprised and flabbergasted! Koch's identity wasn't revealed initially,

not until the official opening, on 26 November 1986, seven months after the first show actually premiered.[18] The Queen came to open the theatre, and that day Koch got on the radio and revealed how he and I had met and discussed the project. The next day, he rang up and asked if he could come round. He drove up in a simple little car with his mom and a dog and some clothes in it, and concerned that there was no place to park asked if he could park on the gravel. He had just built the theatre, for God's sake—he could park anywhere![19]

The RSC administration and governors were stunned by Koch's generosity. Although the total cost of funding has been kept from the public, it is generally thought that it was close to £2 million, which included the construction of the Ashcroft rehearsal room above the auditorium.[20] This was topped off by a vaulting new roof designed to add a soaring, festive air to the skyline of the theatre that, according to architect Reardon, suggests a circus tent or jousting pavilion.[21]

The audience enters the Swan either from Waterside through the old Picture Gallery, spared in its entirety by the fire, or from the Avonbank gardens. The Gallery serves as an antechamber to the Swan, its first floor housing a book and souvenir stall as well as a bar and rest rooms. A staircase leads to the RSC Collection above. Before the 1926 fire, the upper foyer arched gracefully over a narrow roadway below and connected the Picture Gallery and the original theatre. The lower foyer was subsequently built to provide access to the new Swan. An intermediate hallway on the lower level leads to the theatre itself.

The honey-colored Douglas fir from which the theatre's galleries are constructed, the light red brick walls, and the mauve-brown seats provide a warm, inviting ambiance. It is a theatrical environment in which the audience feels welcome and a part of the performance. The height of the theatre, the sense of enclosure, and the proximity of the performers all lend a creative tension to the audience-performer dynamic. Directors exploit the spatial relationships by staging entrances and exits through the audience, utilizing the exposed staircases, and encouraging the actors to play to the highest levels of the audience looming in the galleries above. Michael Bogdanov's roisterous 1993 production of Goldoni's commedia dell'arte classic, *The Venetian Twins,* took full advantage of the space in its use of actor "plants" in the audience, considerable actor-audience interplay, and as much hoopla offstage as on. An exhilarating, almost dangerous sense of farcical expectation was engendered. Adrian Noble's heralded 1995 production of Chekhov's *The Cherry Orchard,* on the other hand, demonstrated equally effective—if more sedate—use of the space. The production was restrained, both physically and emotionally, and the fine line between actor and audience was never breached. The longing, heartbreak, and joy of the exquisitely drawn characters were intimately experienced by the audience.

The Swan allows some degree of flexibility in production, although the general configuration is maintained for an entire season. The theatre was designed with the specific purpose of presenting shows that—given the lack of a fly system, wings, or significant backstage storage—would not need to depend on large-scale design and complex technical production. However, it is a theatrical truism that designers will attempt to fill any given theatre space, and the Swan has seen its share of productions in which the scenery has overwhelmed the theatre. Stuart Gibbons, the Swan's production manager, commented: "The Swan was originally conceived to house 'prop and costume' shows—that is, plays that relied primarily on those design elements and shied away from overreliance on large scenic elements. The space is really quite fragile in that respect, and we don't have the storage space, crew, technical facilities, or budgets to produce larger scenic shows. But despite this, there has been a natural evolution towards bigger shows. Just recently the administration has taken a firmer hand in guiding directors and designers towards more reasonably sized productions. *The Venetian Twins,* for example, was actually designed on a much larger scale and was sized down considerably before it was approved for construction."[22]

The basic wall-to-wall dimensions of the theatre are about fifty by sixty-five feet. The upstage wall adjoins the back dock crossover of the RST. Each designer may choose to design a false rear scenic wall downstage of this to create a small, semipermanent backstage area between the two. The concrete base floor of the theatre is fully trapped, and a three-sided, wood-planked, and trapped stage, slightly less than two feet high, is erected above it. This stage in its most traditional configuration yields a playing space of approximately nineteen feet wide by thirty-three feet deep. The front of the stage narrows at the downstage corners where the voms, or aisles used by actors for access to the stage, cut in from the audience to the stage.

Seating configurations in the stalls can vary depending upon the set, but an audience of close to five hundred total is the norm. Regardless of the configuration, the most attractive feature of the Swan is that no audience member sits more than a few feet from the action. The stage is surrounded by three rows of seats—cushioned and backed brown upholstered benches—on the two long side sections and by seven rows on the short front section. The first rows sit on the "true" floor level, twenty-one inches below the deck of the wooden stage. A wood-slatted, waist-high railing behind the stall seats, with openings at the aisles, encloses the stall section. The stall seats and the platforms on which they are mounted are in turn removable. When the Royal Court's production of *Road* by Jim Cartwright was presented during the 1987 Winter Visitors' Season, all the stall seats were removed and the area was planked over, allowing the audience to walk around the set in what the British refer to as a "promenade production."[23]

Behind the stall railing is another row of seats. This first gallery is at the same height as the wooden stage floor. Directly behind this is a perimeter walkway, "the drum," some six feet wide, surrounding the theatre on the main level. Audience members entering through the main doors in the stage right side of the house use this walkway to access their seats; it is also used frequently by actors. Two aisles, or voms, lead from the drum to the stage at its downstage corners.

Wooden columns support the galleries above the stalls. The second and third galleries, built directly above the first, accommodate two rows of seats each; the third and fourth galleries extend around the full perimeter of the space. The upstage section of the third gallery can be used as a musicians' loft or as part of the acting area; the fourth gallery, twenty-seven feet above the floor of the theatre and encompassing all four sides, houses the stage manager and the lighting and sound technicians, and it offers access to three catwalks that span the stage. Behind the upstage wall on the third gallery level are a musicians' room, a recording studio, a master electrician's room, and a sound engineer's office. The upper galleries are reached by wooden staircases, exposed to the audience, at either upstage end of the drum. Stairways backstage and in the house provide additional entrances.

The grid itself offers adequate overhead lighting positions, and a batten for lighting units circles the theatre from below the third gallery. Master electrician and frequent Swan lighting designer Wayne Dowdeswell usually installs about two hundred seventy-five instruments. The policy of hanging a rep plot, from which only a designated number of instruments can be refocused or recolored by each show's lighting designer, applies in all the RSC theatres. If designers were able to refocus all the instruments in the lighting rig for their shows, changeovers between performances of different shows in the repertoire could never be accomplished in the few hours allotted.

The Swan was intentionally designed without a flying system. Frequently, however, designers and directors choose to fly chandeliers, props, small scenic pieces, and even the occasional actor. To accommodate them, a few relatively simple solutions can be employed, such as using a winch or rigging yachting lines for flying smaller pieces.

The basement serves as the primary location for scenic storage during the season. However, air-conditioning duct work generally hampers the easy movement of scenery, especially taller pieces, during changeovers, and a small container is often placed outside for a season in order to offer more storage space. In the downstage section of the deck and theatre floor, a trap, roughly six feet square, has been cut. The flooring and stage sections can be removed and a hydraulic lift installed to raise or lower actors or scenery.

The flames that engulfed the original theatre still burn in people's memories in Stratford, and that has engendered a cautious approach to the use of fire in the spaces. The wooden galleries in the Swan are more susceptible to fire than the plaster and brick of the RST, and although fire codes are strictly enforced in all spaces, the Swan is kept under special supervision. The wooden structure was coated with a transparent flameproofing material at an expense of some £90,000. The fire marshal is consulted every time a set might impinge on audience exits or when the production might use pyrotechnics. Initially, even so much as a lit cigarette was forbidden by the fire marshal, but in recent years, there has been a cautious relaxation of the policy.

The Swan opened in April 1986 with a performance of *Two Noble Kinsmen*. The theatre was an immediate success with artists, critics, and audiences. According to artistic director Adrian Noble, "It's an extraordinary space. There's a harmony between actor and audience, a sense of occasion created from the moment you walk in. I think it reveals plays at their best, and plays *sound* good in it."[24]

The Other Place

A few hundred yards down Waterside and south of the Swan, at the riverbank of the serene Avonbank gardens, a hand-cranked chain skiff ferry still makes the brief crossing of the Avon for fifty pence per person when weather allows. Across Waterside stands The Other Place. The "other-ness" of this theatre is more than just nomenclature; it reflects an explicit philosophical approach to production that distinguishes it from the two theatres down the road. The articulation and implementation of this artistic policy over the years have caused the little experimental theatre to undergo significant shifts in policy, programming, and location.

In 1963, the company erected an aluminum hut on a site a few hundred feet down the street, nearer the RST. First used as a storage space, then a rehearsal hall, Michel St. Denis's actors' studio, and a Stratford home for the RSC's short-lived educational touring company, Theatregoround, this hut became The Other Place in 1974.

In 1967, a twenty-year-old director arrived at Stratford as an assistant to John Barton, one of the company's associate directors. This energetic and visionary young woman, Buzz Goodbody, in just a few short years established a reputation as a director of challenging, politically charged pieces for the RSC and helped to orient the theatre in a new direction. These works, most notably her 1971 staging of Trevor Griffiths's *Occupations,* starring Ben Kingsley and Patrick Stewart, were first performed in a London studio—The Place—that was employed by the RSC for a few seasons of experimental work. And though she was committed to the works of new playwrights as a means of galvanizing public awareness of key social issues, she also found considerable sustenance in the complex politics of Shakespeare's plays.[25]

Goodbody saw enormous potential in this dilapidated Stratford hut. She convinced artistic director Trevor Nunn to allow her to develop a season of plays there on the most meager of budgets. She was fervent in her belief that shoestring budgets would ensure the new theatre's financial stability and continuity, and the first shows were allotted no more than £150 each. According to her manifesto, the new studio would serve six purposes: to allow younger actors to get better roles, to allow assistant directors an opportunity to work on their own projects, to perform new plays by contemporary writers, to produce more experimental work than was possible in the RST, to reach a new audience, and to serve the community.[26]

Goodbody realized that she would be challenged in finding audiences in Stratford that would attend new, experimental work. She characterized the place as a "sleepy Midlands market town that has come to be a shrine for international theatre" and its residents as conservative white-collar workers. But she counted on the fact that a large local student population and the many tourists who were unable to get tickets to RST productions might be induced to form the nucleus of a new audience. Without a significant base of blue-collar workers or hip younger audiences attuned to the fringe works now becoming increasingly popular in other cities, Goodbody realized that the staple of this new theatre would have to be Shakespeare.[27]

In 1974, The Other Place opened with Goodbody's specially edited production of *King Lear* designed for students. That opening followed a heated debate within the RSC administration as to the advisability—from both fiscal and artistic standpoints—of undertaking a formally announced season at a second theatre. The crucial point was that the theatre had to be financially self-sufficient. The theatre's name, chosen from a long list of submissions, captured the simplicity and ingenuousness implicit in Goodbody's venture and forged a link with the pioneering work she did at The Place in London. Implicit in the name was that an alternative approach would be employed in the work that was done there.[28]

A year later, Buzz Goodbody committed suicide. A shaken Trevor Nunn refused to let this tragedy sound the death knell for the new theatre, and initially he took over the supervision of The Other Place himself. He later handed the reins to Ron Daniels, and a succession of RSC directors has overseen the work done there to this day, with Steven Pimlott presently in charge. The work and schedule were integrated into the repertoire system employed in the main house. Company members were generally eager to work in this venue that stood in stark contrast to the RST. They were now offered the chance to work in other genres and styles that were unavailable in the main house, given the imposed programmatic constraints of the Shakespearean canon. The new theatre's three-quarter configuration thrust performers virtually into the audience's lap and engendered a different set of expectations for actors and spectators alike. The stylistic adjustments to performance and the cross-pollination between theatres kept the actors artistically vibrant. Ironically, because company members so eagerly embraced The Other Place, by the early 1980s the little shack, as run-down as it was, had lost much of its coarse, countercultural aura and had become an integrated part of the RSC establishment.

Work continued apace during subsequent RSC seasons, but the building—never designed as a performance space—continued to deteriorate. It was decided that a new theatre should be built, one that could accommodate not only the new Other Place but the additional rehearsal rooms that would allow the company to rehearse plays simultaneously for its three theatres. A temporary, modular rehearsal building had been built next to The Other Place in 1985, during the construction of the Swan and the Ashcroft rehearsal hall, but now that the RSC had three theatres, the company needed to expand again. The Stratford tennis club, just down the street from the original Other Place and next to an eighteenth-century grain barn, was secured as the new site, and the clubhouse was converted into a home for the RSC's education department. Swan architects Michael Reardon and Tim Furby were hired to design the building.

The new facility, which opened on August 7, 1991, at a cost of about £1.5 million, is a simple red brick affair. The theatre is set back from the sidewalk a few dozen feet behind a small stone patio formed by the placement of a few large wooden flower planters and a kiosk announcing the performances. The building houses the box office, administrative offices, three dressing rooms, the maintenance wardrobe room, the scene dock, and two rehearsal halls. The adjacent grain barn, connected to the main structure by a short corridor, was converted into a two-story hospitality facility. The lower level is used as a lobby during intermissions—there are bathrooms and a refreshment stand—and its walls are often decorated with photos and production notes. Upstairs is a comfortable greenroom for the actors.

The audience enters from the street through double doors and passes through a tiny foyer into the theatre. This theatre's greatest feature is its flexibility in accommodating a variety of audience-stage relationships. Frequently, the theatre has been used in a thrust configuration, seating about 130 on the main level, although it can be arranged in a number of ways: full arena, traverse staging—with audience sections on only two sides—or, as it is currently configured, with a single bank of seats facing upstage accommodating 113. The theatre frequently used a second, gallery level, eight feet above the deck, with two rows of an additional 106 seats, but problematic sight lines from above forced their removal for the 1998 season. In keeping with The Other Place's goal to produce theatre that is more in the spirit of fringe theatre, the seats are unnumbered, and audience members seat themselves on a first-come, first-served basis.

The walls are built of a light-colored brick. A false wall is sometimes constructed for masking and scenic purposes and is set just downstage of the back wall. The enclosed scenic dock behind it is used as a cross-over. Actors can enter through one of nine sets of doors set in the four walls. The two sets of doors in the wall to the left of the main entrance open onto a hallway that leads to a staircase and the second floor's three communal dressing rooms. At the end of the hallway are the Michel St. Denis and Buzz Goodbody rehearsal rooms. The former is used primarily for Swan shows, the latter for Other Place productions. RST shows usually rehearse in the Ashcroft Room atop the Swan. These rehearsal halls were designed with the size of the theatres in mind and are bright, wood-paneled, high-ceilinged rooms with good acoustics and well-sprung floors.

The two sets of doors in the wall to the right of the main entrance open onto a covered, open-sided walkway; actors must walk—or run—outside the building to enter through these or the center doors. A car park is located next to the walkway. On days when RST or Swan shows end earlier than Other Place shows, a stream of audience members can be seen heading towards their cars when those doors are opened during performances. The deck is trapped in a T pattern six feet deep, accessible from the scenic dock. The grid above features a catwalk system for easy access to lighting positions and can also be used by actors or to hang simple flying rigs.

The scenic dock upstage is used for minor repairs and scenery storage. According to John Bluck, who has been a carpenter at The Other Place since 1974, the dock's height unfortunately is about six feet lower than the grid height of seventeen feet, so scenic pieces and drops of full stage height cannot be stored upright in the dock. In addition, if the crew needs to work on scenery during the day, they must often move pieces outside to have access to more space, and the noise can be heard in the house during rehearsals or matinees. Bluck also pointed out that the intricate system of air ducts below the theatre's ceiling prevents the efficient rigging of adequate flying systems in the grid.

Trevor Nunn's production of *Othello,* starring Willard White, Imogen Stubbs, and Ian McKellen, was the last show produced in the old Other Place in the summer of 1989. The new theatre opened on August 7, 1991, with Nunn's production of Pam Gems's version of the Heinrich Mann novel *The Blue Angel.* Chris Parry designed the lighting for both productions.

Parry, a lighting designer who won Tony and Olivier awards for *The Who's Tommy,* has been associated with the RSC since 1976, when he joined the stage lighting crew at the RST. He has subsequently designed more than twenty shows for the company. In 1988, he moved to California to teach and pursue a design career in the United States, although he returns to England regularly to design at the RSC and the National. His RSC credits include *Les Liaisons Dangereuses* as well as Adrian Noble's heralded productions of *The Winter's Tale, A Midsummer Night's Dream,* and *The Plantagenets.* Parry recalled the time he first worked in the old Other Place in the early 1980s, when master electrician and designer Leo Leibovici, who created the lighting rig there, went on vacation.

The old theatre had a homemade feel. You were seeing theatre that was being staged in spite of the building. That's not to say the building was unfriendly—it was very cozy, actually—but it wasn't designed as a theatre. Everything had to be adjusted to make it into one.

But it was informal, especially in contrast to the main house. It felt flexible, full of possibilities, but also full of problems for the designers and crew. If you looked at the grid, it seemed like a cat's cradle of cables, ropes, and gaffer's tape up there, all from years of improvising. The entire lighting rig grew just like Topsy. As a result, some

people didn't want to work there. It wasn't as well supported technically as the RST, and you felt very much on your own down there,
isolated a bit from the rest of the company. But that could actually
be very exciting—it gave you a certain sense of freedom to experiment. You were more or less left to your own devices; there was no
real supervision, and you had to be a self-starter to succeed there.[29]

Parry credits Jean Moore, the first administrator of The Other Place,
and Bronwyn Robertson, her successor, with setting the tone and
atmosphere so crucial in maintaining Buzz Goodbody's vision. But
Parry noted that the theatre's very attractiveness and utilitarian nature almost did it in.

> It was in danger of destroying itself. We were all trying to do more
> than the space could handle. You always were tempted to do some-
> thing bigger and better than the last time. Although shows had got-
> ten more complex, the audiences' expectations for design grandeur
> and comfort were still lower than they were for a show at the main
> house. The "regulars" brought seat cushions with them. There was
> no air-conditioning, no fans, and they expected to broil in the sum-
> mer. In the winter, they knew they'd freeze; we had only a few space
> heaters mounted on the ceiling, and although they didn't get very hot,
> if you looked up you thought you were in a toaster. And when it
> rained!—the building had a tin roof, and the downpour just about
> drowned out the poor actors. You couldn't flush the toilet during the
> show or it would be heard; crew had to walk through the dressing
> room and interrupt the actors to get to the control booth. It was very
> primitive, but the audiences loved it.

When the decision was made to build a new theatre, the staff was
concerned that it might not reflect the dynamics of its predecessor.
Parry, however, thinks that architects Michael Reardon and Tim Furby
did a superb job in designing the new space. "They were very successful at reproducing, without actually copying, the old theatre's interior ambiance. The old building had neutral black walls, and the new
has a warm red brick, but there is still much in common. From the
audience's perspective, there is still the same feel, the same relationship.
From the technical point of view, the new space is a huge improve-
ment. It was custom-built, so it's considerably more user friendly."

Tony Hill is a former high school drama teacher whose first main
job at the RSC was heading the education department. In 1990, Noble

appointed him director of projects to produce the season at The Other Place. In 1995, Hill articulated two problems that have beset the small theatre, one involving the notion of flexible space, the other indicative of changing attitudes towards minimalism.

The producing work is good fun here, but there's another problem wrapped up with the theatre, and that's the folk memory and the reality of the old space. The folk memory is that the old TOP was this interesting tin hut where it was hot in the summer and cold in the winter and where simple yet innovative shows were done. It's like freedom and liberty, you can't be against it, you have to be for it, but so what? Certain people remember that, and so they either dislike this auditorium because they think there's something really virtuous about having to get in line in the rain to get in or about being uncomfortable in the theatre, which I can't see. It seems to me if the theatre's uncomfortable and you can't do anything about it, okay, you put up with it—and we've got bad sight lines in the new space from upstairs. But I believe you fix what you can. I want to ease that problem, I want to rip out the balconies and put bleachers in, not because I'm particularly fond of them, but I've gotten fed up with chairing production meetings where we argue about whether we can take this or that seat out, can we reblock a scene to avoid this bit of seating, and it's a colossal waste of time. The problem is we say that this is a flexible space, and it's patently not, it's an inflexible space, and if we want to make it flexible, we have to remake it.

Another problem, and this is a worldwide phenomenon, is that young designers especially are no longer attracted by the notion of "poor theatre"; they don't want to do things in black boxes. Why should they? They want to do more elaborate things. Now, I think it's great to have the space and staff and budgets challenged; I think they should be pushed, but if what we're trying to do is put up Swansized shows in a house of this size, then we rack up all sorts of problems. First, because people are hard working, they want to make it work in here, and it burns everyone out. And then you've got the run crew problem. With a three-person stage management team and a two-person stage crew, two on wigs and makeup, two on wardrobe, it's a hell of a time running the show with that crew. We have to try to find a creative way of dealing with all that.[30]

To a certain extent, Hill's concerns about flexibility were addressed in 1998 when the theatre's balcony was removed. His concern about production excess in a theatre understaffed and ill-equipped to handle it is the greater issue, one that demands considerable diplomatic skills as the producer seeks to establish and maintain reasonable production parameters.

Bronwyn Robertson, The Other Place administrator, has been associated with the RSC since 1971, when she worked in the press department, and with The Other Place since 1980, when she assumed her current position after Jean Moore, the founding administrator, retired. "My job description, in 'cold terms,' is to administer the building according to the artistic policy and per the budgets available," she said.[31] But it is clear that Robertson's passion for the theatre transcends the temperature of the wording in her brief. She was instrumental in overseeing the development and planning of the new facility, supervises the staffing and building maintenance, and with the theatre's artistic director—now Steven Pimlott—develops strategies to make The Other Place accessible to touring companies, conferences, and other events. "I used to work twenty-hour days in the beginning," she admitted, "but I couldn't do that indefinitely. I handed off the production management and front-of-house responsibilities to the staff down the road," she explained, nodding in the direction of the RST. "It was necessary for me to do so, but it brought The Other Place a bit closer to the other theatres and helped erase some of the differences." It was obvious that she was ambivalent about this development.

> It's different now, with the new theatre. Bricks and mortar have made it different. The expectations, both the theatre's and the audiences, are different from those in a tin shack. The old philosophy was "we have a right to fail." We were trying to find a new audience, to do high-class plays at cheap prices; it was shoestring theatre on a tiny budget, and the space was consistent with the philosophy and the goals. Everybody worked differently when they were at The Other Place; stage managers had to prop the shows themselves with virtually no money.
>
> During the '80s, things started to change. There was more money for shows, so there were more glamorous productions. We had established a solid audience base. The "regulars" actually liked the "pioneering spirit" and didn't mind queuing up in the rain. But we had to shut down the old theatre; romantic though it might have seemed, it was falling apart, and it wasn't worth the money it would have cost to bring it up to code. We needed to make some changes, like installing decent heating and air-conditioning systems.

The RSC charged the architects to improve the facilities when they designed the new theatre but not to unnecessarily increase them. The addition of new rehearsal spaces was essential, but the use of communal dressing rooms was continued, and a small office was built rather than a larger one. Reardon and his colleagues realized that the most important factor to consider was the audience-actor relationship, and they attempted to maintain the intimacy that had been a hallmark of the original theatre. They spoke to actors, audience members, and other artists, and all gave essentially the same answer: intimacy was crucial, and the immediacy of the event should be preserved by requiring audiences to enter the theatre directly from the street, without passing through a lobby. It is generally accepted that the architects were successful in duplicating the essential dynamics of intimacy and simplicity of the old space. But there were trade-offs, such as the poor sight lines from the gallery and the loss of the homespun ambiance. What some of the RSC staff didn't foresee was that it would be impossible to stand still and recapture the past. But Bronwyn Robertson described the predicament.

> With a new facility, the old system of expectations didn't work. Now, queuing in the rain for unnumbered seats is no good. It has gotten a bit stuffy, and we have to turn that around. But the real problem is that we're too close in style and methodology to the other theatres. We're no longer the "bastard stepchild" that we used to be, and while we've gained bigger budgets and more support, we've lost that aura and that sensibility. We're still doing Shakespeare, still doing classics and new plays, but we're doing fewer productions than before and fewer workshops and experimental things. In the last few seasons, the company has produced its own little "fringe" festival of workshops in the rehearsal rooms when all the shows in the repertoire are already opened, and it's been very exciting.
>
> I'd like to see more performances of the shows we do and like to see other things brought in. There's something sad about a theatre that's dark. I'd like to see more work done for young audiences. We do almost no children's work. In the old Other Place, we had a Saturday morning children's storytelling session, but it was discontinued a few years ago. Perhaps we could commission a playwright to write a new show for kids.
>
> I'd also like to make The Other Place more available to the community, in keeping with Buzz Goodbody's vision. We should have our

actors do volunteer work, like "confidence building workshops" for high school graduates on job hunts. We should invite school groups to perform their Christmas shows here. We need to really get the name of The Other Place out into the community. It's amazing, but some of the local people still don't know we exist!

Robertson's concerns were shared by others in the administration, but a key stumbling block was the inability of one small theatre to be all things to all people. Tony Hill articulated some of the core problems that faced The Other Place as it continued to define its own identity.

The problem in practice is that if we made TOP into just a laboratory for creative exploration by the company but didn't open it for public performances, as some members would like to see done, then it loses credibility as a building, as a theatre. But if you put on five productions a year, as the company sometimes does, then where do you do the experimentation and put on the other work? You've got no time. So, what we decided was that we would split the difference, we'd compromise, we'd probably go for only three or four shows per annum. This would leave us some time and money where we could do other work. So far, the theory is very good, because you're saying, "we will have real theatre coming out of this building, we'll have vibrant, exciting work which is suitable to the space."

The problem is that even though you then have release time and extra money, you don't have the actors. Because when you have a repertory system and an ensemble company, then what happens is that whether they're performing in a show here or not, whether they're rehearsing a show here or not, the first eight or nine months in a twelve-month season are spent in rehearsals. So, that means that, sure, you can slot in the name of a Polish or Japanese director that you'd like to do a showcase one Sunday, or you can do some one-off piece [one-time performance] occasionally, but you can't do substantial pieces of work. And so what we found was that we did one hell of a lot of work at the back end of a season. You'd come up here, and there was a workshop on. But what seemed impossible to do was to translate Adrian's brief to use this building to develop the skills of our artists in a year-round program.

And so what's happened over the last few years is a couple of things. On one front, what we're doing is investing more time and effort into some of the production work and some of the producing function. But it's like all handcrafted pieces of work, it's amazingly time-consuming, expensive, and you are brought up in the end against questions like "Well sure, but if we can find the £200,000 to do this, or whatever it might be, should we spend the money on that or should we spend it on this?" So, you're back into value judgments, which are quite difficult, and the time that it absorbs, because it doesn't neatly fit in. I don't think that the RSC is a kind of culture factory, where you just stamp the product out. But there is a kind of production line mentality, whereby you have production manager A and workshop B and producer C, and you can put the components together, and if you've got good enough people doing their jobs, you can say, "Do your job on this," and they'll do it. If you then come up with a project that you can't neatly pass over to them, we find that we're centering that work on different people. At that point, at least, you're in danger of trying to reinvent the wheel, and at worst, you're in danger of providing too much focus on something that maybe in itself is inherently not worth it. It's not as bleak as that, but we've spent a lot of time looking at the actual work that is going on here and how we're doing it, but it's still actually impossible to solve the problem, and I think we're aware we're not solving it. In the meantime, it's not a disaster, the building is not empty, there are plenty of things happening here, there's lots of life, but it's not the life, the activity that I think I'd like to see, that I think other people would like to see.[32]

At the time Hill spoke, he had reached the end of his excitement in producing for the company and soon moved back to a position in the education department. To address the issues Hill raised and to reexamine the artistic purpose and possibilities of The Other Place, Adrian Noble re-created the position of director of The Other Place in early 1996 and appointed the newly named associate director Katie Mitchell to the post, which she occupied until late 1998. Barely in her thirties, the intensely committed young director, responsible for several striking productions in The Other Place, realized that her appointment to the RSC's administration could offer her more than just a salary and a title; it could allow her the chance to revitalize The Other Place as a venue in which the usual RSC parameters of plays and process were redefined. One of her immediate concerns was to articulate for the company and the public the primary artistic functions that the black box theatre should assume. "When it was just the main house and The Other Place in Stratford, The Other Place had a very clear function. But as soon as you put the Swan in there, you had to be very careful you didn't duplicate and make one of them redundant. That was always the problem, the tendency in certain years to produce pieces that could have played the Swan. I think it short-circuited the audience's understanding of the function of our theatre, which is why eventually we thought we should go for programming that was very much engaged with young people's issues, as a way of creating a different sense, a different definition, and creating an open-door policy across the board."[33]

Mitchell, who credits Hill with being an exceptional and passionate administrator, was aware that The Other Place needed an overseer who was a working artist and understood firsthand the problems and processes of the people in the rehearsal room. But the dual talents of artist and administrator rarely coexist comfortably in the same person, said Mitchell. "You might argue that artists should never be given any administrative function beyond their rehearsal rooms, and why people think that because they can direct a play they can also run something is complete madness. You might put an administrative personality in place because the artist is eventually going to go mad, like I did, but finally it's very hard if you don't know what the experience is all about, if all you respond to is a product, and you actually have no inkling of how difficult it is to make it, the complexity of what goes on in rehearsals."

Mitchell resigned her position as director of The Other Place in fall of 1998—she retained the title artistic adviser—in part because of the administrative demands, but her tenure helped to continue the necessary evolution of The Other Place's role within the RSC.

> I wanted to use it [The Other Place] as an access point to get my generation of directors, who weren't associated so much with classical work, in through to the main belly of the company, to the main house. There seems to be a lot of directors of my generation who can be rather scathing about the RSC, without having experienced all that it can offer. I think it's an "attitude vogue," because it's not really supported by practical experience. One key thing at The Other Place was to create a creative haven for my contemporaries. We created a very strong philosophy that we would bend whichever way we needed to as far as we could, even if we went into conflict with the ideology of the overall organization to get the artist what he or she wanted. That manifested itself in terms of being more flexible in terms of design deadlines, so we could cope with a design being developed organically.

We had to develop a remit and draw up guidelines so we could say to people who brought us projects, "No, we can't do this, because we've done projects on this and can't repeat them." We would bring over major practitioners, like Augusto Boal. We would have a centerpiece that would in effect be Stanislavsky work, a counterpoint to the big preoccupation of the RSC of language for language's sake, and we would do interactive work with the community, when possible, with blind and deaf and handicapped people—although in fact we never got that initiative off the ground. And we would try to create a situation where the doors of the building would be open to the community, so we made strong contacts with the local sixth-form college; they're now resident at The Other Place when we're dark there. We would do big coproductions with companies that specialize in children's theatre over the Christmas period.

Finally, we came down to realizing that The Other Place provided the actor with what, sadly, because of the scale of it, nothing else at the RSC could provide. We proposed several things for them: big projects as well as small, specialist work like Alexander training or a cappella work, physical training. We reacted to whatever they wanted, so if someone wanted a certain practitioner, we would bring that person in. We also tried to open the doors and look at the meeting ground of other mediums, and we developed a video facility to train actors and technicians. We made about six short films, very high quality, and it was one of the most beautiful projects that happened, because it brought together people from all departments.

In 1997, Mitchell introduced into The Other Place's season a series of events linked by the exploration of cultural and theological issues that, according to the RSC season brochure, "examine the preoccupation of pre-Shakespearean Britain including ideas that might have inspired or transformed Shakespeare's work." The theatrical centerpieces were Mitchell's own two-part refiguring of the medieval telling of the Creation—*The Mysteries*—and codirectors Kathryn Hunter and Marcello Magni's interpretation of *Everyman*. These productions were complemented by a series of art and photographic exhibitions, mixed-media projects, musical presentations, and workshops of lesser-known medieval and Elizabethan plays, all interspersed over the six-month run of the two plays. Along with other, unrelated events— Edward Petherbridge's tour de force performance in *Krapp's Last Tape*, a one-woman show by Jane Lapotaire, a number of open-house discussions by RSC artists—they contributed to shaping a provocative season at The Other Place.

Maintaining the Theatres

Graham Sawyer is the theatre manager and licensee of the Stratford theatres. He first began service at the RSC in the capacity of house manager for the RST in 1969, and after a two-year stint at the South Bank Centre's Festival Hall in London returned to Stratford in 1974. Sawyer oversees the front-of-house facilities and services, compliance with town ordinances, and a host of other responsibilities.

The Stratford District Council issues a license for the operation of each of the three theatres, specifying codes and restrictions for electricity, safety, fire, and other physical plant concerns, and Sawyer is named as the licensee on the council's document, which must be re-evaluated annually. The maintenance of the company's other properties also falls under Sawyer's purview. A staff of carpenters, electricians, plumbers, and gardeners tends to the various holdings and the immaculate, frequently photographed gardens. Much of the RSC's real estate portfolio was acquired over the years through bequests, and many of the properties are occupied by freehold tenants under ninety-nine-year leases. The RSC owns close to fifty flats and townhouses that it uses as artists' residences—the company rents a number of additional units for this purpose—and Sawyer ensures that each is meticulously maintained. He endeavors to make the company's stay in Stratford as pleasant as possible. "These artists become family. They're away from home, thrown into the pressure cooker of a small town with a big company reputation—a size out of sync with the town itself—and we must do all we can to free the artists of worry about mundane matters so that they can focus on their creative work. If artists don't feel positive about their lives, it will somehow adversely affect their work."[34]

Sawyer spends considerable time overseeing the repair and refurbishment of all the apartments. Some of the actors are RSC veterans, and Sawyer tries to take into account his knowledge of their tastes and habits. Again, making them comfortable is his goal. "Actors are under so much stress here. It's a small town. I've seen actors accosted on the street by long-term audience members who demand to know why the actor said a given line in a certain way in *Hamlet* two weeks ago; he'd probably seen the play twenty-five times before!"

Sawyer's group also maintains the theatres themselves, although the technical stage work is left to the crews. In the winter of 1993, for example, he oversaw the RST's first refurbishment since 1977. New seats and new lights were installed; stainless steel rails were fitted in the balconies; the side balconies were reconfigured; the stonework in the foyer was redone; the steps to the dress circle were repaired; and new floors were laid in the River Terrace restaurant. All this was accomplished in four weeks.

During Sawyer's tenure, he has perceived differences in the methodology and vision of the artistic directors. However, one common theme unites them—their devotion to the company ethic. And it is the needs of the company that Sawyer attempts to serve, albeit with appropriate flexibility. "There's no rigidity about process around here. We all have to accommodate the artistic vision."

London

And now to London all the crew are gone . . .
—Earl of Warwick, *Henry VI, Part 3*

*P*rior to the 1960s, plays that were performed at the Shakespeare Memorial Theatre were occasionally transferred to London, but it was at the start of Peter Hall's tenure as artistic director in 1960 that London was targeted as a second permanent base for the RSC. Hall's ambitions for the company included thrusting the RSC into the limelight of the national theatrical arena in order to maintain a competitive edge over, perhaps even to supersede, the planned National Theatre.[1] The move to London would ensure the company's national reputation, and by virtue of the expense, guarantee the government subsidy that Hall believed was crucial to the RSC's financial welfare and the company's inevitable growth. But Hall encountered considerable resistance from London commercial theatre owners and producers who looked unfavorably upon this competition, and it took some cagey maneuvering for him to secure a lease for the Aldwych Theatre on the edge of London's West End, near Covent Garden.

It was Hall's goal to present primarily new plays at the Aldwych. However, many English playwrights of the time were writing small, intimate works, and the RSC's London company, comprising more than fifty actors, would have been seriously underemployed if its main thrust were the production of small-cast plays. Hall was compelled to stage larger, epic works, such as Anouilh's *Becket,* in those first seasons before the company developed a different approach to the repertoire in Stratford and London.[2] The company opened in December 1960 with Peggy Ashcroft starring in a production of *The Duchess of Malfi.* The 1961 season continued with a London remount of Hall's *Twelfth Night* and productions of John Whiting's *The Devils* (the company's first commissioned play), Giraudoux's *Ondine,* and a John Barton compilation, *The Hollow Crown.* It was a successful first season, although Whiting's new play was the only one that seemed to excite the critics.

There was an explicit distinction made in the early years between the philosophies that guided production in the two cities. Stratford would produce Shakespeare, and London would produce new plays and works by playwrights other than Shakespeare. But financial exigencies were such that although the Aldwych earned its reputation as the RSC's home for new plays, transfers of popular Shakespearean work from Stratford were added to the repertoire to bolster box office revenue. These transfers increased in the 1960s when Hall saw the practical and financial advantages of easing the constraints on the Aldwych repertoire. Audiences in London, like those in Stratford, wanted to see the Shakespeare plays for which the RSC was best known.

Hall was breaking new ground with the establishment of a permanent London base. Actors were signed to three-year contracts to ensure a continuity critical to the life of a repertory company. Two companies of actors were performing in two cities simultaneously, and two physical plants had to be maintained. Although Stratford would continue to be the RSC's spiritual and administrative center, London demanded its share of attention and maintenance, and this polarization placed additional stress on a staff that was literally pulled in opposite directions. Hall had initially hoped that actors could work in both cities during the *same* season, shuttling back and forth between the two. This was theoretically possible within a repertory system, but in practice it placed too great a strain on the commuting actors and was quickly abandoned.

In 1962, Hall presented six plays in Stratford at the RST—the only RSC facility in Stratford at the time—and nine at the Aldwych. In addition, he leased London's Arts Theatre for an additional seven plays. The Aldwych season was exhilarating and richly varied, including transfers of *As You Like It* and *Troilus and Cressida* from Stratford, a revival of the previous season's hit, *The Devils*, and new productions of Brecht's *The Caucasian Chalk Circle*, Pinter's *The Collection*, Strindberg's *Playing with Fire*, Whiting's *A Penny for a Song*, and an adaptation of an epistolary novel by Choderlos de Laclos that John Barton, the director and adapter, entitled *The Art of Seduction*. This novel would again be adapted more than twenty years later by playwright Christopher Hampton to become one of the RSC's most popular works, *Les Liaisons Dangereuses*.

As the Aldwych began to grow in popularity, a philosophical shift could be detected in the RSC. No longer content with staging Shakespeare spoken in well-rounded tones, the company was exploring new styles of production and daring to interpret Shakespeare's plays in radical ways. It undertook the production of new works that were radical in both politics and performance style. Peter Brook's highly experimental and harrowing production of Peter Weiss's *Marat/Sade* in 1964 exemplified this shift towards experimentation and forever shattered the image of the RSC as a "Shakespeare museum." Hall wanted to prove that the company was in the vanguard of theatrical innovation. The move to the Aldwych and the establishment of a London base was the first, essential step in creating this new image.

In those first years at the Aldwych, two shows rotated in performance for several weeks, at which time two new plays were introduced. There was hardly ever a dark period. Although the company enjoyed many successes at the Aldwych, its financial agreement with the owner, Prince Littler, was such that he earned 25 percent of the gross, guaranteeing that the company would operate in the red for most of its stay there.[3] In 1966, the RSC governors implored Hall to economize because the company was now running under a deficit budget. Government subsidies, which had only recently begun to trickle in, were insufficient to stem the flow of red ink, and there were considerable losses, mostly incurred by the seasons at the Aldwych. Hall, committed as he was to the work in London, took a different tack than expected by both RSC insiders and Arts Council executives. He economized instead by mounting only one new production and four revivals in Stratford that season, along with eight new works and one revival at the Aldwych. Although he would subsequently moderate this policy, it underscored just how important the Aldwych—and the work being produced there—was to Hall.

Maggie Roy, now retired after a long career as a member of the RSC's production staff in London, joined the company in 1961 as a green room employee at the Aldwych. She recalled the old theatre fondly but remarked on how the RSC's particular needs placed unusual demands on the building and the staff.

> It was a cozy little theatre. It afforded us a "company feeling." We outfitted the theatre with a minithrust stage that reached to the third row of seats so that we could re-create as closely as possible the dynamic of the RST. We established lighting and sound board controls in enclosed stall boxes on opposite sides of the house, and we didn't move the lighting board to a booth at the back of the upper circle until 1975.
>
> But life at the Aldwych was not easy for the staff. Storage was nonexistent, and space had to be rented behind the paint frame at Theatre Royal Drury Lane, a few blocks away. Sets would be wheeled down the street in the middle of the night for changeovers—in all weather!—and then lowered eighteen feet by ropes and pulleys to the Aldwych's loading doors. I assure you that this could prove to be an unpleasant task in the dead of winter.[4]

The staff learned to adapt, and things ran relatively smoothly at the Aldwych until the RSC's last production, Terry Hands's *Richard II,* starring Alan Howard, closed there in early 1982. In May, the company moved to its new home in the Barbican Centre.

In 1965, the City of London had announced that it would lease to the RSC the theatre being built in its new Barbican Centre, which was planned as an enormous urban arts and housing complex to be built within the bounds of the City of London as part of its plans to revitalize the East End. The city would fund and build the theatre, and it was hoped that the RSC could take occupancy by 1970.[5] Although no one knew then just how wildly unrealistic this date would prove, it gave Hall and the RSC great hope for its future in London and for its ability to compete with the National Theatre, which had been promised space in the new South Bank Centre.

When Trevor Nunn became the artistic director in 1968, the Aldwych was playing at only a fraction of capacity, and shows were being budgeted on the basis of 40 to 50 percent of box office potential. The work at the Aldwych was being eclipsed by that of the hugely popular new National Theatre, at the time playing at the Old Vic, across from Waterloo Station.[6]

Nunn sought to make several adjustments in the RSC's company system and in the nature of the repertoire of the Aldwych. Rather than focusing on new plays and largely to justify employing a sizable company of actors, the Aldwych would primarily house productions of large-cast, relatively unknown classics and a greater number of Shakespearean transfers from Stratford.[7] This scheme would prove to be the most viable and successful for the RSC, and despite the construction of new theatres, the policy would continue—to a greater or lesser extent—until 1995.

After the first years of glowing success at The Other Place, it became apparent to Nunn that a second London theatre would be necessary to accommodate transfers of shows from the smaller Stratford theatre. This decision presented certain immediate obstacles. The Other Place's charter required it to be self-sufficient, and the new theatre would be placed under similar constraints. But the considerably higher operating costs in London would initially make it difficult for a small theatre there to be solvent. Sets for all RSC theatres, including the Aldwych, were built in Stratford workshops, which were running at capacity and unable to take on any new work. Additional sets would have to be built in contract workshops in London, entailing higher labor costs.[8]

The RSC hoped to debut in a new theatre in the summer of 1977, although a space had not been found. It had been determined that this theatre, under Howard Davies's direction, would share a casting pool with the general London company, work in repertory with the Aldwych, and present productions of new British plays as well as Other Place transfers. But finding the right space was not simple. Maggie Roy remembered the process.

First and foremost, we needed to find a theatre that could somehow
re-create the feel and the sensibility of The Other Place. That would
be hard to do, as that space was one of a kind. And there were obviously some drawbacks to The Other Place that we wouldn't *want* to
duplicate. But Howard and Trevor thought it important that somehow the new theatre should engender in the audience and the company that feeling of intimacy and lack of formality so vital in The
Other Place. Also, there were practical considerations. We had to find
a theatre near enough to the Aldwych so we wouldn't knock ourselves
out going back and forth. We finally found our space in the Don-
mar Warehouse in Covent Garden, just a few blocks away from the
Aldwych. We had been using it as a rehearsal hall before our new space
on Floral Street was ready. It had been a film studio, fruit warehouse,
and dance theatre in its "previous lives" before we took it over. It wasn't
perfect—Lord, there were problems!—but it had the right ambiance,
and we made it work.[9]

It took considerable effort to bring the theatre up to code and to
adapt it to the needs of the company. Eventually, it was fashioned into
a space that, if it did not exactly replicate the dynamics and ambiance
of The Other Place, at least created a similar sense of intimacy. The
Other Place's stage had two long sides and one short, whereas the
Warehouse stage had two short sides and one long. It was cramped
and provided poor audience access, and there was virtually no storage space. As uncomfortable as it was, however, the Warehouse enabled the RSC to finally establish a commitment to new plays and
new playwrights in London.

Meanwhile, work proceeded slowly on the construction of the
Barbican Centre for Arts and Conferences, which had first been
planned in 1955, when the thirty-five-acre site in London's East End
was still in a state of devastation from the Blitz. The term *barbican*,
meaning an outer line or defense of a city or castle, referred to the fact
that the neighborhood had been built above the ruins of the ancient
Roman walls of London. As the Guildhall School of Music and Drama
had been promised new premises by the city, it was decided that this
site would be the ideal place for it.[10] The Corporation of the City of
London decided that a planned neighborhood, including housing
projects and an integrated arts center, would revitalize the depressed
East End neighborhood. Events moved slowly, however, and in 1968

the architects Chamberlin, Powell, and Bon submitted a report that considerably enlarged the scope of the original plan. The Barbican Centre would comprise several theatres, a library, a concert hall, cinemas, an art gallery, and ancillary facilities. In addition, a housing complex of some two thousand units would be built by the city as council flats (subsidized housing) with an upmarket flair. Half would be rented, and half were to be sold as co-ops.[11] The city approved the plans for the entire project, and construction began in October 1971. In addition to the housing towers, the complex includes the following facilities:

- Barbican Hall, seating 2,026, serving both as the home of the London Symphony Orchestra and as a fully equipped auditorium for conferences
- three cinemas, seating 280, 255, and 153, respectively, also suitable for conferences
- a fifteen-thousand-square-foot art gallery plus an open-air sculpture court
- a city library
- five seminar rooms, each with seating for as many as 80
- special function rooms, catering areas, two public restaurants, employees' restaurant, and parking for five hundred cars
- foyers providing nearly fifty thousand square feet of space for bars, buffets, information and reception desks, cloakrooms, book and record shops, informal displays, and exhibitions
- two trade exhibition halls, with a combined display area of eighty-six thousand square feet
- the Guildhall School of Music and Drama, with a 400-seat music hall, a 300-seat theatre, rehearsal halls, and classrooms
- the Barbican Theatre, seating 1,166, designed as the London base for the RSC
- the Pit, seating approximately 200, also used by the RSC

Completing the Barbican Centre was no simple task. Labor strikes caused delays. The excavation required constructing an enormous retaining wall to keep the tricky London clay from giving way; later, the wall itself began to slip. A line of the London Underground had to be moved to clear the excavation site. The complex, budgeted at £106 million but completed for £153 million, was opened in stages, and the RSC began performances there in May 1982 with *Henry IV,*

Parts 1 and 2, directed by Trevor Nunn and starring Patrick Stewart as Henry, Timothy Dalton as Hotspur, and Joss Ackland as Falstaff.

As the RSC is only a tenant at the Barbican Centre—its current lease expires in 2007—there have been difficulties over the years in working with the Centre's staff and the Corporation Council (the local governing authority for the financial and commercial heart of greater London), exacerbated recently by the RSC's decision to shrink its presence there from eleven months to seven. Graham Sykes was the RSC's administrator of the Barbican theatres from the opening until 1998, at which time he took a position with the English National Opera. He reflected on the challenge of running such a large enterprise under tenancy status.

> This is a difficult theatre to supervise. In Stratford, everything is much more cut-and-dried—the RSC owns the spaces and deals with no one else but the Stratford council. Here, there's a difficult balance to strike, as we have to share facilities with other tenants and interact daily with the Barbican administration. The Barbican Centre must have a licensee who is directly responsible to the city. Each of the tenant organizations in turn then has a licensee representative, and I'm the RSC's.
>
> The relationship between the Corporation of the City of London and the RSC can be stormy. The RSC was facing a major financial crisis in 1990, and we needed aid from the city. They refused to give us more than we had; the Arts Council responded in similar fashion. It was decided by the RSC administration to close down our theatres at the Barbican in order to cut our severe deficit; we would save on the cost of mounting two new productions. It was also a bit of a bluff to get a better deal from the city. Well, they called our bluff, and we didn't back down. We needed to make a savings somewhere, and this ploy accomplished that; the move also helped publicize our financial plight in a very dramatic way, in addition to a saving us money. We closed in November of 1990 and reopened with our new season in March 1991. As the RSC then operated fifty weeks a year at the Barbican, this represented a sizable chunk of our season. However, the city finally responded, and we were able to negotiate a more favorable tenancy agreement.
>
> Prior to 1990, the RSC rented the space and paid additionally for the ancillary and plant services—the Barbican staff, the air-conditioning, those things. It was a "fully repairing lease," in which we were responsible for all maintenance costs: for example, seating, decora-

tions, and the like. The theatres themselves were, and still are, staffed completely by RSC employees. In 1991, the Corporation started giving the RSC a subsidy. This is, of course, an important source of funding that was hard fought.[12]

Perhaps it is a tribute to Shakespeare's enduring power that he is at home in every environment, for this glass, concrete, and steel monolith lacks the warmth or charm present in many older, more traditional theatres or in more thoughtfully constructed modern ones such as the Swan. It was not situated on the banks of a placid river but was plunked down in the midst of a crowded and nondescript section of the city, surrounded by office buildings and banks. The neighborhood lacks the colorful bustle and pace of the West End and offers few dining options outside of the complex's own facilities, with their modern menus but institutional setting. The Centre's hulking brutishness desperately begs some compensating feature—even the equally depressing National Theatre complex in the South Bank benefits from stunning views of the Thames—and the trees and fountains in the Barbican courtyard do little to mitigate the oppressive feeling. Although Shakespeare's work was originally performed in an urban environment far grittier, the Barbican Centre's size, scope, and institutional appearance do little to greet the audience with any sense of the festive. The theatre spaces themselves are functionally accommodating venues, but they must work all the more to recapture theatregoers who are often alienated or confused by the complex's labyrinthine layout and size.

The Barbican Centre is accessible by car—though driving in the city can be confusing, even for Londoners—as well as by taxi and by Tube. The two Tube stations, Moorgate and Barbican, are just far enough away to make audiences feel that it is an effort to walk, especially in poor weather. A first-time visitor can easily get lost trying to follow the yellow line pavement markings that point towards the theatre. Peter Cadley, the Barbican theatre manager, questioned the wisdom of the siting of the theatres.

> The Barbican [site] has all the disadvantages and none of the advantages we would hope for. The city gave the RSC a lot of money to come here. What a coup for them, to get one of the most successful companies in the world! The one thing they missed that would

have transformed our time here is putting a Tube station closer. I've been down with the engineers. Underneath the Pit is the Tube line that runs from the Barbican to Moorgate. You can actually get down there—one of the guys who was head of engineering here told me, if he was late going home, that he would just go down to the Pit and through a set of doors and stairs and walk to Moorgate through the Tube walkways. What would it have taken to move the Barbican Tube stop a quarter of a mile to here? "I'm going to the Barbican tonight." "Oh, good luck following the yellow line when you get there!"

The problem is that so many people arrive here complaining because they had a terrible journey. They couldn't park the car, the Tubes were bad, whatever. If you had a focal point where they could arrive, they could get out and say, "Ooh, it's a lovely building." A lot of people who come here regularly love the place. It's got restaurants in different price ranges, the food's not bad, there are two art galleries, three cinemas, a concert hall, a library, people can spend a day here, as I did as a student.

Another problem is that restaurants and pubs didn't spring up here over the years. The area just east and north of here, it's not one of the nicest areas in London. The entire area is a cultural and culinary desert, really, and we're the oasis in the middle.[13]

Cadley's associate, Tim Smith, house manager of the Barbican and Pit theatres, agreed. "People walk in with a bad perception of the Barbican, that it's an unpleasant place, and that's been ingrained in people. The Centre was a gift to the nation, and it's like receiving a present and being ungrateful. In a lot of ways, the Barbican is a great place, and perceptions need to be changed."

As a result of the Barbican Centre administration's growing awareness that attending an event there could be a potentially intimidating or unpleasant experience for patrons, they created the "Total Experience." Although most patrons would be unaware that such a scheme was in place, it represents an intent to alter public perceptions of the place by training staff to make a greater effort in terms of customer care. Staff now wear badges to make them more identifiable, customer comment forms are available, and customer letters are answered within seventy-two hours. As one RSC staffer commented, "The Barbican [administrators] are keen to lose the image that the badly designed building has got them. No matter how many fantastic pieces of art we put on, be it at the RSC or London Symphony or in the Gallery, people's perception the moment anything goes wrong is, 'Well, that's the Barbican.'"

Approaching the complex's main entrance on Silk Street—which provides the most convenient access to the RSC's theatres—one is confronted by an imposing, hunkering jumble of stressed concrete and glass towers and atriums. Neither the Barbican Centre's logo prominently displayed high on one concrete wall—a square of four large, highly polished aluminum letter *B*s, which at a quick glance bear an unfortunate resemblance to a swastika—nor the center's name spelled out in large brass letters above the entrance in any way identify the place as the home of the RSC. The entrance is adjacent to an underground parking structure and is dwarfed by a bowed canopy of milky, frosted glass spattered with red and blue paint and framed by black steel. Audiences must walk down a short tunnel past the loading dock to enter the foyer.[14]

In 1994, the architectural consulting firm Pentagram was hired to redesign the Silk Street entrance—long considered a problem since there was little there to herald the presence of the theatres inside—and assess the facility's decor, signage, and access. This very expensive venture resulted in the installation of a wall of tiny mirrors dangling near the entrance and gold statues of the Muses perched atop the canopy. The odd combination of styles and materials struck glaringly incompatible notes with an already poorly designed facade. In 1995, former RSC administrator Graham Sykes commented on Pentagram's £10 million efforts.

> The Silk Street entrance has always looked like a drab entrance to a car park, since taxis emerge from the underground parking area adjacent and nearly knock you down. Pentagram created what they call "a path of light" that is supposed to guide you towards the Centre. It's made of a lot of little mirrors hanging down from the ceiling, and they move in the breeze and twinkle and are supposed to be inviting and enticing—we nicknamed them "budgie mirrors," since they look like the mirrors in budgerigar cages—and it's now a bright, garish entrance. The canopy they built and the Muses atop are supposed to give the place a sense of importance and give one a sense of arrival—but if you arrive by taxi or car, you miss the Muses and the look completely. I think everyone, including the Corporation, agrees that the Silk Street entrance and "path of light" have been totally unsuccessful and

should be changed. They could replace the mirrors with a real path of light, up lighting from the floor, but that would be very expensive.[15]

In 1997, John Tusa became the Barbican Centre's managing director, and according to theatre manager Peter Cadley, he decided that the Muses and mirrors presented an inappropriate image for the entrance and promptly had them dismantled. "Actually, most of the mirrors fell down. Lorries would knock them off. The Muses were sold off to a reclamation yard near the theatre," said Cadley.[16]

One unnecessary refinement had been removed, but the Barbican can still be considered an unwelcoming venue for audiences. The RSC uses the same lobbies and foyers as do the other tenants in the building. Although there is no lack of amenities—four restaurants, coffee carts, bars, RSC bookstalls, a Dillon's bookshop, plus sofas and tables and the like—their layout and the shortage of signposting make them difficult to find, and one can easily get lost. Although Pentagram installed semimobile "You are here" maps to guide visitors to their destinations, refitted the elevators, and installed new carpeting, lighting, and murals, the place is still a multileveled, confusing admixture of ramps, staircases, garish carpeting, harsh lighting, and unnatural proportions. Graham Sykes had these thoughts:

> We generally don't approve of much of what Pentagram did. The idea was to draw you towards the auditorium, but I think that's failed. What the Centre needs is rich colors. The foyers and lobbies need to be about what is going on in the concert halls, the theatres, the cinemas, and at the moment it's just a bland statement by the architects and designers. It needs to be a place full of black carpeting, graceful lighting, banners, greenery. It needs to be enticing and inviting, and it's none of that. There was an opportunity to get it right, and they got it absolutely wrong.
>
> The decor and ambiance don't put the audience into the right frame of mind for a performance. I think, in point of fact, that it actually alienates them. There are problems in finding the place, in parking, in getting a drink and going to the loo, and especially on people's first visit, they get exasperated, and it makes the actors' jobs doubly difficult to get them to enjoy themselves and what they came to see.
>
> If you look at the main house's foyer, you see we've put up all these large production photographs near the entrance, but if you look across

the lobby, there's nothing telling you what's going on inside. We're not allowed to extend ourselves beyond this point—there's a lot of compartmentalization and segregation of the various tenants of the Centre—and that makes it problematic to create a sense of occasion here. For one season, we put up colorful banners, but then the Centre put up security cameras, and the banners got in the way, so they came down. I would love to see the company doing platform performances, doing preshow events out here, create a lively atmosphere, roughen the place up a bit, set out secondhand bookstalls, make it more streetwise. When you go to the National Theatre, you see people sitting around on the carpet, there's a sort of buzz around the place. The Barbican feels like an airport lounge.[17]

The RSC, during its tenancy, occupies approximately 25 percent of the Barbican Arts Complex, with its offices, dressing rooms, and theatres spread over nine windowless levels of the center. The Barbican Theatre's foundation is sunk so deep that the fly rail is located on the fifth floor, which is street level.

Each floor of the RSC section of the complex wraps around the stage space in a rectangular, continuous hallway. The second basement houses the green room and staff cafeteria, the musicians' room (situated much farther from the stage than at the RST, so the musicians view the action via video monitors), access to the Pit and the cinema (there were originally two cinemas, but one was converted into a storage area behind the Pit), the rehearsal hall, and the Pit Bar. The second level is the Barbican stage. The third level, "Minus One" in confusing Barbican-speak, provides access to the Barbican stalls and houses a bar, coffee cart, ticket desk, lounge, cloakroom, and other public amenities as well as a level of dressing rooms. On successive levels can be found a Dillon's bookshop, other restaurants, more bars and coffee carts, a first-aid room, a sculpture court, two more cinemas, conference suites, and the RSC's administrative offices. It is a maze of arches, ramps, counters, booths, overhanging mezzanines, and performance platforms.

Since the RSC's premiere at the Barbican Centre in 1982, vociferous critics have decried the complex as a soulless enclave. Some have urged the RSC to pull up stakes and move elsewhere. Former artistic director Terry Hands responded by observing, "It would be ridiculous to pull out. We could never find a landlord as generous as the

City of London. And we must have a London showcase. If we don't have a London showcase, the top actors will not come to us."[18]

Although there was wisdom in Hands's statement, a few years later the RSC administration reordered its priorities. In what was viewed by many as the most radical decision in its producing policy since Peter Hall engineered the company's move to London some thirty-five years earlier, the RSC announced in 1995 that it would curtail its presence at the Barbican and reduce the season there from eleven months to six. Adrian Noble and his staff believed it was critical for the RSC to establish a more profound national presence, and in a risky gambit chose to reduce its output in London, create an additional residency after Newcastle, and devise a greater—and more costly—touring schedule. Not only would the RSC now have less visibility in the capital, it would also produce fewer new plays there, where previously as many as eight or ten new productions were added to the repertoire during the Barbican season. Actors, who at that time made a two-year commitment to the RSC—at least in spirit if not by contractual letter—relished the chance of performing for a year in London, where television, radio, and film work could be found to augment relatively modest RSC salaries. This new vision of the company's mission would occasion a chain reaction of events, which will be explored in greater detail in subsequent chapters.

Once the decision was made to vacate London from spring through early autumn, the Barbican Centre needed to fill the void in the theatres. In 1998, it developed BITE, the British International Theatre Event, which continues as an annual festival. In its first year, BITE presented a smorgasbord of international theatre and dance, including: a pan-European *Measure for Measure;* the British premiere of a Robert Wilson and Philip Glass collaboration, *Monsters of Grace;* the Maly Theatre of St. Petersburg's version of *The Possessed;* Japanese director Yukio Ninagawa's *Hamlet;* Peter Sellars's production of *The Peony Pavilion;* a Romanian production of *Oresteia;* the Merce Cunningham Dance Company; and many other works. Featured in the festival was "Staged America," comprising a number of plays performed by American companies or exploring American themes and issues, including *Miss Evers' Boys, A Huey P. Newton Story, 2.5 Minute Ride,* and Steppenwolf's production of *The Man Who Came to Dinner.*

The RSC's presence in London has always presented problems for this bifurcated company. Although there is constant dialogue and communication between the two cities and one set of administrators overseeing the RSC as a whole, communications problems arise. One former RSC Barbican staffer explained the feeling shared by many London colleagues about their relationship with Stratford: "Stratford is still 'head office.' The administrators often don't come down here. It's not ill will, but Stratford is the company's theatre, and we're just lodgers here. The city doesn't allow us to do what we want without their permission. Now, we here believe that London is where it's at. For many years, we have had a longer annual season than Stratford, we did more shows, and we don't have production shops here and have to build them at outside shops. It's all very different from Stratford, a lot less cozy, maybe, but more exciting. In Stratford, there is a sense amongst many of the staff that 'Oh, Dad worked here, now I do.' Here, we don't have that."

A current RSC Barbican manager concurred with this observation and noted that many in the administration were Stratford-centric in their views of the company. "They don't believe that anyone could not actually want to be in Stratford, although many of the actors refer to it as 'Brigadoon.' But Stratford isn't the center of the universe; it's not Broadway or the West End. Until that changes, there will always be a problem."

The RSC and Barbican Centre staffs, too, were slow to fully integrate over the years. A multitude of problems, such as restrictions on RSC advertisements within the theatre and lack of knowledge about RSC programming by Barbican Centre box office staff, contributed to the RSC's perception that they were never truly at home there. With the advent of the shorter season, they discovered they were inventing an imperfect relationship anew. Barbican theatre manager Peter Cadley said, "We've worked hard recently to liaise with the Barbican. In the past it was always seen by the Barbican that we were a separate entity, and in our own snobby way, the RSC felt the same about the Barbican. But now we have regular meetings with Barbican staff to talk about how we make it work for the customer."[19] But obstacles remained, such as the Stratford box office computer's inability to communicate with the Barbican Centre's computer (RSC Barbican tickets are sold by the Barbican-run box office) and the maddening impossibility of one venue selling tickets for the other. Cadley elaborated on the efforts to develop greater rapport between the Barbican and RSC administrators.

> We did a training session with Barbican staff, showed them around, to make them realize that we're separate parts of the same entity. We now have internal e-mail between the departments, so we can call up everything on the computer from the box office. For years, we had no access to look at reservations—I guess they thought we might start fiddling around with them—and now it turns out that we could have had access all along, they could have done it with a flick of the switch, all we had to do was to guarantee we weren't going to start selling tickets on our own. All we had wanted to do was to look at a performance and say, "Oh, look, there are all these reservation indicators, we now know what's going on." In the past, we had to call up or e-mail to find out what was going on.
>
> But we made our own mistakes. We were too supercilious with the Barbican in the past, because "we are the RSC," and we realize that in today's economic climate, we need to let them know what is going on. And the more we let them know, the nicer they are to us. They really want to help now. It does seem to be working.

The Barbican Theatre

One of the greatest concerns for Peter Hall, set designer John Bury, and the then general manager, Patrick Donnell, all of whom were instrumental in the planning and design of the Barbican theatre spaces, was that a theatre of the requisite size should offer the best sight lines possible. The RSC had done what little it could to ameliorate the sight line problems in the RST, but a new theatre allowed them the chance to ensure a better design from the outset. As a result, no seat in the house is more than sixty-five feet from a central point onstage, located eight feet up from the edge of the forestage. To achieve these sight lines and relative proximity to the stage, the architects had to design a fairly wide auditorium.

The house seats 1,166 and is configured with a raked stalls section seating almost 700 and three narrowly built circles, each stacked directly above the next, which wrap around to raked side boxes, with a combined seating capacity of about 475. Each circle contains only two rows of seats, and this sense of intimacy compensates for the very wide and open auditorium. Although the topmost audience circle towers above the stalls, sight lines are excellent from all vantage points. A fourth circle high above the theatre is used for technical equipment. The first three rows of stall seating can be removed to create an orchestra pit, but this is rarely done for RSC shows because the company prefers to maintain the income from selling these seats. Seating is arranged in continental fashion, in unbroken rows stretching from one side aisle to the other. Behind the stalls is a series of partitioned booths with windows for the deputy stage manager who runs the show, the light board and sound operators, projection equipment, and the director's and designers' viewing rooms. Victor Glasstone, writing for *The Architects' Journal,* noted that, "Whereas so much of the grandiose scheme [of the Barbican Centre] entombs the aspirations and pomposities of the 1960s in worthy solemnity, the theatre seems fresh and newly minted—Brighton Pavilion set down in Whitehall."[20]

Each row of seats is accessible through doors on both sides of the auditorium. The doors are controlled by an electromagnetic system that automatically triggers their release at the start of each act. The interior decor is a rich, dark brown with walls of Peruvian walnut. Fitted bronze sconces and chandeliers provide appropriate illumination.

The theatre was designed with the newest technology of the time: a flexible proscenium, computer-controlled fly system, cavernous backstage areas, and hydraulically controlled floors. However, the architects had to balance the company's desire to replicate the RST's dimensions in order to accommodate transfers with the need for a wider stage that would offer better sight lines.

As a result, many artists who work there feel that the space lacks defined character and believe that the planners failed to successfully grapple with the problems of easily mounting transferred productions. Although there is ample backstage storage space, some of the high-tech components were either not properly installed or proved problematic or unnecessary. According to lighting designer Chris Parry, it seemed as if the dynamics and dimensions of the RST were never taken into account when the Barbican was designed. "Since we do so many Stratford transfers, there was no need to diverge so radically from the RST configurations. We're constantly reinventing the wheel every season. Too many of the Barbican's initial elements had to be redone or compromised to get the space to work the way we need it to."[21]

Unlike the RST's small proscenium opening, the Barbican stage combines a generous thrust with the potential of a deep proscenium theatre, although there is no proscenium arch. The side walls of the auditorium end at the downstage edge of a cavernous open stage, some seventy-three feet wide. Immediately upstage and onstage of the walls are side assemblies, similar to those in Stratford, that flare out towards the three-sided thrust. These wedge-shaped assemblies may be left on house floor level, stepped up to the stage, or raked. As in Stratford, these areas are most often used as transitional spaces from the thrust to the wings.

The thrust itself is an odd, pentagonal affair that initially angles upstage from the black legs erected at the side walls, then downstage, and then across. This front edge is twenty feet wide, three feet above the house floor, and four feet from the first row of seats. As in Stratford, the stage floor is usually raked, more to duplicate the look and feel of Stratford transfers than for sight line purposes. A false proscenium arch is formed at a point fourteen feet upstage of the thrust's edge by moving tracking black flats into position. These flats, or "house legs," are not set in a fixed position for the season but can be moved onstage or offstage for each production. Usually an opening of no less than thirty-two feet is used, to mimic the Stratford proscenium arch. The height of the stage opening is flexible as well. Conforming to the irregularly shaped thrust, and just upstage of it, is an electrics bridge for lighting instruments, masked on the downstage side, which can be flown to different heights to form the top of a makeshift proscenium arch.

One striking, innovative feature of the theatre is the fire curtain. A one-foot gap between the house floor and the downstage edge of the thrust follows the shape of the stage around to the auditorium walls; there is a similar gap in the house ceiling. During the intermission or before the start of a one-act play, a highly polished and elegant corrugated steel fire curtain is formed as two sections, one rising up from the floor and the other lowering from the ceiling, meet like a pair of stainless steel jaws. This unique, highly effective "curtain" strikes a handsome, contemporary note, and the house lights play dazzlingly

off its reflective surfaces. However, as the curtain must be displayed
at every performance, any scenic piece that extends downstage past
the curtain line must be mechanized in order to disconnect from the
main stage when the curtain moves into place.

Four enormous concrete pillars support the mass of the fly tower
and upper levels above the stage and create a forty-eight-foot-deep
octagonal acting space of three thousand square feet. As the grid was
installed to conform to the octagonal dimensions of the acting area,
the battens hanging from the one-hundred-seven-foot-high grid vary
in length. Of the sixty-seven battens, the farthest upstage measures
just eighteen feet across, while the longest, at midstage, are forty-four
feet. The grid terminates at the upstage end of the acting area. A
twenty-seven-foot-high dropped concrete ceiling overhangs the upstage storage space and crossover, and these combine with the wings
for an additional six thousand square feet of space. The octagonal grid
poses one significant problem for designers. Although the upstage area
is rarely used for staging, it is the point at which a backdrop or scrim
or cyclorama would be hung. However, the eighteen-foot width of the
battens at that point is insufficient for a rear drop, and designers must
rig them along a curved line, utilizing several battens. Side fly galleries offer reasonable lighting positions. Built at the same height as those
in the RST, these galleries were retrofitted after the Barbican opened
and it was discovered that the original galleries were too far from the
stage to be of any use.

Nestled between the two stage right pillars is a floor measuring
thirty-one by thirty-four feet, referred to as "the equalizer." Built upon
a hydraulic lift, it can be tilted to almost any angle—all four corner
points can adjust to different heights simultaneously—to facilitate the
moving of scenery from the distant storage bays onto the raked floor
of the acting area. The rake itself is laid over the entire stage floor and
extends to the backstage side walls to allow easy movement of scenery. The floor of the acting area is built on full screw jacks and can be
raised or lowered, either fully or in sections, but its use is cumbersome,
and the carpenters prefer to install a constructed raked stage instead.
Far offstage right is a truck lift. As the Barbican is sunk well down
into the London bedrock, the architects had to create a mechanism
for trucks to unload scenery and other equipment directly into the

theatre. The largest eighteen-wheeler can park on this lift, adjacent to the stage door and main entrance on Silk Street, and be lowered to stage level.

The much-vaunted computer-controlled fly system proved to be problematic, however. Nigel Love, the former deputy production controller, explained the difficulty.

> The theatre was originally built with a steel grid and a power fly system that we didn't like. It was too problematic, too finicky, and just didn't work right. We decided to replace it with one of our own choosing. The Corporation of London had an obligation to replace the original system. Our systems department selected a new system, but the subcontractor went out of business, setting off a chain reaction that caused considerable delays. Finally the systems department took over the project themselves, and the entire overhaul, which should have taken twelve months, took three years. And we're still not happy with it. It won't pick up heavy loads—each line set can lift only five hundred kilograms—and no one quite trusts it, as the system is not well calibrated for loads at the top end. Most of our flymen want to use chain hoists for really heavy stuff, but they're too slow and noisy. In a counterweight system, like in the RST, if your load is overweight you would join two battens together and take advantage of their combined power. You can't do that here, as the mechanized battens don't travel at exactly the same rate. In the case of malfunction, there is a manual override, but it works only if the fault is in the software, not if the fault is electrical. In that case, you have to hand crank or override with a winch, both of which are tedious and problematic.
>
> Additionally, the battens in the Barbican are square, whilst the ones in the RST are round. This is one additional little headache to be taken into account when shows transfer; you need different hardware to attach scenery here than in Stratford. The whole fly system here has lots of potential. It could be truly wonderful, but it isn't.[22]

The original lighting system and instruments were purchased and are owned by the Barbican Centre, but the equipment soon grew obsolete. The current inventory of some six hundred instruments was later bought by the RSC. The original equipment must be stored, though, according to the agreement with the Barbican. The master electrician hangs a rep plot of about four hundred instruments for the season, and as in the other RSC theatres, only a portion of them can be focused or colored by the designers for each show.

The costs of outfitting the Barbican with its own scenery, paint, and props workshops would have been prohibitive. Although there is a metal shop on the premises, most maintenance work on the set is done onstage or on the loading dock. Sets and costumes for new shows produced at the Barbican and the Pit as well as redesigned pieces for transferred shows are occasionally built in the Stratford workshops, but since those shops are usually already working at capacity, the construction is almost always contracted out to London workshops.

The Barbican Centre recently spent about £3 million to refurbish the stage mechanics, hydraulics, traps, wheelchair access, and two orchestra pits. Although these were necessary expenditures, the Centre refrained from spending an additional £1.5 million to replace the seats in the auditorium, something that will be needed in the immediate future.

The Pit

When the Barbican was designed, the company's productions in London were limited to the Aldwych, and therefore only one theatre was necessary at the Barbican. When the Warehouse was added as a producing venue in the mid-1970s, the RSC was faced with the problem of creating a similar theatre in the Barbican. It was too late to design additional space to house a second theatre, so existing space would have to be converted. The City of London had no financial obligation to pay for this new theatre, and the RSC had to earmark funds for this purpose. It was no easy task to create this second theatre, which was converted from one of the RSC rehearsal halls under construction at the time, and a ten-foot-thick concrete wall had to be broken through to create a public entry. The Pit, while a venue for artistically invigorating work, is cramped and uncomfortable and is saddled with a number of inconvenient features that stem from its late devising.

The Pit, located below the Barbican Theatre's orchestra pit on level one of the complex and thus aptly—if not altogether happily—named, is reached by elevator or stairs. An intimate lobby, shared with one of the cinemas, is outfitted with salmon-colored walls, brown leather banquettes, and track lighting. A box office, rest rooms, telephones, and a food and drink counter provide the needed amenities. Audiences enter the Pit's yellow foyer through a set of doors in the lobby, and two vom aisles, used by audience and actors alike, lead from the foyer into the theatre. Like the Swan and The Other Place, the Pit is most frequently used in a three-quarter configuration but can easily be set in full round for a maximum seating of two hundred. The black walls and low-slung ceiling and cramped, dark blue seats create a claustrophobic atmosphere. This dynamic can serve some plays remarkably well, but despite the intimacy of the space, it can be uncomfortable to sit in for three hours.

Sally Barling first worked with the RSC as a stage manager in the 1960s. When the Barbican opened in 1982, she was appointed assistant administrator of the Pit and later served as manager of the theatre, until 1998. She objectively assessed the Pit's viability as a performance space.

> We've outgrown the auditorium. In 1982, there were lots of studio theatres, and students would come to pay cheap prices to see good new plays in small theatres, but when we moved to the Barbican, a lot of our younger audiences were put off. They just hated coming here and finding their way. It might have been better if the Pit had its own entrance, but it doesn't—one has to use the lift—and we lost a lot of our audience. We did move from plastic seats to bench seating, but they're still uncomfortable and cramped. Ticket prices have gone up, but we haven't changed the seats. Our audiences, who now tend to be well heeled, are not happy about that.
>
> But it's not just about seats. The whole audience needs to be rebuilt to give more depth to the seats, more legroom, but this would involve losing seats. There was some talk years ago about breaking through the back wall of the theatre and taking over some of the rehearsal room space, but because of the air-venting duct work hanging from the ceiling, you could gain depth but not width, so it would be a very strange space. We could do something major here, in terms of revision, but it would require a lot of money.
>
> However, because the seating is so low and tight, the atmosphere can be fantastic. In The Other Place, the seating is broken up into an upstairs and downstairs, so there's less of a sense of inclusion, but here the claustrophobia can actually help. I've seen audience members almost pass out from the excitement and intimacy when they've been living the play. *Les Liaisons Dangereuses* is a great example of a play that worked well in here.[23]

The acting area is approximately twenty-two feet wide by thirty-

two feet deep and reflects the improvised nature of its birth. There
are eight rows of seats in the short front section, and four rows of
varying lengths in the longer side sections. Another long section of
seats is added for shows that perform in the round. The center and
side sections are separated by the vom aisles, and actors can also enter from upstage left and right. Upstage left leads to a corridor behind
the rear of the audience that accesses the downstage voms. There is a
small quick-change costume booth just off this passageway. When an
entrance from upstage center or a quick crossover behind the set is
desired, a false upstage wall must be built to create a backstage area.
Actors must use an elevator to reach their dressing rooms five and six
levels above the stage. Behind the last row of the center seating section is an eight-foot-deep platform, accessible by a ship's ladder from
the back of either vom. This houses the deputy stage manager's position as well as the sound and light board operators.

The height of the ceiling varies due to the Pit's location beneath
the Barbican. The floor of the auditorium above is itself built on a
rake, so the ceiling of the Pit is built along the angle of that rake. The
right side of the Pit (stage left) is set under the front of the Barbican
stage thrust, and the ceiling there is lower than at the other side of
the Pit, located under the Barbican audience. This creates an odd sense
of imbalance, apparent when the house lights are on but quickly for-
gotten once the theatre is darkened. The ceiling is strewn with a network of lighting pipes, sprinkler pipes, and air-conditioning and heating ducts. This massive duct work proves problematic for designers,
as every foot of grid space in the small theatre is valuable.

The grid itself is low, hanging at an average of only thirteen feet
above the deck and creating obstacles for lighting designers seeking
steeper and more attractive angles for the one hundred twenty instruments used in the Pit. The lighting designer's problems are compounded by the presence of the nine-foot-square air-conditioning
system hung smack in the middle of the stage. This unit is only ten
feet off the deck, so none of the higher hanging grid pipes can traverse
that area. This eliminates the most desirable center stage lighting
positions, forcing designers to compensate by hanging more units on
the side sections of the grid.

The floor of the Pit cannot be trapped, as this is the lowest level of
the theatre. A thin wooden deck rests on top of the concrete slab, and

individual show decks can be laid on top. Behind the permanent upstage wall is a mirror image of the Pit, initially intended for use as a rehearsal hall. A small room to the side was earmarked for scenic storage, but as it also houses the air-conditioning and heating works for the main building, it proved inadequate for the ever-growing scenery used in the Pit. As the company's rehearsal rooms in the south London neighborhood of Clapham provided a viable alternative for rehearsal needs, the larger space behind the Pit was subsequently employed to house both scenery and the Pit musicians.[24]

The Pit was originally conceived as a transfer house for Other Place shows as well as for a portion of the Swan repertoire. The lack of a third Barbican theatre to directly accommodate Swan transfers has been an obstacle for directors, designers, and production staff since the Swan opened in 1986. There was neither extra space at the Barbican nor funding to build a third theatre, so Swan productions were redesigned for one of the two Barbican stages. Neither theatre proved ideal, as scaling up a show to play in the Barbican was expensive and time-consuming, and scaling down a show for the Pit was fraught with its own problems of redesign and restaging. The Swan and the Pit both employ thrust stages but with completely different sizes and shapes. Swan productions often exploit the traps in that theatre's deck, but the Pit doesn't have a trapped floor. The bouncy, comfortable ambiance of the Swan is the polar opposite of the Pit's. Currently, the prohibitive cost of rebuilding Swan shows to the larger Barbican scale have resulted in transfers of Swan shows to the Pit or an off-site rental theatre, such as the Young Vic. Other Place productions almost always move to the Pit when the company shifts to London.

Chris de Wilde was the production manager of the Pit for several years. He offered his opinion of the theatre's strengths and weaknesses.

> It's very actor-friendly. Once you have an audience in, it's a very difficult place technically but very nice for the actors. It has a bit of flexibility, but other than deciding whether to play three-sided or in the round, the flexibility is minimal. It's not like the Cottesloe, at the National, which can play massively different-shaped spaces. I have to say, though, that I find the space enormously likable. It does no favor to a designer whatever, except for the fact that audiences do get a good focus on the center of the acting area from all points in the house.

One of the main problems here is that the stage floor is built right on top of concrete, so there's no way to put in traps. And that is a fundamental problem for Swan transfers, since it is something you can do there; you can even do it in The Other Place, with a certain amount of effort. It's something that's exploited by designers in Stratford and something they have to deal with here. Anything that used to come up from below now has to be brought in from the sides. Sometimes, when a show is reliant on traps in Stratford, it's completely redesigned, from scratch, for the Pit, since there is no effective way to adapt without completely reconceiving the staging and scene shifts.[25]

The budgets for the Pit are considerably smaller than those for the Barbican. According to de Wilde, this is understandable, given the size disparity between the two spaces, but often problematic when drastic design measures are needed to accommodate transfers. "I'll be contentious about this. The Pit, compared with other RSC theatres, has been underbudgeted for a number of seasons in a fairly serious way, to the point that it's affected the productions. They're asking the Pit to do more. Budgets for the other spaces haven't gone up much, but ours have actually gone down a bit during a time of belt tightening. But the size and scale of the shows seems to have gone up massively during that time."

De Wilde's observations have been validated by other RSC production staff, but budgetary decisions are based on many factors. The Pit is the smallest of the RSC theatres and is thus given the lowest budgets. Now that the Young Vic and Lyric Hammersmith are being used for larger-scale transfers, some of de Wilde's concerns about budgetary constraints have been relieved.

When the existing rehearsal space in the Barbican Centre was earmarked for other purposes, adequate rehearsal facilities were needed. Across the Thames and twenty minutes away via the Underground's Northern Line is Clapham High Street, site of the RSC's London rehearsal halls since 1987.

The RSC begins rehearsals for its first few Stratford shows in Clapham. It is more convenient and less expensive for actors to rehearse in what is the home town of the majority of the company, as their housing stipend for Stratford usually proves inadequate to cover the full cost of rent there. It is also desirable for the administration to rehearse in London during the first hectic days of the company's life when casting is still under way. During the rest of the year, the Clapham studios are used by the Barbican company for rehearsals of new productions or by other theatre companies that sublease the space from the RSC.

The rehearsal halls are housed in an imposing white stucco Victorian building set back from the High Street. It had previously served as a cinema, a temperance hall, and a storehouse for auto accessories before the RSC leased it. "It took a lot of hard work to make it into a viable studio space, but it was worth it—they're very good facilities and serve us nicely," said Graham Sykes.[26] Within it are three large rehearsal spaces, a production wardrobe room, wardrobe storage, rooms for the voice department, and other administrative offices. The building is light and airy, a pleasant change from the Barbican's windowless gloom. But Clapham borders Brixton, long considered one of London's more dangerous neighborhoods, and this causes some unease among the company traveling to and from the studios. "There has been some vandalism, and one does happen upon some undesirables late at night, but rehearsal space of this size is difficult to find in London, and we have no immediate plans to move," said Sykes.

The Season

The seasons change their manners . . .
—Prince Humphrey, *Henry IV, Part 2*

*T*he town of Stratford initially saw relatively little theatrical return on the Flower family's financial investment. From the inaugural festival of April 1879—consisting of *Much Ado About Nothing, Hamlet,* and *As You Like It* as well as a reading of *The Tempest* and a program of Shakespearean songs—until eighteen years later, theatrical performances at Stratford lasted just one week each year. In 1897, Frank Benson, the actor-manager whose company performed annually during the festival, enlarged the scope of the proceedings to two weeks, during which time a rather ambitious slate of twelve productions was mounted.

It was not until 1919 that the Memorial Theatre had its own company of actors and no longer needed to rely on the inconsistent talents of star packages and imported companies. It was in that year that William Bridges-Adams was appointed artistic director of the Memorial Theatre and charged with forming a resident company in Stratford. Although there was little time to rehearse the six plays presented in the festival that season, the groundwork had been laid for the Memorial Theatre's evolution some forty years later into the complex producing organization that would be the Royal Shakespeare Company.[1]

Today, the RSC performs throughout the year and can be seen at various times in Stratford, London, Newcastle, Plymouth, and a multitude of other cities and towns throughout the United Kingdom and the world. The modest few performances of those first seasons have metamorphosed into a formidable repertoire of two dozen or more plays presented in the company's two home bases. The evolution of the RSC season continues today and reflects a number of signal changes in the nature of artists' aesthetics, audience taste, and theatre employment trends. The character and structure of the RSC season have undergone radical revision in recent years.

The RSC repertoire is selected each year by key members of the artistic and administrative staff. It is not arrived at easily, for it represents a vision for the following two years. Former general manager David Brierley, who oversaw the RSC's fortunes for two decades, enumerated the factors that contribute to the complex decision making. "The selection process takes into account an artistic directorial overview, individual directorial aptitudes and preferences, performer availability (especially for the major, production-carrying roles), the 'mix' of any season to produce a balanced repertoire, our duty to produce all Shakespeare's plays from time to time, the period between new productions of Shakespeare's plays, the economic requirements of any season to produce a salable selection, our commitment to the presentation of new plays and historically lost plays, and a few other factors, too!"[2]

RSC staff members who participate in the process agree that it is an annual period of fevered wrangling, with continual discussions between directors, producers, financial staff, workshop staff, planning office, marketing department, production management, and casting directors. Agreement on a workable schedule can take months. In April 1997, artistic director Adrian Noble observed, "The planning never really ends. I've been planning next season, the one that begins in Stratford in November, since last January, and we're only three-quarters through it. It's very easy to schedule the first half, not too difficult to get the next quarter, but there's usually one final piece that lingers, sometimes for months, to get into place."[3]

The slowness of the decision-making process is compounded by the availability of the desired artists. Directors are often booked more than a year in advance of certain projects. The RSC believes that the most compelling repertoire consists of shows that directors hunger to do, so well in advance of the selection process, Noble and Michael Attenborough solicit wish lists of plays from colleagues, which are thrown into the hopper for consideration. As Noble noted, "Directors can be difficult, but actors fall out, too. It's a constant process—getting the right title, people wanting to do certain plays, myriad reasons—and it never seems to end. You can't do certain plays without certain actors, but actors won't commit until late in the day, and you can't do *Othello* without an Othello, so if your Othello drops out, which happened to us last year, you dump the play. You can't say, 'I'll go out and shop for an Othello.'"

Although the RSC tries to cast an ensemble that remains constant for the duration of the season—and there are sometimes as many as seventy-five actors each in the two cities' companies—all RSC members are not created equal. Some few actors are considered for a handful of plum roles in a season, while most fill out the supporting roles, understudy assignments, and walk-ons. The staff has to consider actor availability in deciding the repertoire. Competition has grown stiff among the RSC, the National, the Almeida, the new Globe, the commercial West End producers, and the television and film industry for the services of "name" actors like Derek Jacobi, Diana Rigg, Ian McKellen, Alec McCowen, Antony Sher, Eileen Atkins, Kenneth Branagh, Susannah York, Michael Gambon, Judi Dench, Jeremy Irons, Sinead Cusack, and others. Virtually every well-known actor with any classical experience in Britain has appeared at one time or another with the RSC, and most used to find it appealing, schedule permitting, to return to the cozy environs of Stratford to tackle another major Shakespearean role or two.

In the mid-1990s, theatre journalists as well as RSC administrators began to observe that the RSC was attracting fewer actors with box office draw. Although the company has continued as a launching pad for new, successful careers, most recently those of Ralph Fiennes, Toby

Stephens, Alex Kingston, Emily Watson, Alex Jennings, and Joseph Fiennes, it did not seem to feature the same number of choice, star actors as the National. The reluctance of established actors to join the RSC was largely due to the time commitment demanded from them, a commitment that was generally unequaled in the ranks of major British theatres. The RSC staff is fond of publicly making the point that the RSC makes stars but does not hire them. For example, the actors forming the nucleus of the 1970 company—Alan Howard, Janet Suzman, Patrick Stewart, Helen Mirren, and Ben Kingsley—were relatively unknown at the time but today are stars of considerable magnitude. Privately, however, RSC personnel acknowledge the need to feature at least a few prominent names each season if the company is to fare well at the box office.

Popular performers are generally booked long in advance of a season, and their contracts must be negotiated as much as a year before the starting date. For plays in which an actor in a "title" role—Hamlet, for example—must carry the show, the artistic directorate will first offer the actor the role before committing to producing the play. When attempting to secure a star, Noble and colleagues will sometimes solicit the actor's input on the choice of director. According to retired general manager David Brierley:

> The factor which slows down the process of announcing the season is the decision-making rhythm of the British actors. They are short-termist, with their minds now very much influenced by the fact that the greater part of most actors' earning power lies in television and films, for which, on the whole, offers are made relatively close to recording dates, and for relatively short engagements. Pro-rata, however, they are likely to be much more lucrative than theatrical engagements—and especially engagements in the subsidized sector. So actors delay until the very last minute their acceptance of an offer for a season in Stratford—however prestigious that may be—and part of the reason for this delay is, of course, that once taken, the commitment is for more than a year's cycle of work.[4]

Questions arise as to whether the paucity of big names has attributed to the RSC's falloff in box office revenue. In the late 1990s, frequent appraisals by both theatre journalists as well as company members considered the wisdom of the long-term commitments the RSC

used to require. Peter Hall demanded an initial two-year commitment
in the early 1960s, and that was maintained as the general rule of
thumb for almost three decades. When the RSC bowed to pressure
from British Equity and reduced the contractual commitment to eighteen months, the company acknowledged that it was making a necessary, if unwelcome, concession to the changing nature of employment in the entertainment industries. Now, however, the RSC finds
itself forced to offer even shorter contracts in order to attract leading
actors to the company, not by Equity, but by the continuing transformation of the actors' perspectives of contractual obligations. This
has resulted in two drastic reconfigurations of the RSC season in the
last few years.

The actor, director, and playwright Simon Callow, whose ambitious
stage version of the French classic film *Les Enfants du Paradis* premiered at the Barbican in 1995, expressed his concerns about the current state of ensemble theatres in England in an editorial, published
in November 1998 in the *Independent,* prompted by Trevor Nunn's
announcement that he would seek to return the National to an ensemble repertory company. Callow observed that true ensembles,
working together for long periods of time and often able to create
theatrical magic, no longer exist in Britain. He cited a number of factors as the cause, and his indictment struck at the very heart of the
issue: "It is more expensive, without question, to keep a group together
than it is to cast from play to play. And for a group to function at the
level that the RSC reached under Hall and then Nunn . . . the inspi-
ration, whether from an idea or from an individual, needs to be white
hot. Somewhere, they lost their power to inspire their members to
think of themselves as . . . an ensemble. Being a member of the RSC
or the National became just another job; a rather less well paid job
than the one in the West End or in television or film."[5]

Although the RSC operates on the company system, implicit in
Callow's article is the observation that a company is not necessarily
synonymous with an inspired and focused group of artists with a
shared vision and purpose. Other journalists have recently criticized
the RSC for failing to find the alchemical formula that would transform the company into a golden ensemble. Adrian Noble has answered this in part by altering the nature and duration of the season

to attract a group of more high-powered artists, and his maneuvers will be examined later in this chapter.

As difficult as it is to identify the most appropriate actors for the company and then secure them contractually, there are additional factors, cited by Noble in 1997, that contribute to the protracted nature of season selection.

> It's difficult to find the right balance in the repertoire. About this time last year, I was aware that the new play titles that I was wanting to do weren't going to come in time for this particular Stratford season. I was working with The Other Place's artistic head, Katie Mitchell, on developing a new season there, and we decided to not do any new plays at Stratford this year. I wanted to do *Little Eyolf, Camino Real,* and *The Mysteries* down the road at The Other Place, so we had to balance that work with the work done at the other theatres. This year, The Other Place's plays are very much linked by theme, but in the future we may not have that, although I do hope it continues to present plays with strong, intellectual thrust.[6]

If the RSC is to fill seats in Stratford—and with the building of the Swan and The Other Place, there are many more seats to fill than in the days of Peter Hall—the repertoire has to balance experimental work, or work that is less immediately recognizable, with those Shakespeare plays that traditionally attract large audiences. If the RSC staged four different Shakespeare play every year in Stratford without recycling, it could theoretically present each play every nine years. In practice however, that is not done, as not every Shakespeare play can attract a significant audience; *Titus Andronicus* is rarely considered a crowd pleaser. In the 1998–1999 season, the RSC staged the historically low box office–drawing *Troilus and Cressida* as its regional tour (it also played the Pit and the Swan) but balanced it with *Richard III,* featuring Robert Lindsay, the popular star of *Me and My Girl.* However, *Richard III* had played in Stratford as recently as the 1995–1996 season. The argument can be made that frequently reinventing these rich classics can result in artistic innovation as well as the introduction of new audiences to the Shakespearean canon. Conversely, one can argue that the more often the most popular plays are offered, the smaller the likelihood for staging the lesser-known works. But perhaps that is as it should be, for not all Shakespeare plays are of the same caliber. And while a mixture of new plays and classics offers a greater range of artistic challenges for both artists and audiences, it is difficult for a theatre, even one as large as the RSC, to be all things to all people. Still, Noble is resolute in his desire to continue to stage those works of Shakespeare that are less well known or considered more problematic.

> In 1996, I started to stage some of the more difficult plays of Shakespeare on the main stage. We started it with *Troilus and Cressida,* continued this season with *Cymbeline,* and will continue in the future. And audiences have not responded to these shows as well as we'd like. But it seems to me that you have to look pretty long term at this. I think if I put *Merchant of Venice* or *Twelfth Night* on instead of these two plays, our box office would be considerably higher, but I don't think that's the way we should proceed. I think we should be taking risks and educating an audience into some of the most beautiful plays in the language but not always the most popular titles. And I think we have to break that circle of pop plays, high box office.

Along with the consideration of the drawing power of various Shakespeare plays, the place of new work in the RSC season must be factored into the seasonal mix. With the cutback to a six- or seven-month season in the Barbican, new play production was guaranteed to be eclipsed by established works. Critic Michael Coveney, writing in the *New Statesman* in the spring of 1998, took the RSC to task for the dearth of new plays in London.

> New work is no longer risked on the Barbican main stage. Where once there was *Les Misérables* playing against an important Howard Barker season in the Pit in the mid-1980s, there is now no definable tension or gritty planning in the programme.
>
> There has been no major new play on the Barbican stage since the debacle of *Columbus* by Richard Nelson several years ago. It is as though all creative faith in the public dimension of new writing there has evaporated.[7]

Coveney's assertions as to the number of new plays produced cannot be denied, but it must be taken in the context of the RSC's evolving mission. As will be seen later in this chapter, a series of decisions made by Noble and the administration dictated against the likelihood, at least in its current incarnation, that the RSC will produce as many new plays as it had a decade ago.

Michael Attenborough is passionate about the need for the RSC to continue its varied production season, but he also acknowledged that the RSC faces an ongoing struggle to define its artistic identity.

> To have a company performing a new play, say *The Broken Heart* by Anne Devlin, one night and *Measure for Measure* the next, you've got a richness of artistic language that vastly stretches the resources of the company, both actors and others. And I would argue that it gives our audience a range of opportunities of plays to see. It's hard to do this kind of work and stay afloat financially. Although we did eradicate a £3.1 million deficit between 1990 and 1995, I sometimes think we're to some extent swimming against the tide. Ten years ago, young directors all wanted to do new plays, and now they all want to work on the classics, because they rightly see that's the only way to make a splash for themselves. I think a lot of the most talented directors have had an affinity for classical work and have found a lot of contemporary work too influenced by film and television. But it's harder now than it was twenty years ago to persuade the really exciting up-and-coming actors and even the more established ones to come and spend a year in Stratford to do classical work. You have to shell out for accommodation; you live away from home, wife, and kids; and it's hard work. You've got to have a particular bent for that, to say, "I'm sorry, I'll probably be subsidizing the RSC, and I'll miss my kids like mad, but I *have* to play Othello." Nowadays, careerism and instant opportunity and instant success have tended to take the place of the much more structured sense of how you become an accomplished actor, which existed twenty years ago. I don't think it exists nearly to the same degree now, and that makes life difficult for us. But we remain committed to the ideas we believe in.[8]

The Changing Seasons

It was fairly easy to describe the RSC's production season prior to 1996. There were innovations and revisions in season selection and scheduling over the decades, many occasioned by the building or renovation of new theatres, and by the early 1990s, a certain pattern was set that responded to the administration's perception of company and audience needs. But since 1996, the season has been in extreme flux while an earnest attempt is made to craft the most sensible approach to producing in a rapidly changing landscape. An examination of the older scheme will show how recent exigencies, in tandem with Adrian Noble's vision of the RSC's mission, have forced the company to radically reinvent itself.

The RSC is a repertory company, rotating a number of productions, usually on a daily or per-performance basis. Prior to 1996, it was typical for the RSC to cast a company of actors for a season in Stratford composed of four or five slots of plays, each slot comprising one play in each of the theatres. Actors, who were usually cast in several plays over the season, could be cast in only one play in a given slot, since these plays were always performed at the same time. Rehearsals for the first two slots began in January in the Clapham studios in London, and the two slots of plays (usually two shows in both the RST and Swan, and one in The Other Place) opened within a few weeks of each other in late March. Shows rotated so that on a matinee day—Saturday, for instance—one could see two different performances. A visitor to Stratford could, in a couple of days, see all the shows running at that early point in the season.

The company remained in Stratford until late January of the following year, performing anywhere from eleven to thirteen or more plays (four or five each in the RST and Swan and three or four in The Other Place). Often, a regional touring show with a separate cast performed in the Swan or The Other Place, departed for its tour, and returned to Stratford at the end of the season to give more performances. Roughly 75 percent of the company was cast at the start of the season, with the rest added after the first slot of plays opened. Plays opened periodically throughout the year, so many actors in the company both rehearsed and performed on a daily basis for much of the time.

After the Stratford season closed in late January, the company moved to the industrial center of Newcastle-upon-Tyne in northeast England, where it performed the entire Stratford repertoire in three theatres over a five-week period. The Stratford offerings were performed in separate, straight one-week runs, a simpler and more cost-effective means of presenting so many shows in a short time span. As the shows were performed for a largely resident audience in Newcastle, there was no advantage in employing the more expensive rotating repertory system there.

While the company was away, the Stratford theatres received necessary refurbishing and annual maintenance and then opened for about six weeks of Winter Visitors' Season performances of touring companies, one-person shows, and local amateur groups. In March, the cycle began again with the arrival of a fresh company from the Clapham rehearsal studios in London.

It was at the end of the Newcastle engagement that the actors' initial sixty-week contract ended. David Brierley referred above to the actors' two-year commitment to the RSC, but that was a commitment in the spirit—rather than the letter—of the law. The RSC had sought a contractual obligation for a full two years, but British Equity ruled that sixty weeks was the maximum period of time it would sanction for initial contracts, to allow the actors some flexibility should other opportunities arise. Although some actors would invariably decide to leave at the end of the first contractual cycle—which usually fell after Newcastle—the majority did sign on for another tour of duty, usually in six-month increments. But gradually a change could be detected in actors' enthusiasm for a long-term contract, according to David Brierley.

> Not long ago, the idea of a two-year cycle of work at the RSC was quite the news, but it no longer is. People no longer want to sign up for two years; they don't even want to do it morally, they want to feel free to get on with a different sort of life before the two years are up. If you look at what's happened in the Barbican in the early and mid-nineties, you see that they've really been broken seasons. We have been able to hang on to the services of the original Stratford company there till about September, and then there seems to be a complete transfusion, and almost another company has had to be raised to finish off the Barbican season. Making the arrangements for that had become disproportionately burdensome, taking an immense amount of casting and directorial and other resources to try to finish off the season in what is a good, solid, quality way.[9]

After Newcastle, the company then moved to London in March and opened at the Barbican. The entire Stratford repertoire was performed on the two Barbican stages—with openings staggered throughout the year—until late February of the following year, at which time the Barbican closed briefly for maintenance. In the rare instance that the administration viewed a particular show as both an artistic and financial failure, it was dropped from the repertoire before the company arrived in London, but plays considered weak at the box office but artistically worthy were almost always allowed to play for some period of time there. The Barbican and the Pit each offered the Stratford

transfers as well as one or two new productions mounted specifically
for London. This infusion of new work late in the cycle energized the
actors when their artistic spirits were beginning to sag and renewed
the interest of critics and audiences.

The three or four new productions that debuted in London closed
at the end of the season, transferred to a commercial engagement, or
toured. They were rarely performed in Stratford. In 1993, Adrian
Noble experimented with a new approach to scheduling. Production
manager Geoff Locker explained the motivation.

> There was always a logjam at the beginning of the year, what with
> the end of the previous Stratford season, the Newcastle tour, the open-
> ing of the Barbican season, and the scramble to cast the company. It
> was Adrian's idea that we could start the season with two plays in the
> RST and the Swan that had originated at the Barbican or on tour. One
> of them, the RST production, would have a star in the leading role.
> These plays would run for six to eight weeks in straight runs; when
> they closed, these casts would disband, and then the new Stratford
> company would begin performing the next two slots as in previous
> years. This would guarantee a smoother opening in Stratford, as we
> wouldn't be trying to keep too many balls in the air at once, and
> would alleviate some of the pressure at a critical time in the season.[10]

Previously, shows had rarely transferred from London to Stratford,
and it had been decades since a straight run of several weeks had been
attempted during the season. But it was viewed as a worthwhile experiment. A critically successful, star-driven production would likely
sell out quickly and launch the season with great publicity fanfare.
Locker admitted, though, that "in reality all it did was push the casting problems back from January to March. We still had to put a company together."

In 1993, the Stratford season opened in the RST with *Hamlet*, starring and directed by Kenneth Branagh. This production had been the
last play to open at the Barbican in the previous season. According
to David Brierley, "it was the first time in the company's history that
a Shakespeare play had opened in London and transferred to Stratford."[11] The Swan opened with *Richard III*, with the RSC's rising star,
the chameleon-like Simon Russell Beale, in the title role. This note-
worthy production had played in Stratford the previous summer at
The Other Place before departing on an international tour. Noble

correctly predicted that Kenneth Branagh had sufficient drawing power to lure theatregoers who had traveled to Stratford for *Hamlet* to also see *Richard III.*

The two productions opened in mid-March and played simultaneous straight runs of seven weeks, after which the two casts were disbanded and the RSC reverted to its traditional seasonal schedule. The repertoire opened in the RST and the Swan, respectively, with *King Lear,* starring Robert Stephens in a career-reviving turn, and T. S. Eliot's *Murder in the Cathedral,* with Michael Feast as Becket in a stark, austere, pre–World War II Canterbury. Two weeks later in the RST, David Calder, Penny Downie, and Owen Teale debuted in *The Merchant of Venice,* set in a contemporary world of cutthroat corporate traders; and Michael Bogdanov's darkly comic version of Carlo Goldoni's *The Venetian Twins,* with David Troughton in the eponymous roles, opened in the Swan. At the same time, Katie Mitchell's electrically charged production of Henrik Ibsen's *Ghosts,* with Jane Lapotaire and Simon Russell Beale, launched The Other Place's season. By the first week of June, five plays were running in the repertoire. In early August, the next slot opened. Audiences saw Alec McCowen and Simon Russell Beale in Sam Mendes's production of *The Tempest,* Max Stafford-Clark's delightful production of the Restoration comedy *The Country Wife,* and David Thacker's contemporary spin on *Julius Caesar* in the RST, the Swan, and The Other Place, respectively. *Julius Caesar* was cast outside of the main company, because it would have to leave for a national tour after its summer run. In mid-October, the fourth and final slot debuted with Daniel Massey in *Love's Labour's Lost* in the RST, the world premiere of David Pownall's *Elgar's Rondo* in the Swan, and Ron Wooden's adaptation of *Moby Dick* in The Other Place. The season ended in late January 1994. The balance and mix of plays is representative of a typical Stratford repertoire. The straight run of two plays at the start of the season proved a successful and effective means to inaugurate the year and was repeated the following January with the enormously popular Derek Jacobi and Cheryl Campbell in *Macbeth* in the RST and with Alan Ayckbourn's *Wildest Dreams* in the Swan.

This new system offered a viable solution to starting the season smoothly, said David Brierley, "only if we had a major name actor in the title role. It's essential to have a star if you're going to attempt a straight run of several weeks in Stratford. As it might not always be feasible to attract such an actor, we couldn't guarantee that this scheme would continue indefinitely."[12] In 1995, the RSC reverted to its normal system and began the season with several plays in the repertoire.

Although the RST continues as the premiere venue for producing Shakespeare, the 1998 season opened with a production of Richard Brinsley Sheridan's *The School for Scandal* in a straight run, followed by *The Lion, the Witch and the Wardrobe* in the repertoire—two rare occasions that the RST's stage has seen the work of other playwrights during the season. Similarly, the Swan has drifted from Trevor Nunn's original intent as a site to stage the works of Shakespeare's predecessors and contemporaries. In the 1997–1998 season, for example, the Swan housed productions of Shakespeare's *Two Gentlemen of Verona*, the world premiere of Robert Holman's *Bad Weather*, and only one play by a Shakespeare contemporary, Ben Jonson, *Bartholomew Fair*. In recent seasons, it has offered the works of Tennessee Williams, Henrik Ibsen, Anton Chekhov, and a world premiere by Richard Nelson.

The New Season, 1996

In 1995, the administration announced sweeping changes to the RSC schedule that would reverberate throughout the company and the British theatre community. Chief among the new guidelines was the abbreviation of the London season to a tightly packed six months. Revisions included shifting the Stratford calendar from a March through January cycle to one that ran from November through August. Newcastle would now receive the repertoire in September as opposed to February, and London's new season would run only from November through early May. The RSC would seek out, in addition to Newcastle, a second residence city (soon identified as Plymouth, in the southwest, for at least the first three years of this new paradigm) in which to perform in October. The company also announced that it would increase the scope and frequency of its touring productions. According to Adrian Noble, this shift in seasonal policy was occasioned by a number of factors.

> This has been a period of massive change. In my first few years, I wanted to get the company back onto stable artistic and structural

financial footing. It then seemed to me that we were faced with a choice. Did we want to carry on doing what we did, which was fine, or did we need to respond to a shifting world and a shifting artistic agenda by a process of diversifying around the company but refocusing at home? The shifting world is one in which it is more and more difficult to run a repertoire or ensemble in what is essentially a freelance world. It's a shifting world in which we must rethink the idea of the RSC as a national resource. We have to try to focus our work, and that is very hard to do if one is as big as we are.

We had to redefine the idea of a national theatre and to refocus our work with less. I think it will ultimately affect us very positively. Such changes take a bit of time, around three years to work through the system, to stabilize it, and it's difficult for audiences. To be honest, I think the key is the creation of quality work. If that work is created in Stratford-upon-Avon, we can then be seen by an extraordinary number of people. If you look at England, Scotland, Wales, and Northern Ireland, 75 percent of the nation will be able to see RSC work within forty-five minutes of their homes—and that includes the wilds of Scotland! If you were to stay just in England, it's about 90 percent. And I think you literally start redefining the idea of what it means to have a national company, as long as that work is being generated out of Stratford to the highest quality.[13]

Ensuing howls could be heard from RSC Barbican staff who were anxious, with good reason, about their prospects for employment during the almost six months the company would be absent from the capital. Some in the administration feared that a shortened London season would result in a significant loss of revenue unlikely to be made up elsewhere. Directors worried that the elimination of half the London season would alienate actors for whom the time spent there was recompense for a season in Stratford. There was consensus among the company that a truncated London residency would vastly diminish the RSC's stature in the world of theatre. David Brierley, who had presided over many previous RSC shifts in policy in his almost thirty years as general manager, explained the reasons for the new approach to scheduling.

An artistic director should, absolutely and fundamentally, look ahead to try to decide what the company ought to be doing for its best and for the nation's and the audience's best in years ahead. There are two issues which have been driving us as we've been making these deci-

sions. The first is the view of the British at the moment and especially the supply of large-scale classical productions. We now are the
only company, literally, dedicated to doing large-scale classical productions. Companies like the Prospect and the Renaissance and the
English Shakespeare and the Compass, they're all dead and gone.
Occasionally, a commercial producer will take a chance on a Shakespearean play; the regional repertory theatres, which used to do quite
a lot of Shakespeare, now are hard pressed to do just one—and it's
quite often cut down in scale. And what's left of the big touring
theatres, about twenty-eight of them, the Palaces and Hippodromes
around the UK, don't have access at all now to productions like this
because it's not being offered. We believe, given that we're the company that's dedicated to doing these plays, that that's something we
must address.

Now, we haven't exactly been slouches at touring the past few years,
but it's been irregular, it's not been an integral part of our life. We
feel that we have to build it into the fabric of life in the same way that
Newcastle has been, and we should do one more city in Newcastle-
style residency each year. We have to make touring a part of life, we
have to maintain our regional tour, which we take to auditoriums as
a regular part of life, and we have to add the ability to take out Swan
shows into comparably sized theatres with similar dynamics. But the
driving issue is the supply of large-scale classical theatre throughout
the UK. It's badly disrupted, shrunken, and we have an obligation
to do something about that.[14]

True to Brierley's word, touring did increase. In 1995–1996, the RSC
gave 112 performances of one production on tour throughout the
United Kingdom; in 1996–1997, that jumped to 246 performances of
four different productions. Brierley also explained that the new policy
finally responded to the increased reluctance by actors to commit to
a not-for-profit company for lengthy periods, regardless of its international stature.

Actors have been telling us, through their actions, that they don't
want a two-year contract. So, we will cut down the cycle of what
we're inviting actors to participate in, to something like eighteen
months, during which time they'll have the chance to play Stratford,
Newcastle, Plymouth, or another city and then London for six
months, during which time all the Stratford work will be seen, which
is important for both the audiences and the performer. And there will
be perhaps one slot of new work integrated into that, rather than what

we previously did. That was essentially adding six months of new work halfway through the London season, after the Stratford repertoire had been running at the Barbican for a while, and everyone had their value out of it. That's the story. Actors' lives have changed much more of late, influenced much more by the possibility of short-term TV and film engagements, which we can't match in terms of money, and a general unwillingness to be tied up for any length of time. And this is not peculiar to us, either. In the West End, people are looking for investment in a vehicle with performers of importance, and they'd usually look for a twelve-month commitment, but now they're more than likely to get three months from these people. And you can't break even in three months.

The London production of Yasmina Reza's hit play *Art* in the late 1990s served as a good example of what Brierley described. Cast changes in the three-character play were announced every few months, and after two years, the play was healthy and profitable. The long-held belief that two sets of rules existed for the not-for-profit institutional world and the commercial sector was quickly proving obsolete.

One significant result of the shakeup in the season was the reduction in new productions, often of world premieres, at the Barbican. Noble sought to remedy this by emphasizing more new works at the Swan and The Other Place and an expansion of the work done at the Young Vic. When the new season was announced, Michael Attenborough elaborated on the issue of attempting to produce so many plays and produce them well.

> When I came to the RSC, you could put most of our problems down to one thing: we were doing too much. Simple as that. If we're to be a company, rather than a factory, those of us at the top must be in touch with the work. If we lose touch with it, if everything just spins off into satellites everywhere, which to a degree it has, you lose the sense of company and of quality. It's curious to note that all the people who have complained about this decision are in London, and all the people who have rejoiced about it are outside of London. But in the end, as I said, we will do less. There will be fewer productions. Now, that's a deeply unsexy thing to say, and some people get worried when you say you're going to do less, but I'm absolutely convinced the standard of the work will rise, and we won't be heading for the nearest padded cell out of sheer exhaustion. This certainly means a greater focus and concentration on Stratford, which is excellent, and to a

degree that means a greater concentration on the classical texts, since that is where it originates. It's a bit of a blow to new writing in London, and there will be fewer outlets for new plays, but we will continue to do new plays, and maybe if there are fewer in the repertoire, it will mean that the really good ones get in.[15]

In the late spring of 1998, after the London season closed, the RSC sent the best of its repertoire to both the Brooklyn Academy of Music and the Kennedy Center in Washington, DC. The company hoped that the income from the tour, combined with the benefits of initiating new audiences to its works, would have a salubrious effect. The productions sent over were Matthew Warchus's controversial, cinematic *Hamlet,* starring Alex Jennings, a linchpin of the company in the mid-1990s; Gregory Doran's acclaimed *Henry VIII,* with powerful performances by Paul Jesson and Jane Lapotaire; Adrian Noble's staging of the seldom-performed *Cymbeline,* infused with a mythical, Japanese flavor; the surprisingly successful production of the rarely performed medieval classic *Everyman,* directed with clean simplicity by Théâtre de Complicité's codirectors Marcello Magni and Kathryn Hunter; and Edward Petherbridge's acclaimed performance in Samuel Beckett's solo piece, *Krapp's Last Tape.* The productions were greeted by mixed reviews in New York, although they fared better in Washington. Vincent Canby posed the question "Does Shakespeare Really Need B-12 Shots?" in the headline of his *New York Times* review of the three Shakespearean productions. Although he found *Henry VIII* to be a compelling and vivid production of a lesser Shakespearean play, he upbraided the company for what he considered a lackluster showing overall.

> Though this tour was designed to show off the R.S.C. to advantage (and could, if successful, become a recurring event), it also demonstrates why London press support for the company has eroded. Some English critics argue that the R.S.C. isn't adventurous in either its choice of plays or approach to the productions it chooses to stage. They also worry that many of its productions simply aren't good enough. . . .
>
> Thus the Americans' surprise and disappointment when the R.S.C. comes over and, in addition to the seldom seen *Henry VIII,* presents fancified though indifferently performed productions of *Hamlet* and *Cymbeline.* Even its production of Samuel Beckett's *Krapp's Last Tape,*

starring Edward Petherbridge, is a letdown. It is a perfunctory staging of the classic.[16]

Undeterred by this criticism, the RSC sent another slate of plays
over to the same theatres in the spring of 2000. T. S. Eliot's *The Family Reunion,* Friedrich Schiller's *Don Carlos,* and *A Midsummer Night's
Dream* were presented to generally better reviews. Ben Brantley in the
New York Times lauded Gale Edwards's treatment of the Schiller piece,
titling his review, with some degree of admiration, "Vintage Soap
Opera (as in Castile Soap)." He observed that "Ms. Edwards brings
out the Jacobean blood and thunder in Schiller, plus a nerve-strain-
ing sense of the corridors of power as minefields. . . . The director is
not shy in underscoring her intentions, coaxing perilously heightened
performances from her very adroit cast members."[17]

1998 and Beyond

A press release was issued by the RSC on May 13, 1998, trumpeting
yet another shift in the seasons at the RSC:

**Two Stratford Seasons
Will Broaden RSC Repertoire**

**Shorter Contracts Offered to Actors
Actors will choose between six and twelve month seasons**

Adrian Noble today announced plans to broaden the RSC's repertoire by staging two seasons in Stratford each year. He claimed that
greater programming flexibility would prove attractive to actors and
be popular with audiences in Stratford, London, and around the nation. Building on his remodeling of the company which began two
years ago, Adrian Noble said that these changes represent the next step
in the essential modernisation of the Royal Shakespeare Company.

The new Stratford Winter Season was inaugurated in the RST in
early October 1998 with *The School for Scandal,* the RSC debut of the
popular Cheek by Jowl company's artistic directors Declan Donellan
and Nick Ormerod. It played for two weeks there and then opened
the Barbican season with a four-week run. At the end of October,
Richard III, starring Robert Lindsay, played three weeks in the RST,
followed by a large-scale national tour and a limited commercial engagement at the Savoy Theatre in the West End. In late November,

The Lion, the Witch and the Wardrobe opened in the RST, and Turgenev's *A Month in the Country* opened in the Swan. In early December, the *Lion* actors began performances of *The Winter's Tale* in the RST, and the Swan actors commenced playing *Troilus and Cressida,* which had debuted in October in the Pit. This represented another considerable departure from previous seasons, as two distinct companies were now playing in Stratford simultaneously, with no cross casting between the two. The runs continued until the middle of February, when the Swan productions left on a regional tour. The two RST shows, *The Lion, the Witch and the Wardrobe* and *Richard III,* then moved to the Barbican in March 1999, joining the Barbican season of previous Stratford shows and new works, and performed until the end of the London season in early May. Although these shows played London after their runs in Stratford, that may not be the case with future Stratford winter productions, which are now designed to play Stratford and then either close, tour, or perhaps transfer to a commercial venue. In this last instance, new contracts would be negotiated.

In March 1999, the newly configured Stratford Summer Festival debuted after rehearsals for the first two slots in Clapham. Ten productions opened in the three theatres between March and August and played until mid-October. They were then presented in Newcastle for a month and moved to London from December to April 2000, joining a handful of productions that had premiered in the new London season in November. Subsequent to the London run and the Plymouth residency, three of the productions toured to New York City and Washington, DC.[18] This company adhered to the traditional contractual commitment of sixteen to eighteen months. The new template was designed in part to restore the RSC to its greatest level of activity in Stratford in the summer months, which occur at the height of tourist season. In the previous few years, the season ended there at the beginning of September, losing a potentially lucrative late summer box office.

The May 1998 press release continued, now quoting Adrian Noble:

> These changes will maintain the RSC as the world's leading classical theatre company, with a redefined repertoire ensemble at the heart of its success. Remodeling the repertoire will give opportunities for actors who really can't come for long periods of time to join

us, and encourage those actors in particular to tour. . . . I believe that as we move into the next millennium, the RSC will continue to work with Britain's finest actors, presenting plays by Shakespeare alongside a broader programme, to the widest number of people across the country. Despite the difficulties of the past, and uncertainties over future funding, I intend to enfranchise rather than constrain the repertoire and, on this basis, forge an artistic policy for the future.

The shorter contracts proved to be immediately successful, with such actors as Alan Bates, Nigel Hawthorne, Margaret Tyzack, Michael Gambon, Kenneth Cranham, Eileen Atkins, Antony Sher, Robert Lindsay, and Frances de la Tour being drawn to the RSC stages between 1998 and 2000.

Another benefit deriving from the split season was the opportunity to attract younger audiences to the theatre in the winter holiday months. Although *A Christmas Carol* had formed a staple of the Barbican's holiday offerings for a number of seasons, Noble believed that other shows could successfully draw children to the RSC and introduce them to the world of the theatre. As he noted in an interview in the *Independent,* "It's fantastically important to get young people into the theatre, to own it, to celebrate it. *Lion* has been amazingly good for the company. We hope it will broaden our audiences in the long term. In the main house, we always had just Shakespeare and we rarely did anything that was just for families. From now on, every season will have something purely for family audiences."[19] Noble correctly predicted that the C. S. Lewis work would be successful, as the RSC proudly announced that it attracted forty thousand new theatregoers to Stratford that season. Continuing this policy into the 2000 Winter Season, the RSC presented the English premiere of the musical *The Secret Garden* in the RST.

Some RSC employees as well as journalists initially characterized Noble's reconfiguration of the production season as a gambit designed to address the RSC's worsening financial health. The RSC had been on a course towards solvency in the mid-1990s but saw its deficit balloon to almost £2 million by the end of 1998. This could be attributed in large part to the multiyear freeze of their Arts Council grant and very poor box office receipts for a number of productions. It is also possible that the absence of stars and the growth of the media's perception of a decline in the company's acting contributed to the significant falloff in box office revenue. Though financial factors contributed to the decision to revamp the season, the reconfiguration did result in a greater ability to cast the casting net wider and add more variety to the seasonal offerings. It also appears to have had its desired fiscal effect, if measured by one critical barometer of a theatre's health: the accumulated deficit was reduced to approximately £500,000 by the middle of 2000.

For some, Noble's attempts to address the serious issues facing the RSC were perhaps insufficient. A month before the May 1998 press release, *New Statesman* critic Michael Coveney suggested a drastic remedy deriving, it would seem, from a desire to remake the RSC exclusively as a nucleus for theatrical experimentation—something it had never envisioned itself. Coveney called for

> an entire dismantling of the current RSC and an immediate reconstitution of a slimmed-down operation based entirely in Stratford and dedicated to investigating Shakespeare and his contemporaries without concepts, designers, marketing strategies or sponsors, and with a hard core of around 20 dedicated, well-paid actors and the active, permanent participation of three or four living dramatists.[20]

While no one in the company takes this radical solution very seriously, it does beg the tantalizing question: what would be the result of a reconceived RSC? A provocative preshow discussion that addressed this very issue was held early in 1998 before a performance of associate director Matthew Warchus's stylized production of *Hamlet* at the Barbican. Panelists included Warchus, director and playwright Stephen Poliakoff, voice director Cicely Berry, and literary manager Simon Reade, with theatre critic Michael Billington as moderator. The heart of the discussion concerned Shakespeare's relevance to today's audience. Not surprisingly, the participants expressed substantially divergent views on how—and, perhaps more crucially, *if*—the RSC should produce Shakespeare.

Warchus, whose *Hamlet* drew fire from journalists and critics by spinning the production in a consciously contemporary, cinematic fashion and excising considerable portions of text, affirmed his belief that our familiarity with the plays breeds a certain ennui when we work on or see them: "I find it exasperating, given that Shakespeare is one of the world's most controversial writers, that everybody knows his stories almost off by heart—I think that diminishes him. I'd like us to find ways of helping him—saving him, if you like." Stephen Poliakoff disagreed, noting that every new generation of actors and audiences needs to be exposed to Shakespeare, but cautions that "we should be wary of re-shaping Shakespeare into something he is not. The plays can be done in many new ways but we shouldn't be making him into 'new work': we should have faith in new audiences changing the context of the plays themselves." He added, "Is it desirable . . . that the plays have to reflect the changing world, all the technology and fashion, which are moving so fast in this decade? Isn't that impossible, and even patronising?" Warchus answered that directors' overexposure to the canon can result in boredom with the work, which can easily affect the audience's experience, and volunteered the solution that perhaps directors should stop doing them. Poliakoff underscored his own position, saying, "There has to be a reason to put on any play—an urgent need, not just market research." Critic Michael Billington restated the obvious when he noted that in order to balance the books, the RSC must continue to stage the most popular of Shakespeare's works. "The nub of the problem is that there is a narrowing of the repertoire to serve the box office, whereas the audience needs to see the whole range of plays." Warchus replied, "We are producing him out of habit, *that's* the nub. Parts of *Hamlet* are actually rather badly written, and we shouldn't be afraid to say so." However, when an audience member challenged directors' reluctance to tamper with the language to make the plays more accessible to modern audiences, all the panelists seemed to agree that this would sound the death knell for Shakespeare. Poliakoff retorted, "Saying that people can't understand the language is patronising." Cicely Berry responded, "Just by speaking the language even quite uneducated people start to feel confident and articulate. That is the magic of Shakespeare's writing; it's not just the stories." Warchus cautioned, "We must celebrate the language but not revere it."[21]

Katie Mitchell, a former associate director of the RSC, offered her considered opinion of the state of the company's work in late 1998, seen against the broader social and economic canvas of the United Kingdom at the end of the twentieth century. Mitchell, whose work is often infused with subtextual ripples of class conflict and political struggle, continues to sound contemporary notes in her investigation of classical material. She is most concerned with the RSC's awareness of its place and its necessary function in the cultural landscape of the moment.

> George Steiner said, in a lecture at the Edinburgh Festival in 1997, that there's a natural life span to any institution. He said there came a moment where every institution will die. The point is, how do you stop that occurring? His argument is that it's often when something is at its peak artistically, critically, financially, that the danger bells should start to ring in your head, and you have to ask, "Does the current form reflect the ideas that birthed it, does it have the life, the petrol in its tank to move forward and develop?"
>
> I have a feeling that the last decade of Thatcherism had a fantastic impact on most human beings in this country. What it means yet I don't think we can articulate, but part of the changes which have happened is that these arts organizations don't mean what they meant, either within or outside the profession. Now, that's not anyone's fault, and you can't catch the moments where the meaning changes. We're only realizing now that in the last decade a quarter of the population have become poorer, are below subsistence levels, while three-quarters have become richer in real terms by about 40 percent. Now that's really interesting, if you've got an across-the-board drop in your audience figures, because you've got three-quarters of the population who are wealthier. Somehow, artists haven't been keeping abreast of all these changes, haven't been thinking beyond the immediate horizon about what function or role these institutions and the artists within them are going to have in what has been high-speed, devastating political change.[22]

The RSC directorate has taken steps to address some of the concerns voiced by Katie Mitchell by making more of its work accessible to the public via regional touring, usually at very low ticket prices, and by holding down the cost of tickets at its main-stage venues. As West End and Broadway commercial production costs spiral incessantly upwards, resulting in higher ticket prices, the RSC has maintained its ticket prices as low as it could over the years.

But Mitchell also addressed the issue of finding currency and vitality in the work itself, and the RSC has recently responded to her concerns. Shakespeare's panoramic cycle of eight history plays captures a cycle of medieval madness, folly, devastation, intrigue, and occasional glory that reverberates with discomforting contemporary resonance. Starting in spring 2000, the RSC began presenting them all in chronological historical order—Shakespeare wrote them out of order—as a cycle of plays entitled *This England—The Histories.* The company plans to complete the cycle in 2001. Michael Attenborough, the director of *Henry IV, Parts 1 and 2,* was quoted in an article in the *Financial Times*: "It seemed the right moment to look at the way this man looked at history, the way he considered the questions of national identity, leadership, and social organisation. So we said, 'Well, let's not be modest about this, let's do all eight.'"[23]

Season Slots and Double Casting

Shakespearean plays all require large casts—or a lot of double and triple casting—and as the canon forms the nucleus of the repertoire, the RSC needs to assemble a sizable company for its Summer Festival season. Roughly seventy-five actors are required for a complete season of ten plays, of which usually four are by Shakespeare. Additional companies are cast for the Stratford Winter Season and for the touring slate. As it was in Peter Hall's days, the primary attraction for the actor of working at the RSC is the potential diversity of roles in a mix of genres and styles.

To ensure the most effective performance schedule and to maximize the efficiency of the workshops, production staff, and casts, plays open periodically throughout the year in tandem or singly in specific slots. These slots are scheduled in such a way that every few months all the theatres in one city close down for about a week. During this time, new sets are quickly loaded in, and the plays are put through the paces of technical and dress rehearsals. It is always a stressful period when all the theatres in one city prepare to open within the same week. Each show gives about eight preview performances in a straight run before press night—staggered a day apart for each opening in the slot—after which the other shows rejoin the new production in the repertoire. The RSC is careful to schedule openings in Stratford and in London at different times so that the artistic and production staff, as well as critics, can attend.

Since each actor can be cast in only one show per slot in the regular season, it is theoretically possible for an actor to appear in four or

five productions. This is rare, however, as it is widely accepted that
actors need some time off during the season and cannot long sustain
such a pace. Performances are scheduled so that at any given time all
the plays from one slot are in performance. Otherwise, the entire cross-
casting scheme that governs most of the company could never work.
The beginning of the season, when the first two slots are in rehearsal
at Clapham, is a hectic time, with directors and stage managers bar-
tering for actors' services during the simultaneous rehearsal periods.
This will be examined in greater detail in chapters 9 and 10.

Announcing the Season

Although the RSC develops a projected calendar for both cities in
advance of the seasons and announces most or all of the anticipated
productions at one go, the public receives notice of the specific dates
and times of the season's offerings in installments. Given the inability of even the most experienced planning administrators to predict
the success and drawing power of all the shows in any season, it would
be folly to publish the full season's performance dates at once. The
RSC monitors its box office statistics and then announces new performance schedules in increments of two to three months. Colorful
brochures contain synopses, cast lists, performance schedules, seating
plans, and other RSC information.

Performance Schedules

Marketing surveys have indicated that many theatregoers who visit
Stratford do so for only one day at a time. The RSC's response is to
schedule, when possible, two different productions at the two performance times on a matinee day—usually Thursday and Saturday—in
each theatre (The Other Place, however, is often dark for one performance on a matinee day). This scheduling policy allows a customer
to choose two shows from a possible five or six performances on a
given day. It also enables audience members who prefer one theatre
over another the opportunity to see two shows in one day in the same
space. During the week, when two or more productions are running
in a theatre, shows play at most for two or three performances in a
row and sometimes change over after every performance. The planning staff attempts to maintain some parity so that at the end of the
season, when four shows are running in one theatre, each will get to

perform in the most desirable slots—Saturday night, for example—once a month.

During peak summer seasons, a ninth performance is sometimes added, usually a Tuesday matinee, to take advantage of day tourists. In the unlikely event that an actor or stage manager plays nine shows in a week (most actors are not cast in all slots, so this happens rarely), there is extra pay. The stage crew, which works all performances, is automatically paid a premium for working an additional performance.

In London, however, where most theatregoers are either residents or visitors staying for more than a day, it is rare for the RSC to perform two different plays in one day in the same theatre. This eliminates the need for expensive matinee to evening "turnarounds," in which the crews often have less than two hours to put in a new set, refocus and recolor lighting instruments, switch wardrobes, and set new props. The turnarounds can be tiring and time-consuming. When the 1993 Stratford production of *The Merchant of Venice* was put up or taken down, Shelagh Keegan's modern, sleek, eight-ton, multi-tiered steel set had to be moved in or out of the theatre in less than ninety minutes.

In both cities, turnarounds on a one-performance day are now accomplished during daytime hours. From the Aldwych days in the mid-1970s until 1991 in the Barbican, London crews completed their turnarounds after evening performances—during premium salary time. Despite resistance from the crews, management was able to convince the stagehands' union, BECTU, to accept a switch of turnaround time to the less expensive daytime hours. But some sets are so large and technically complex that when daytime turnarounds were attempted, the curtain had to be delayed. Production management decided that in these cases it was worth paying the overtime to the crews to change at least part of the set immediately following an evening performance.

The beginning of the season is a demanding period not only for those rehearsing the plays but for the production staff as well. Nigel Love, the former deputy production controller at the Barbican, discussed the problems his crew faced installing the season's first shows at the Barbican.

> It's always tight getting the first two shows into the Barbican and the Pit. They come from Stratford via the tour to Newcastle, and we always have to do some redesigning—sometimes, considerable rede-

signing—to adapt them to the Barbican theatres. At the beginning of the season, Stratford's workshops are always so busy getting the first Stratford shows up that they don't have time to make adjustments for the first Barbican transfers. It became expensive, as we would have to go to London contract workshops and pay through the nose. We were very happy when Adrian adopted the policy of kicking off Stratford's season with shows that had already been done either here in London or on tour, like Branagh's *Hamlet;* that way, the Stratford workshops are freed up at the beginning of the season, as the sets for the first Stratford shows have already been built. It was a lot simpler and faster to adapt them for the Stratford stages than to build new ones, as is usually the case.[24]

Transfers

Periodically, the RSC transfers one of its productions to the West End for a commercial run, the most notable of which was *Les Misérables.* This coproduction with impresario Cameron Mackintosh premiered at the Barbican in 1985 and transferred to the West End in 1986, a move that had been planned at the show's inception. Worldwide productions of the musical have earned the RSC more than £15 million in royalties. In the 1990s, a number of RSC productions enjoyed West End transfers: Sir Peter Hall's production of Peter Shaffer's *The Gift of the Gorgon,* with Judi Dench and Michael Pennington; Trevor Nunn's production of *The Blue Angel;* Adrian Noble's version of Chekhov's *The Cherry Orchard,* with Alec McCowen and Penelope Wilton; Michael Attenborough's production of Peter Whelan's *The Herbal Bed,* recounting a slander trial involving Shakespeare's daughter; Matthew Warchus's production of Yasmina Reza's *The Unexpected Man,* with Michael Gambon and Eileen Atkins; and *Richard III,* starring Robert Lindsay. The RSC has also forged a strong relationship with the Young Vic. Given the shortened London season, not every RSC production can be effectively housed in the Barbican. When the Barbican theatres are overscheduled, when a production—most often a Swan transfer—is considered inappropriate for the Barbican or Pit, or when a successful returning tour can benefit from additional London exposure, the company may mount a production on the Young Vic's intimate thrust. In 1999, the venerable Lyric Hammersmith also served as a transfer house for the RSC, with a new production of Pierre de Marivaux's *The Dispute.*

Simon Russell Beale as Oswald and Jane Lapotaire as Mrs. Alving in Henrik Ibsen's *Ghosts,* 1993, directed by Katie Mitchell. Photo by Ivan Kyncl.

Simon Russell Beale as Ariel *(right)* and Alec McCowen as Prospero in *The Tempest,* 1993, directed by Sam Mendes. © Copyright Zuleika Henry.

Left to right: Simon Russell Beale as Edgar, David Bradley as Gloucester, and Robert Stephens as Lear in *King Lear,* 1993, directed by Adrian Noble. © Copyright Zuleika Henry.

Kate Duchêne as Alithea in William Wycherley's *The Country Wife*, 1993, directed by Max Stafford-Clark. © Copyright Zuleika Henry.

Kate Duchêne as Varya *(far left)* and David Troughton as Lopakhin *(seated on floor)*, with Alec McCowen *(standing)*, Penelope Wilton *(center)*, and Lucy Whybrow, in Anton Chekhov's *The Cherry Orchard*, 1995, directed by Adrian Noble. © Copyright Zuleika Henry.

David Troughton as the title character in *Richard III,* 1995, directed by Steven Pimlott. © Copyright Zuleika Henry.

Robert Bowman as Sebastian and Haydn Gwynne as Olivia in *Twelfth Night,* 1994, directed by Ian Judge. From the Shakespeare Centre Library, Stratford-upon-Avon. Photographer, Malcolm Davies.

Robert Bowman as Antipholus of Syracuse in *The Comedy of Errors,*
1996, directed by Tim Supple. © Copyright Zuleika Henry.

Adrian Noble, artistic
director. Photo by
Stephen Markeson,
courtesy of the Royal
Shakespeare Company.

David Brierley,
general manager
(retired). Courtesy of
David Brierley.

Michael Attenborough, principal associate director *(left)*, with actor Ray Fearon. © Copyright Zuleika Henry.

Katie Mitchell, director. © Copyright Zuleika Henry.

Robert Jones, scenic and costume designer. Courtesy of Robert Jones.

Chris Parry,
lighting designer.
Courtesy of Chris
Parry.

Lynda Farran, executive producer.
Photo courtesy of Lynda Farran.

Geoff Locker, head of production and stage operations. © Copyright Zuleika Henry.

Andrew Wade, head of voice. © Copyright Zuleika Henry.

Touring

Travel you far on, or are you at the farthest?
—Tranio, *The Taming of the Shrew*

The RSC, committed by its charter to our greatest playwright and subsidized by our taxes though the Arts Council, has national responsibilities. Indeed, for its own healthy development it needs constantly to reach new audiences. What, nowadays, are the best ways of reaching such audiences through touring?"[1] This question was posed by Sir Ian McKellen in an article entitled "Small Scale Tour" in the RSC's 1978 yearbook. The previous year, the RSC had begun its annual residence in Newcastle, but Trevor Nunn quickly realized that a presence in just the southeast (London), the midlands (Stratford) and the northeast (Newcastle) was insufficient for a company committed to theatre for the entire nation. The RSC had, from time to time, sent shows on tour throughout Britain, but these were primarily large-scale productions that played in established theatres in major urban centers such as Manchester, Liverpool, and Edinburgh. In 1978, under Nunn's leadership, McKellen, then an active company member, was asked to devise a small-scale tour that would travel to towns without access to regular professional theatre. Jean Moore, the administrator who had done an outstanding job overseeing The Other Place, was appointed tour coordinator. From July to October of that year, a tour of *Twelfth Night* and *The Three Sisters* played in established theatres as well as schools, sports arenas, and other venues in twenty-six small cities and towns throughout England and Scotland. The performances were often augmented by student workshops led by company members.

In 1979, directors John Caird and Howard Davies, armed with a subsidy from the Arts Council and sponsor Hallmark Cards, expanded the physical stature of the tour by piling "thirteen tons of seating, two tons of scenery, costumes and equipment, sixteen actors, twelve crew, and two drivers" into two forty-foot trucks.[2] Again, the tour played twenty-five venues with productions of *Much Ado About Nothing* and Brecht's *The Caucasian Chalk Circle,* and the performers conducted workshops with students at schools along the route. The regional tour then became an integral and valuable component of the RSC's production schedule. Adrian Noble's 1995 decision to alter the RSC's profile inaugurated the company's presence in Plymouth as well as a greater commitment to touring.

Similarly, the RSC has a history of mounting large-scale international tours. In 1913, Frank Benson took his Stratford-upon-Avon Players to the United States and Canada, where sixteen productions were performed. After that, with the exception of the years 1932–1950, the company sent a tour to other nations almost annually.[3] One of the most influential RSC touring presentations was the 1965 New York performance of Peter Brook's revolutionary production of Peter Weiss's *Marat/Sade.* This terrifying realization of Antonin Artaud's theories of the "Theatre of Cruelty" caused a tidal wave of critical response, shattered many Americans' perception that the RSC excelled only in productions of the classics, and proved a turning point in the experimental theatre movement in America.[4] Six years later, Brook mounted another production that took America by storm. In a remarkable display of theatrical fervor, critics and audiences alike judged *A Midsummer Night's Dream* one of the finest and most revolutionary interpretations of Shakespeare ever presented, certainly the most extraordinary ever produced by the RSC. In 1981, Broadway audiences were willing to pay as much as one hundred dollars for a ticket to see both halves of the Trevor Nunn and John Caird production of a David Edgar adaptation of Dickens's *Nicholas Nickleby*. One reason the tickets were so expensive was that the complete overhaul of the Plymouth Theatre required to accommodate the massive, six-ton structural set brought the production budget to $1.2 million.

The RSC produces two sorts of tours: small-scale productions of works developed specifically for touring throughout the United Kingdom, which might also play a brief run at one of the Stratford or London theatres, and others that were originally produced as part of the regular season and are subsequently sent on tour. Both categories of tours may play dates at foreign venues. At times, the itineraries for the international tours are exemplars of a globe-trotting frenzy. The 1994 production of Katie Mitchell's *Henry VI: The Battle for the Throne*, developed to tour after a brief run at The Other Place, played four dates in England and then a week in Los Angeles. It returned home for two dates, then played a week in Milan, went back to Britain for seven weeks, and then played Tokyo and Kobe, Japan, as well as Manila. The 1996–1997 tour of Tim Supple's version of *The Comedy of Errors* played Mexico and the Netherlands in back-to-back dates and then returned home—before heading out on the international "road" again.

The small-scale tours are a highly effective means of reaching large numbers of audiences. The 1998–1999 regional tours of *The Herbal Bed, Krapp's Last Tape, Richard III, Troilus and Cressida, A Month in the Country*, and *The Dispute* played to almost one hundred sixty thousand people in forty-nine venues throughout the United Kingdom. Overseas tours played to an additional ninety-seven thousand from Nagoya, Japan, to New York City.

In the spring of 1998, the RSC sent an unusually generous package of five large-scale productions that had just finished their Barbican runs to both New York and Washington for almost two months. The cost of more than £1 million was picked up by American producers and British sponsors and not funded directly from RSC coffers. More often, a corporate sponsor such as NatWest, Royal Insurance, or Allied Domecq will foot the bill for a regional or international tour, and the Arts Council will also periodically subsidize the RSC's touring efforts.

In September 1994, Katie Mitchell's production of *Henry VI: The Battle for the Throne*—consisting essentially of *Henry VI, Part 3*, plus some interpolated bits from other parts of the trilogy and from *Richard III*—took to the road after two months of performances at The Other Place. After some regional British dates, it played a week at the Cerritos Center, a spanking new theatre complex just south of Los Angeles, as part of the UK/LA Festival. Like many RSC small-scale tours, the show was cast mainly with younger actors who would embrace the rigors and demands of a lengthy run on the road. But according to Lynda Farran, the RSC's executive producer, it was perhaps a mistake to send the production to Cerritos, given all the hoopla that surrounded Prince Charles, who was on hand to open the festival. Although the play received generally enthusiastic reviews, there was some criticism that the RSC had not sent its top artists to an event with such large attendance, said Farran. "We should have played one of our large-scale works, because in a sense the regional tour of *Henry*, which Katie directed very successfully, was designed for four-hundred seat auditoriums, to be taken to out of the way places that don't have theatres. Although we were very proud of the work, it was quite possibly the wrong decision to send it to Cerritos. We were showcasing a production with many actors who had never worked for the RSC before, and it was a bit hairy with all this attention, since it wasn't really representative of the kind of first-line work we do on our main stage."[5]

One RSC actor performing in the main-stage company the following season voiced some concern that these regional tours did not always represent the best of the RSC talent, as enthusiastic and well trained as the performers are: "No matter how good this cast is, they're still very young and have not got the seasoning and depth of character needed for the RSC's level of Shakespearean production. It's a bit misleading to foreign audiences, who don't understand the particulars, to sell a show under the RSC banner when the company have never worked there before. When an RSC main-stage show tours, like Adrian's *The Winter's Tale,* it is a different story. In that case, it's the original RSC company that's been kept together after the London run, or in the case of the Derek Jacobi *Macbeth,* after it closed in Stratford. These are higher profile productions and are much more representative of the power of the RSC's work."

That assessment is perhaps unfair, given the usual high quality of the touring productions. The RSC's regional tours that have played large American cities such as Los Angeles or San Francisco have generally garnered excellent reviews. Small-scale regional tours playing abroad may not present the same visual punch as Terry Hands's stunning 1984 Broadway presentation of *Cyrano de Bergerac* and *Much Ado About Nothing,* with Derek Jacobi and Sinead Cusack, but they are frequently excellent examples of RSC work. British audiences understand that there are varying levels of RSC productions and accept the differences. Foreign audiences are usually unaware of the distinctions. The productions are not advertised as secondary efforts, and the RSC name is a powerful marketing tool. A foreign audience seeing the RSC expects a high level of theatrical sophistication and is usually satisfied.

Henry VI: The Battle for the Throne was originally staged in the intimate confines of The Other Place. The set, designed by Rae Smith, consisted of a square wooden platform eighteen inches high, strewn with wood chips and dead leaves. A wooden wall at the upstage end framed massive double doors, shuttered windows, and a weather-beaten painting of St. George. A pendulous cast-iron bell, hung on a rope and struck numerous times by the actors with dirgelike effect, and the gnarled skeleton of a tree completed the sparse set. The few pieces of furniture—a simple throne, for example—were carried on and off by actors. An ingenious snow effect, utilizing a detergent-like compound that disintegrated after contact with the moistened stage floor, added to the stark, wintry atmosphere. The costumes, also by Smith, evoked the fifteenth century but incorporated many contemporary notes, most notably the leather jackets worn by some of the men. The effects of the play's deadly cycles of internal strife and civil war were conveyed with chilling visual simplicity.

The production was built to play British venues used for other purposes, such as sports arenas, factory cafeterias, and school gymnasiums. The tour was a self-contained unit carrying its own set, lighting, costumes, props, sound equipment, and seating modules. On the international portion of the itinerary, where it played traditional theatres, there was no need to ship seating, lighting, or sound equipment. The tour played three types of houses: the nontheatrical spaces, where the RSC supplied every aspect of the physical environment; "bare" theatres in which the company supplied its own lighting and sound equipment; and fully equipped theatres, such as the Cerritos Center, where the house lighting and sound systems were used.

Jasper Gilbert was the tour manager for *Henry VI* responsible for moving the show throughout the United Kingdom and around the world. Gilbert, a graduate of the Central School of Speech and Drama in London, started work at the RSC in 1983 as a member of the stage management team. Because of the highly effective production management staff at the RSC, said Gilbert, "a good RSC stage manager doesn't have to be a good technician and generally doesn't have much opportunity to stretch those muscles if he is. I am a good one, however, and enjoy that part of the work, so I got involved with the tours, where that background is essential."[6]

Gilbert began work on the tour seven months prior to its departure from Stratford. His job, a composite of company and production management, involved supervising the building of the sets and props to ensure easy storage and loading, selecting the lighting and sound equipment, and with the help of the workshops, devising the seating units. He was in touch with each venue, discussing schedules, budgets, housing, transportation, technical facilities, and the like, and he traveled in advance to each city to see for himself just how the show had to be adjusted to work in that particular, idiosyncratic space. He coordinated the travel of the company and the physical production as well. In the United Kingdom, the physical production and seating units were hauled on four tractor trailers; for international dates, it was packed, without the seating, into forty airfreight containers. Four sets were built so that during the international dates one set could remain in the United Kingdom while the other three were shipped to different continents in anticipation of the tour's arrival. These sets were sent on slower, reasonably priced cargo ships. The rest of the equipment—costumes, props, wigs, and the like—was sent by the much more expensive means of airfreight.

The regional portion of the tour was "kamikaze theatre," according to Gilbert, requiring quick adjustments by the cast and crew every week to radically new spaces. Intrinsic to the success of any tour is a high level of flexibility by cast and staff, and for shows playing only in traditional theatres, this is not a major concern. The regional tours, however, being sent to towns in the United Kingdom that often do not have a theatre, were faced with the challenge of fitting the show into an entirely new environment at each new location. This challenge was one aspect of the job that Gilbert relished, for then he had to be creative, adjusting the variables as needed to create the most consistent environment for the performers and the most appropriate and effective seating arrangement for the audience.

On the road, Gilbert is the final authority. "When you're dealing with people who run these nontheatre spaces, there's got to be someone to say yes and no; otherwise, it's a recipe for disaster." The company typically arrived at a regional British venue at 2:00 P.M., and the crew of three stage managers, two carpenters, two electricians, two wardrobe staff, and one sound engineer began loading in the production, working until about eleven at night. Work continued the following day, with the cast arriving at 6:30 P.M. for a 7:30 curtain. This schedule allowed the actors only a quick look around; they had to make their physical and vocal adjustments for the space on the fly, so to speak, during performance. British Equity rules dictate the total number of hours actors are allowed to work in a performance week, and actors cannot be called for spacing rehearsals—often needed to adjust to the configuration of a new theatre—during the day. After the final show, the load-out might take from five to ten hours, depending on the layout of the theatre and access to the trucks.

The production, designed initially for The Other Place, worked best in the three-quarter configuration, and as Gilbert pointed out, "There's no time to adjust, so it's critical in setting up the scenery for me to maintain the same actor-audience relationship in each space." Director Katie Mitchell traveled to California, however, to restage the play for the nine-hundred-seat proscenium theatre at the Cerritos Center, and the actors employed this staging on the tour's subsequent proscenium dates. According to Gilbert, Mitchell didn't make too many adjustments. "On a show like this, which will play so many different spaces, it's important for the director to have the confidence in the production to not make too many changes when it goes into a proscenium house. Given the nature of these tours, it's best to let the actors run with it and adjust as necessary. They usually develop very quickly some very good instincts about how to play the show best in a given space."

Gilbert ensures that everything is where it should be at all times. Sometimes, however, the vagaries of fate take control. On opening night in Cerritos, parts of the set, some costumes, and some sound equipment had not arrived via airfreight from the United Kingdom in time for the curtain. "In these cases, you get on the phone and make a long, maddening series of phone calls to the airfreight people, all the while attempting to maintain your calm. And you just make do. In Cerritos, the house crew were terrific. We didn't have one of our pieces of very sophisticated sound equipment—it was probably somewhere in Guatemala at that point!—and the local sound man found an equivalent piece for us at the last minute somewhere in LA."

Gilbert also oversees the life of the company on the road, booking hotels and travel arrangements. "We don't book housing in the UK, just pay them per diem, as they all seem to have friends in a given town with whom they want to spend a few nights. In other countries, of course, we get them hotels." In a sense, Gilbert acts in loco parentis for these uprooted actors and crew, and deals with all problems with remarkable calm and equanimity. "In LA, two of the company bought surfboards, and I had to spend time talking to the airlines about the best way to ship these back to England." He must be ready for any and all contingencies, including changes in the booking of the tour. The Cerritos date was originally scheduled for September. But Prince Charles, the nominal sponsor of the UK/LA Festival, had to change his schedule, which resulted in the entire festival shifting to the end of October and early November. All the tour's dates through that point had to be rebooked.

The regional tour cost about £200,000 to produce, most of which came from an Arts Council grant. The RSC charged a fee to each United Kingdom venue of about £30,000 a week but didn't take a percentage of the box office receipts, as this portion of the tour was never intended to generate a profit. In the United Kingdom, according to Gilbert, the show lost about £15,000 a week, but the RSC was already charging the most they felt they could. "We make the money up on the foreign dates, which cost an additional £160,000 to tour.

Most of that we received from corporate support. On the foreign dates, we charge the presenting theatres a much higher fee as well." Also, the overseas sponsors in each city paid the company's per diem, airfare, hotels, and other incidental costs, which are considerable. In 1994, English Estates, the RSC's corporate sponsor for previous tours, withdrew its support for *Henry VI,* so the RSC was forced to depend upon the Arts Council grant and venue fees to fund the regional portion of the tour. Allied Domecq, then the RSC's primary corporate sponsor, funded the foreign dates in conjunction with local sponsors.

Despite the hectic pace, Gilbert enjoys the work and takes pride in it. "The regional tour used to be something of a second-class citizen at the RSC, staged by a young assistant director. Now, however, it gets national and international press, we hire a top director—Katie Mitchell, Sam Mendes, David Thacker—and it has a much higher profile." Still, the tour must be cast with a separate group of actors. Because they will leave Stratford after a few months, they cannot be integrated into the regular company. It is difficult to find a group of experienced, older actors willing to spend months playing small towns in the United Kingdom, so the regional tours are most often cast with younger players. Youth aside, the RSC is able to attract the best recent drama school graduates and members of other regional theatres.

In May 1997, the RSC tour of *The Comedy of Errors* played for one week at the Gershwin Theatre on the campus of the University of San Francisco. This was the last booking in a yearlong tour. Despite the oppressive heat wave that struck San Francisco that week—the Gershwin is not air-conditioned, and the small jewel-box proscenium theatre was stifling—Tim Supple's mournful, mystical, moving, yet achingly funny production of a play that is usually performed as an out-and-out farce sold out its run and received extraordinary reviews. Martyn Sergent was the tour manager. Sergent had stage managed for a number of years with the RSC and had taken out several tours. This production had played The Other Place the previous summer, a subsequent regional tour throughout the United Kingdom, and dates in India, Pakistan, Mexico, Holland, and other countries. It was a self-contained unit of fourteen actors, three musicians, eleven technicians, two stage managers, and an assistant director. The spare, whitewashed set, consisting of a raked deck and an imposing upstage wall with

double doors—similar in architecture, if not in style, to the set for
Henry VI—as well as the costumes, lights, sound, and props all fit into
one forty-five-foot-long trailer.

Sergent, like Gilbert, savors the rigors of touring, although he admitted that it was sometimes difficult for one company to work for so long
in such varied and often strenuously demanding circumstances.

> I think the last part of the tour before San Francisco really got to
> us. We played five weeks in India—Bombay, Bangalore, Madras,
> Calcutta, and then Delhi—and it was fine until Delhi. We all got hit
> with an intestinal bug, "Delhi Belly," and were miserable. And then
> we left Delhi and went to Pakistan, and it took some time to recover.
> In Pakistan, we played an outdoor stadium, our only outdoor venue
> on the tour, something like thirty-five hundred seats, and we had to
> do a fit-up in one-hundred-degree temperatures, and that was start-
> ing early in the morning. And it just got hotter and hotter. None of
> us were really up to it, and we really struggled. And of course the cast
> had extra problems to deal with, like the sound of the cricket match
> from the stadium next door and the traffic outside.
>
> But the audiences in India and Pakistan responded remarkably well.
> They were absolutely wonderful. One of the things left as a tradition
> of the Raj was a deep-seated and in-depth knowledge and love of
> Shakespeare, and the audiences were incredibly insightful. They knew
> the text, every joke and nuance, and went absolutely wild. People
> often ask me at home how international audiences respond to Shake-
> speare, and it's always difficult for me to choke back the response of
> "Well, actually, they get on with it a lot better than we do." There's
> something about Shakespeare that is completely international any-
> way. If the RSC is at your doorstep, like in Stratford or London,
> people often don't bother to come, but people will travel miles to see
> us if we're abroad, and the audiences we get are just absolutely phe-
> nomenal.[7]

The show began rehearsing in Clapham the previous spring with
only four actors in the cast who had previous RSC experience. It then
played The Other Place from June until August, when it went on the
road. During that time, Sergent was "zipping around the country,
setting up contracts, 'reccing' venues in Britain, writing to all the
places we'd play abroad, organizing transport, and looking into what
we could or could not do for accommodation." Although Sergent was
also responsible for dealing with ticket revenue and reconciliation of

box office receipts while on tour, most of the dates were sold for a flat fee—usually about £32,000 at home—and therefore wrangling with local box office staff about the complexities of the daily receipts was rarely necessary.

Sergent vociferously advocates the RSC's curtailment of the Barbican season and an enhanced touring schedule not only because it would result in increased employment opportunities but because of a deep-seated belief that it is a critical part of the RSC's mission as a national theatre.

> You're talking to someone who came from a place in Wales with no theatre and no access to it. I'm jumping for joy about this. It's all very well sitting on your bottom waiting for people to come see you, like in Stratford. That's fine for Stratford, where people are *going* to come. But of all companies, if anyone has the ability and the expertise to tour, the RSC should do it, should get in the trucks, play the inaccessible parts of Britain, keep the interest alive in theatre until a better time when these places have more money to put into theatre. And believe me, the interest is there, we see it week after week. People who have never been *near* a theatre in their lives come, because the RSC is turning up at their local sports center. They come in, because it's something to do, and the town has got *nothing* to do, and then they rave about it. They say, "I've never been to the theatre before, I was terrified to come," and we say, "Well look, it'll only be a few pounds, you can afford that." And we try to build an audience, keep the younger generation interested, show them there's something other than sitting in front of the telly all day, and it's an educational process, for them and for us. We learn a lot, an awful lot on tours like this about people. We make these judgments about the people who are the core of our audience, and we're often wrong. People of all classes come to the theatre in Britain, and it's not until you do a tour like this do you realize it's not the middle class who are dominating the environment. This tour certainly attracts all types, and I'm all for it.

Administration

I commit into your hands the husbandry and manage of my
house . . .
—Portia, *The Merchant of Venice*

Work at the RSC always seems to transpire at a hectic pace. Fax machines, e-mail, and an internal phone system connecting Stratford and London facilitate internal communications, but it takes at least two hours to travel between the two cities and longer to reach Newcastle, Plymouth, or any of the dozens of towns and cities to which the company tours. The distance between London and Stratford, however, is more than geographic. Staff members who work exclusively in London complain that they sometimes feel like unloved stepchildren. As Sally Barling, former manager of the Pit, put it, "Stratford is head office, but in the Barbican here we're lodgers; the city doesn't allow us to do anything without its permission, and we feel a bit cut off from the center of it all."[1] Some Barbican employees view the administration as "Stratford-biased" and believe that the theatres there reap the benefits of most administrative and planning decisions. One Barbican staffer explained that, "Although I'm paid year-round by the RSC, I only feel like I'm an RSC employee from October to May. From May to October, although I still answer to Stratford, everything I work on carries the Barbican logo, so from the public's point of view, I'm Barbican staff at that time. So, things have changed." Although the RSC administration has taken great pains to reassure the Barbican staff that they are an integral part of the company, this sentiment is understandable when viewed in light of the 1995 decision to truncate the London season.

The RSC's governance is established by its royal charter, and the company's titular authority is the Court of Governors. Governors are elected by the court and may serve without reelection until the age of seventy. The court's membership cannot exceed seventy-five in number and consists of the successful, the influential, and the famous. They meet twice a year but exercise little authority except as a rubber stamp. The real power lies in the few select committee members whose skills are most valuable in negotiations among the company and the Arts Council and the London and Stratford municipal authorities.

The smaller, twenty-five-member Council is the basic working body of the court. Councilors are elected by the court to three-year terms and may be reelected until their tenure as governors expires. They function like a board of directors since the RSC's bylaws under its royal charter invest them with the responsibility of guiding the company's course. But like most boards of directors, they defer the day-to-day exercise of powers to the professional artists and administrators they hire. David Brierley noted, "When it's reduced to its bare essentials, the Council have only two regular jobs to do: to hire an Artistic Director, and to approve an annual operating budget which he submits to them. They have no hand in appointing any other personnel, and they 'approve' the season's repertoire only in the sense that the Artistic Director will tell them what it is once he has made up his mind."[2] The bulk of the work devolves upon the Executive Committee, usually numbering six members. This committee is in close contact with the theatre administration, and according to Brierley, "They make the bullets for the Council to fire."

The Artistic Director

It is the artistic director's vision that truly guides the company, and his or her force of personality and theatre aesthetics establish the tenor of life at the RSC. The RSC's leaders have all been prominent actors or directors, some conservative and traditional and others fervently innovative. The first individual to lead the Shakespeare Memorial Theatre was an actor-manager of the old school, Frank Benson. In the late nineteenth century, when Benson first went up to Stratford, the role of the director in theatre was in its fledgling state, and it was not until 1919, when William Bridges-Adams assumed leadership, that the theatre in Stratford had its first true artistic director. He developed the first independent company at Stratford (Benson had his own troupe take up residence for the annual festival), undertook the then radical experiment of presenting Shakespeare's plays uncut and with only one intermission, and oversaw the considerable work of rebuilding the new theatre after the fire of 1926. His successor in the 1930s, Ben Iden-Payne, did little to advance the company's stature, at a time when Britain was experiencing the beginnings of cataclysmic events that would irrevocably change the shape of theatre and the nation. After the war, Barry Jackson undertook some necessary administrative reforms to enable the theatre to run more efficiently, but the Memorial Theatre again seemed artistically caught in amber. It was Anthony Quayle, George Devine, and Glen Byam Shaw, working together in the 1950s, who finally succeeded in attracting the best directors and actors to Stratford on a regular basis, enlarged the scope and nature of the theatre's artistic reputation, and resolutely pointed the Memorial in the direction of expansion and modernization. Peter Hall's visionary contributions in the 1960s included the development of a permanent company, the inclusion of new works in the theatre's schedule, and the critical move to London. Trevor Nunn, who was appointed to the post in 1968, continued the work Hall began and was responsible for expanding both the physical and artistic spheres of the RSC, branching into the production of musicals, adding more West End transfers, and increasing international touring. Terry Hands joined Nunn to serve as joint artistic director in 1978 and took the reins himself when Nunn left in 1986.[3] Adrian Noble has been artistic director since 1991. One long-time member of the RSC production staff was candid in appraising the artistic directors of recent decades.

Peter Hall had extraordinary political skill and government backing, which was crucial in establishing the RSC and getting us on our feet. It was his vision that put us on the map. He made us a company and got us going in London. He was a very good and exciting director and was instrumental in developing the high degree of efficiency in speaking the verse that our company possesses. He had a nice personal touch and lots of enthusiasm. We were all one big family with him. I think one of the reasons he left was that the job was so draining and he was so very tired.

Trevor Nunn is a terribly shy man, but he is one of the best directors I've seen, with keen vision and artistic vigor. You see a lot of emotion and a real humanitarian quality in his plays, and that quality transferred to his administration, too. He got the Swan built, pushed The Other Place and the Warehouse along, developed the Newcastle season, and oversaw the building of the Barbican. He broadened the RSC's spectrum in a wonderful way. But the theatre became too big for him, and his outside work kept growing, so he needed Terry Hands's help as joint artistic director. His idea was that he and Terry would rotate each year as primary supervisor of the work in each city, and David Jones would directly supervise the work at the Aldwych. But when Trevor started really hitting it big, with *Cats* and the like, he decided to move on.

Terry Hands is a very private person. He had a positive attitude about the company and the work, and the atmosphere was all right. Terry wasn't artistic director for long enough to effect any real changes in policy—he more or less kept the status quo.

Adrian Noble was very shrewd in initially focusing on communication and examination of policy. He is approachable and friendly, with a good sense of humor. He's really interested in the production process. He's not the type to just okay a designer's request for more money, for example, without examining it in detail and referring it back to the various administrators who deal with budget. Adrian is a little more willing to drop a show from the repertoire upon transfer to London if it appears it hasn't been up to snuff in Stratford. Adrian also was instrumental in developing the producer scheme, which has had a very positive effect on the way we work.[4]

The 1990 appraisal report by an external group of theatre professionals, written as part of the Arts Council's ongoing evaluation of its funded organizations, made the following observation the year before Adrian Noble became artistic director: "The RSC enjoys a close knit, very high caliber senior administrative team which has remained stable for a number of years. Partly as a result of the fact that the management team is so close knit and effective, practices have arisen which appear to result in poor downward communication and a sense in middle management of a lack of participation in the management process. It remains to be seen how the style and structures of the organisation will change following appointment of new senior management to succeed Terry Hands."[5]

Hands considered the RSC too large an organization for one person to oversee effectively. He proposed that the RSC governors allow his successor to appoint a joint artistic director to participate in the administration of the company, much as he had enjoyed with Nunn, and that the RSC establish the position of a producer "in the Broadway impresario sense, who would be a fixer, with a proper understanding of actors and producers."[6]

Although a joint directorship was not reestablished when Noble took the reins, he did implement the position of executive producer. One of Noble's first internal decisions was to refine the process of communication among the various levels of administration and between Stratford and London. Task forces and committees were established to report on the state of the company and to encourage dialogue across departmental lines. While it may seem that this theme's bell is struck frequently at the RSC, clear and precise communication in a company with so many employees in several sites around the nation is critical to the theatre's health and very existence. The 1990 appraisal report criticized the RSC for "a tendency for the decision making to be unusually centralised, which may be to the detriment of the participation, consultation, good communication, and the development of the next generation of RSC managers."[7] Graham Sykes, a former London administrator, characterized Noble's efforts to overhaul the communication process: "He gave the company a great boost when we needed it. New blood raises new hopes and expectations. These may not always be met, but in Adrian's case we have the feeling that his word is being backed up by his actions. He's approachable and believes strongly in talking—to everybody. He set up excellent channels of communication and more effective line management in the development of the positions of executive producer and resident producer. He encourages upward and downward communication. We have frequent interdepartmental meetings in both Stratford and London to disseminate information, attended by all middle management heads of departments. It's a very effective way to run a theatre of this size."[8]

Many institutional theatres rely on tradition—most often oral—to perpetuate their methodologies and procedures, eschewing written guidelines as evocative of corporate culture. All too often, the artistic temperament supersedes the pragmatic, and it is left to the midlevel production staff to impose restraints on directors and designers. The RSC has learned that the best way to support artistic vision is to articulate its purpose and vision and to admit the limitations and constraints under which it must work. Adrian Noble articulated his principles in the foreword to the 1993 information packet distributed to company members at the Barbican.

> The Royal Shakespeare Company is and must remain the finest classical theatre company in the English Speaking World. . . .
>
> Why do we do classics? Surely because they so often talk about the very frontiers of human experience. And because they contain within them the spiritual, intellectual, and emotional history of the nation. That is what the RSC should be trying to refresh.
>
> I believe we should do new plays not because they're new, not because they make points, but because they excite and amaze people, because they make them emotionally more literate, because they open mental doors.
>
> Wherever the insignia of the RSC appears—for example in the RST, The Other Place, the Pit . . . on the road, at home or abroad, we must all make a contribution, and our work must bear the stamp of the highest quality. One space does not have priority over another, rather the priority is the quality itself.
>
> We are, above all, a company. Our health and unity as a company is very important; in order to achieve and maintain the above aims, we must provide the means whereby all of us, management, artists, craftspeople, etc., are properly trained, regenerated and refreshed.
>
> Equally important we must never forget that the centre of everything we do is our audience. Our focus must be to provide, in whatever way we can, the finest, the most enjoyable, most complete ex-

perience of going to the theatre. In this, as in everything else, we are all crucial to the success of that challenge. We are a company for the people and the service we provide for them must be second to none.

Finally it is my firm belief that the best work comes from those who enjoy what they do. It is my intention that we should all have the opportunity to enjoy our work and I shall do everything in my power to ensure that that is made possible.

Although the position of artistic director officially includes the responsibilities of both senior artist and head of administration, detailed supervision of the theatre's daily operation itself is too overwhelming for any one artistic director. Authority must be delegated, and because of the size of the RSC's production output and physical plant, a large, interdependent organization has grown over the years to keep the company running smoothly.

The two administrators on whom the artistic director relies most heavily are the general manager and the executive producer. The former has always been a key RSC position; the latter was created when Noble implemented Terry Hands's suggestion. The current general manager is Christopher Foy, who was appointed in the autumn of 2000, following William Weston's departure earlier that year. For almost three decades, however, David Brierley occupied that position and was universally considered the guiding force of stability in the theatre's evolution. It is the general manager who administers the budgets, physical plant, workshops, company and stage management, and the technical production process among other areas, and Brierley presided with grace, rectitude and patience.

Brierley attended Cambridge, where he began to study acting but soon turned to theatre administration. He became president of the Amateur Dramatic Club at the time when Peter Hall had just left the university. Brierley went on to receive his certificate of education at Cambridge and taught English and economics at the King's School, Macclesfield. He joined the RSC in 1961, in the salad days of Peter Hall, spent two years stage managing in Stratford, and became company manager at the Aldwych in 1965. In 1966, he returned to Stratford to become Hall's administrative assistant and assumed the role of general manager in 1968.

Brierley identified confidence and trust as the guiding principles in his relationships with the four artistic directors with whom he had worked. Effective communication "is a process of osmosis," he said; without extraordinary efforts in both directions, the process can quickly degenerate.[9] It is largely a tribute to Brierley's skills that the RSC has weathered so many crises, including the early closing of the Barbican in 1990. The 1990 Arts Council appraisal report succinctly praised his contributions to the company: "The role of David Brierley, General Manager for years, is particularly important. His management skills, diplomacy, his grasp of the business of theatre, and the capacity to maintain an overall view of the complex workings of the RSC, have enabled the company to survive and succeed over the years."[10]

Adrian Noble established the positions of executive and resident producers to relieve the artistic director and to share responsibility for the supervision and decision-making process of production. Before this, since the days of Peter Hall, a corps of associate directors—all of whom were long-standing RSC members—was appointed and served, in Brierley's words, as "the artistic director's main artistic cadre" who would advise on casting, design, and other critical artistic issues.[11] Noble himself had been an associate director under Terry Hands.

But perhaps it had grown too exclusive, mused Brierley. "Adrian felt that the group needed to open up to a more catholic group of directors. He removed the confined collaborative support and opened the artistic director to a broader spectrum of directorial input." When Noble assumed the top position, he initially eliminated the formal body of associate directors—but maintained a core group of directors upon whom he relied for advice and feedback that would eventually transform itself back into a more formal group of associates by the late 1990s—and he developed the key role of resident producer as the new overseer of the production process.

The RSC's extensive schedule makes it impossible for the artistic director to adequately respond to the needs and problems of every production in the repertoire. Under the leadership of the executive producer, the resident producers—usually two or three in number—serve as a conduit for artistic and production dialogue on the shows to which they are assigned. They have the artistic director's endorsement and authority in the decision-making process throughout the life of a production, working closely with directors, designers, casting direc-

tors, workshops, and especially the production controller and production managers. "It's had a large, positive impact on the production
controller and the production managers. Now there is a concerned body
of people interested in both production matters and the RSC as a
whole. They're not partisan to the play *or* the theatre," said Brierley.

Geoff Locker at first questioned the need to insert yet another layer
of management into the production process. However, after a period
of adjustment between production managers and producers in the
early 1990s, Locker became convinced that the new relationship works.

> Initially, the producers were tacitly given budgetary oversight for the
> shows, and I felt that was a mistake. For all their concern for the shows
> and their charge from Adrian, they still didn't have the specific de-
> sign and technical knowledge of the nuts and bolts of a given the-
> atre that the production managers have. Now, the budgetary respon-
> sibility has swung back to the production managers as part of the
> evolution and ongoing definition of the producers' job.
>
> The producers do serve an important function. It's crucial for
> someone to have a long view of the show. Shows start in Stratford,
> but they have a life beyond, on tour and at the Barbican. The pro-
> ducer can provide the follow-through that was missing before, when
> each production manager would hand a show off to the next one. It's
> hard for the production manager to have a vision for the show that
> extends beyond the duration of its life in his theatre. The scheme is
> a good one, and I think it's all working out for the best.[12]

Almost a decade after the introduction of the producers into the
RSC, there are still those company members who contend that it is
an unnecessary layer of management. If the RSC produced plays in
just one venue, the producers would largely be redundant. But the
RSC's unique production process demands oversight that the production managers cannot provide, given their dedication to one specific
facility. Tony Hill, a former director of projects and a producer at The
Other Place, offered a producer's perspective on the relationship with
the production managers.

> I think in a way the responsibilities and roles of the two haven't
> changed over the few years the producers have been here. I think the
> producer is there to help the production manager. They're not there
> as a kind of senior production manager, though. Geoff Locker doesn't
> need someone to help his relationship with the workshops; I mean,

you might ask Geoff to help *you* with *your* relationship with them. But if Geoff turns around and says to you, "I have a problem with so-and-so," you'll listen, because your basic respect for the man's abilities is such that if he's telling you he has a problem, you want to help. But in the past, if he'd had a problem, he'd eventually have to see Adrian about it, and that could be a lengthy process in which the problem could fester and go bad. Now, he's got access to the producer, who's got the delegated authority from Adrian to sort it out directly, and in the unlikely event they can't, could ease access considerably to Adrian.

I think anyone is bound to raise an eyebrow when another level of management is inserted above you, but I think that we are there to do a complementary job to the production manager. In the past, it was hard for a production manager to say no to a designer; there would usually be some long process of negotiation. It's much easier for a producer to say, "No, you can't do that, you cannot have it, and you can stamp and scream as much as you want to, but you're still not going to have it." Hopefully, you're not going to have too many of those situations, but we have Adrian's backing in those events and also the diplomatic skills to make sure it doesn't happen.[13]

Lynda Farran, the executive producer, occupies a central and complex position within the structure of the RSC. In addition to coordinating the producers' assignments so that every production in the season is supervised, the executive producer assumes the responsibilities of deputy artistic director. She assists Noble and Attenborough in determining the RSC's overall artistic strategy, general policy, and future planning and maintains an overview of all RSC activities and standards. She has special responsibility to oversee the casting department, the literary department, the press, marketing, and publicity department, and the social and physical environment of the company and the audience. The executive producer also line-produces a certain number of productions and sits on the Executive Committee, the Council, and the Court of Governors of the RSC. When Michael Attenborough served as the first executive producer in the early 1990s, he directed seasonal productions as well. Attenborough admitted, in an interview published in the RSC's magazine, that his producing role was made easier by virtue of his work as a director. "It means that when I sit down for a note session, with, say, Adrian or Peter Hall, I'm not just reacting to the production, we're talking things through as fel-

low directors. Of course, you have to be tactful."[14] Attenborough left
the position in 1995, but he is still intimately involved with RSC administration in his role as principal associate director.

> When I came here, I had just had a foray into commercial theatre
> and had also run two theatres as artistic director. As executive pro-
> ducer, I found that I was more of a producer who might direct than
> a director who might produce, which made me slightly uncomfort-
> able, since I'm primarily a director. It was a misnomer for me in terms
> of how I identify myself, but it was a perfectly accurate description
> of what I did here. After five and a half years of this, I came to the
> conclusion I didn't want to do this anymore, and after long discus-
> sions with Adrian and with my chairman, I stuck to the view despite
> their trying to convince me otherwise. It's not true that I didn't en-
> joy producing, though when the problems begin to revisit themselves
> on you year after year, you begin to tire of them.[15]

In 1993, David Brierley cited the inbred nature of the associate directors and Noble's desire to start his tenure with new personalities
and policies as motivations for the development of the role of the
producers. In 1995, Michael Attenborough described how Noble, who
had eliminated the associate directors, was in the process of reinventing them.

> Adrian said to me, "I don't want to see you go, what do you want to
> do?" I said, "I don't want to produce at all, I just want to concen-
> trate on directing plays." He responded, "Well, you can do that with
> us, we'll form a team of associate directors, just come and work for
> us and direct plays full-time." So, for me, that's bliss.
> The return of the associate directors has arisen organically out of
> the work we've done for the last five years. Steven Pimlott, myself,
> and a few others are being asked to step into those positions. We're
> people who have worked here with Adrian, we know the company.
> The world has changed again. Bill Alexander, Barry Kyle, those folks
> were here with Trevor and Terry when everyone worked permanently,
> more or less, at the RSC; this is unlikely to be the case now. Even
> my contract, which indeed is a permanent one, has a clause that states
> that I have the right to work free-lance, at which point my salary here
> would be adjusted accordingly. Adrian has the desire to have a think
> tank, a source of ideas. I want to take over The Other Place for six
> months and put on plays from a specific period. I think it's impos-
> sible to run the largest theatre company in the world with two resi-

dent directors, and Adrian and I can't do it. Every problem came to me as executive producer and now comes to Lynda. I was directing plays, had all the Board responsibilities, sponsorship meetings, entertaining people, and fund-raising.

Lynda Farran's previous work included stints with various fringe theatres, the Joint Stock Company, the Cambridge Theatre Company, and the Royal Exchange Theatre, Manchester. Initially a resident producer under Attenborough, Farran took over as executive in 1995. Her first task was developing a relationship with the artistic director.

I talk to Adrian—a *lot*. I have gotten to know his taste. It seems to work very well. I certainly ask him all those questions of what he wants out of the company and where he wants it to go and what he's trying to achieve. I am, of course, much more on the ground than he can ever be. Although he normally spends a lot of time with the company, as executive producer my job is to spend as little time behind the desk as possible and really be out there, working with the directors and designers and everyone else. He wants me to be around, company-wide, with my ear to the ground. I won't produce as many individual plays as before, but I will certainly do some, since that's the best way to stay in touch with what's happening in our enormous company.

What we do as producers is work with the artistic director and help with the planning and programming of the season, so that's repertoire choice. And we also help decide which directors do which work and work on principal casting. We're involved from the very early stages. One of my responsibilities is working with the literary department on new writing. Basically, I work on Adrian's behalf to pull it all together, and I set the wheels in motion. Adrian obviously makes all the strategic phone calls and all the final decisions, but I do all the maneuvering and work on the planning and how it all fits together. Once we've decided on the season—and that's a complex process, because we're planning the whole season and trying to get it to land in one go, maybe a dozen productions in Stratford to start—we as producers take on a number of productions that we have overall responsibility for.

Last year I worked on thirteen productions, including the Stratford rep, new plays in London, touring, West End transfers, overseas, occasional filming, you name it. Each producer then gets on board with the director and discusses the team of people who'll be working on that show. Sir Peter Hall is very clear as to whom he wants on his shows, but some of the newer directors are less knowledgeable about

who is out there and what the options are, so part of our role is to
make sure we know who is out there and to broker marriages. Having done that, we're part of the casting process. We sit with all the
directors—and there can be a dozen of them—and the casting department, working together on casting the company of some seventy-five or so actors for Stratford. Most of the directors are hopefully present for most of the process, but it takes several months, and
each actor has to agree to a line of parts, not just one role. So, there
has to be common ground for at least three directors in that room
who are not directing in conflicting slots. That's quite a lengthy and
difficult process.[16]

While serving as the head of special projects at The Other Place,
Tony Hill, who worked under Farran's supervision, credited her with
the ability to keep everything she described above running smoothly.

Lynda ran a very large—albeit smaller than us—company before
coming to the RSC, so she knows how to see from day to day how
"large consideration A" needs to be wrapped up against "large consideration B" and not get lost in the minutiae of how we're going to
get this particular problem solved on the show. She's very good at
dealing with some of the stuff that threatens to drag a producer down,
like a workshop saying, "We can't get this particular piece of material at this price, and you need to solve the problem." She's much
quicker and good at being able to say in response, "No, what I need
you to do is find the places where we can use *any* material, and *you*
need to do that, this is your job, you're very good at it."

Nicky Pallot, one of the other producers, had enormous experience with new writing, and although the RSC produces a lot of new
work and has a dramaturg and a writing policy, to have somebody
suddenly working there, in a producer function, who's been doing
this for twenty years and who's really on the ball with contacts with
new writers and directors . . . that gives you a different perspective. I
hope the producer role does work, although it's hard to tell show to
show. You do certain shows where you meet the creative team in the
beginning, have a couple of conversations with them, make sure the
casting's okay, go along to the read-through, maybe have supper four
weeks later with them, go to a run-through, it's fine, go to the first
couple of previews, wait for press night, it's fine, good-bye.

You have *other* shows where you've already gone through most of
the ingredients for a pretty solid nervous breakdown before you've even
gotten into the rehearsal room. So, it's very difficult to tell; different

directors and designers and projects need different things, and it's kind of hard to work out sometimes what the flow of work will be.[17]

Health and Safety

Largely because of demands made by the European Union (EU), all British theatres are now required to adhere to more stringent standards of safety. It is the safety manager's job to ensure that the RSC follows the rules, maintains the codes, and protects its employees' health on the job. Until 1996, this position was held by Kevin Sivyer. With a background in chemistry and a bit of experience as an amateur producer and director, he joined the company in 1989 and was responsible for maintaining, as he put it, "a global view of safety at the RSC."[18] The safety manager is a constant presence at most technical and dress rehearsals and at load-ins and "floats" during performances from space to space. Responsibilities include attending to all details of safety in every department in the theatre. Once the designs for a show are approved by the artistic and production staff, the safety manager scours the plans for likely problems and discusses solutions with designers, production managers, and workshop heads and works closely with the local building and fire inspectors to maintain standards and codes. But despite the best efforts, it is still difficult to guarantee a high standard of safety on productions. Watchdogs such as Sivyer face the chronic problem that theatre practitioners, especially the older generation, often refuse to seriously consider issues of day-to-day safety, believing instead that they are a breed apart, a notion that is partially nurtured by the make-believe nature of the whole proceeding. Sivyer noted:

> There is a lot of intransigence on the part of many of the people here, especially the older crew and staff, with regards to safety and rules. There is a pervasive attitude not just here but in theatre in general that implies "we're theatre artists, therefore we're somehow special; we have been doing it this way for decades, we're invincible." The problem is that as technology gets more sophisticated and potentially more hazardous, safety awareness generally doesn't keep up. It's very hard to change old habits. Not enough attention is paid to small details. The stage managers have got to learn to develop better vision for problems on- and backstage. They should, for example, spend time walking the set with the cast prior to tech, but the director and

everyone else are breathing down the SM's neck to get started and not waste time, so the cast is often unaware in advance of the problems on the set of a given show. And matinee to evening turnarounds are a big problem, as the crew is often pressed to the last minute to make the change, and expediency, rather than safety, is the byword.

Sivyer identified the use of pyrotechnics, smoke, fog, and haze as an issue that continues to divide theatre practitioners. Directors rely on these effects for atmosphere and mood, and lighting designers frequently utilize haze and fog to create visible beams and shafts of light. But as technology grows and theatres try mightily to develop effects that can rival those in film, actors, stagehands, and musicians are increasingly subjected to harmful inhalants and other dangers, according to Sivyer.

> *Grease* was running in the West End, and the producers were sued for £10,000 because they use dry ice, and the operator in the basement who was working the machine in a confined space wasn't getting enough oxygen—there was too much CO_2 being given off—and he passed out. We once did *Henry VI* and used a lot of pyrotechnics for the battle scenes. When we first teched, actors and crew were all keeling over feeling sick. Hydrogen sulfate was being given off, which in small doses is worse than cyanide. The pyro industry said, "Look at the health specs." Most of these things are made for external use—you can shoot it off in the park with no problems, but it's not made for indoor use when the director and designer want flash-bang wallops.[19]

The safety department has no working budget; when Sivyer identified a project that needed funding, he would approach the production controller and submit a request. "I'll tell people that something needs to be done, and when they agree, money is usually found to do it."

As EU policies continue to evolve and performing unions develop more stringent guidelines regarding the safety of their members, company members will likely need to reevaluate production practices.

Finances

Thou hadst need send for more money.
—Sir Toby Belch, *Twelfth Night*

*T*he RSC, like most not-for-profit theatres, wages a continuing battle against a budget deficit, struggling for an increase in government subsidy, corporate sponsorship, private donations, and audience. This bleak but familiar financial landscape is traversed by artists and administrators in theatres throughout the United Kingdom—and in the United States as well. The RSC at times has been forced to adopt a policy of budgetary brinksmanship in an attempt to stem the growing tide of red ink. With its national subsidy eroded in the mid to late 1990s by a freeze on its Arts Council grant—which only recently received a slight boost—the RSC's financial affairs have generated significant artistic and administrative policy changes. But it must be noted that the financial affairs of any theatre tend to run in cycles, and despite some recent seasons in which budgetary issues were a greater concern than usual, by summer 2000, the RSC was enjoying a healthier fiscal outlook than it had in recent years. That might not always be the case in the future; it certainly has not always been so in the past.

The RSC, operating under a royal charter, is a registered non-benevolent charity—medical charities, for example, are considered benevolent—and is eligible for local and national arts funding and enjoys tax-exempt status. Any income the company generates from charitable purposes—the making of theatrical productions—is not subject to corporation taxes. Income from activities that fall outside the definition of charitable activity, such as selling merchandise, is taxable, but this is handled through an ordinary-income business structure that donates the profits to the RSC, so that taxes are avoided—a fairly common practice in these circumstances in the United Kingdom. The RSC does, however, pay value-added tax (VAT).

In 1983, Clive Priestley, a government official, was instructed by the Minister for the Arts to evaluate the financial affairs of the RSC, the Royal Opera House, and Covent Garden. At that time, the RSC was operating under a budget deficit of slightly more than £1 million. Yet in his report, Priestley noted that "The Company is doing work of fine quality; is demonstrating to the admiration of its audiences not just an impressive virtuosity but also the power of a great Company to exalt as well as to entertain," and he concluded that at present "the financial affairs of the RSC are well ordered and that the Company is not willfully extravagant."[1] The Priestley report pointed to many factors that contributed to the ballooning deficit at the RSC in the early 1980s, such as the directorate's decision to spend more on the physical elements of productions. Trevor Nunn and his associates believed that their reluctance to do so in the past had cost them dearly at the box office in Stratford, and they were determined, in 1982, to inaugurate the Barbican with a production that offered visual pomp and circumstance. But increased production costs generally do not affect the finances of a theatre so much. The most significant contributor to this deficit, according to Priestley, was the chronic underfunding by the Arts Council of Great Britain, or ACGB (now the Arts Council of England). He pointed to historical antecedents. "For 20 years, until the recent supplementary grant, the funding of the RSC lay under the shadow of a qualification entered by the Treasury when the

RSC was first grant-aided to the effect that if the RSC came to London and operated at a 'national' level, it should not have the same size (or rather scale) of grant as the National Theatre. That qualification now no longer applies but its effect is still felt because the base for funding has never been established to the intellectual satisfaction of both the RSC and the ACGB."[2]

Since its inception, the Royal National Theatre always received more substantial government support; in 1980–1981, 65 percent of the National's expenses were covered by grants, as compared to 38 percent for the RSC. The Shakespeare Memorial Theatre, subsequently the RSC, had been in existence for almost a century before the National arrived on the scene and had been doing well enough to succeed without such assistance, although Peter Hall had long noted the need for aid if the RSC were to expand its producing capabilities. The National Theatre, though, was being birthed—with a new, expensive theatre complex on the South Bank—so its subsidy was considerably larger than the RSC's. Priestley, however, noted with considerable prescience, "Although the disparity between them is wide and will remain a justifiable grievance unless now narrowed, it is unnecessary to look to a direct comparison. . . . The principal necessity is to decide on policy towards the RSC."[3]

Nick Paladina, the financial controller at the RSC, recently amplified this issue. "When we first got Arts Council funding, for many years it was on the basis that we might not get it the next year. The Arts Council were very loath to provide that level of funding to a regional theatre. It's been a long time to get away from being seen as such, to be seen as a national theatre. That's one of the reasons that Adrian got us out of London and out on the road more. And we're much more national than the National, both in terms of outreach to taxpayers—taking our work to them—and in representing this nation's dramatists."[4]

The RSC's financial fortunes in the 1990s were to some degree representative of the travails of all British not-for-profit arts organizations. Arts Council freezes imposed by the Tory government took their toll annually in the face of inflation and increased production costs. In the preface to the 1990 RSC appraisal report, generated in accordance with Arts Council procedures, the following appeared:

The RSC now faces a budgetary crisis. In the current year, operations at the Barbican have been curtailed from November 1990 in an
attempt to save £1.3 million from an estimated deficit of £1.7 million
for a full year's operation. RSC management estimate that the full
year cost of operating at both Stratford and the Barbican with the
current modus operandi will be £10 million before grants in 1991/92.
The intimated grant for the Arts Council is £6.26 million.

This deficit has arisen for several reasons, the most important being failure to achieve high box office targets, declining public subsidy in real terms, declining revenues from exploitation, and expenditure increasing above the rate of inflation.[5]

The consequences were grave, and the appraisal team was succinct
in describing the options available. "The RSC can only see two possible long term solutions to their current financial crisis: either the Arts
Council provides an additional £3.8 million to finance a year round
operation at both the Barbican and Stratford, or the company will be
forced to withdraw from the Barbican permanently. It is the RSC's
view that there are neither the economies to be made within the current operation to bridge this gap, nor sufficient opportunities to increase earned income. The Team concur with that view."[6]

These were disturbing financial revelations, but even more troubling
was the RSC's threat to shut down the Barbican from November 1990
until the following season's opening in March 1991, unless they received greater funding. Never before had the RSC had to consider,
let alone implement, such a radical course of action, but the situation
had grown desperate. It was certainly not a bluff, and the theatre followed through on its declared intent to close down for lack of subsidy. The action was seen by many as both a power play against the
Arts Council and the Corporation of the City of London, as well as
a move to generate public sympathy for the RSC's financial plight.
After this radical maneuver, the RSC emerged from the crisis with increased support from the Arts Council and with a first-time subsidy
from the City of London. David Brierley, in a letter to the author dated
August 7, 1992, expanded on this event.

> We had been in discussion with the funding bodies some three years
> before we had to close down the Barbican, trying to cause them to
> understand that the erosion of the value in our subsidy which had
> been taking place annually since 1984/85 was rapidly pushing us to

the point of unviability and potential insolvency, if it was required
that we should continue to operate on the same scale as we had hith-
erto. The enforced closure of the London operation—without which
we should, in 1990/91, have run up an unhandleable deficiency—
clearly focused the reality of this condition, and the net result was
that for 1991/92 our subsidy increased by just over 50%—of which
half came from the Government via the Arts Council, and of which
just under half came from the City of London—our landlord at
the Barbican, to which we pay rent, but which had never previously
offered us annual revenue funding. This increase of subsidy virtually
brought us back to that balance between subsidy and self-gener-
ated revenue that was agreed to be appropriate in 1984/85, after the
Priestley report.

The RSC's accumulated operating deficit continues to fluctuate
depending on a number of factors, such as box office receipts and
government and corporate support on the income side of the ledger
and on the number of productions, tours, capital expenses, outreach,
and marketing on the expense side. In spring 2000, the deficit had
been reduced to about £500,000, but the anticipation of the production costs of *This England—The Histories* in 2000–2001 led Nick
Paladina, the financial controller, to predict that it might grow to more
than £1 million by 2001.

In the mid-1990s, RSC administrators lost confidence in the Arts
Council's ability or willingness to increase funding. David Brierley
pointed out that the Arts Council had seen its own budget for 1994
slashed by some £5 million, and government appraisals recommended
even further shrinkage of the council's role and funding allotments
in the future.

After John Majors's government decentralized the ACGB in 1993,
Alexander Patrick Greysteil Hore-Ruthven, Earl of Gowrie—the Tory
arts minister who had commissioned the Priestley report in 1982—
became chair of the newly organized Arts Council of England. According to an article by John Rockwell in the *New York Times,* Lord
Gowrie took steps to bolster the council's sagging fortunes and de-
flated spirits, including the appointment of a number of Labour-af-
filiated arts activists (among them Trevor Nunn) to the council. Lord
Gowrie denied that the Tories were hostile to the arts—David Brierley
had commented that "Labour is almost always more sympathetic to

the arts in general"[7]—and tried to dismiss the notion that the £5 million cut to the council's budget would have significant consequences for recipient organizations. The *Times* article quoted Lord Gowrie: "The problem is political. At a time when they are closing factories or hospitals, they don't want to be seen as giving more money to the ballet. When I was arts minister, Mrs. Thatcher was always prepared to smuggle me money, as long as I didn't crow about it."[8] He believed that the reversal of international financial fortunes would generate greater corporate and private support for the arts and was hopeful that the new National Lottery would be a major benefactor, with one-fifth of its proceeds going to support the arts. However, lottery funds were earmarked for supporting capital expansion and improvements. According to David Brierley, this resulted in the building and refurbishment of arts facilities for organizations that lacked sufficient funding to adequately inhabit them.

Have the arts fared better under a Labour prime minister? Tony Blair's administration's policies, especially in light of the exorbitant budget for construction of the much maligned and controversial Millennium Dome in Greenwich, have endured some sustained fire from arts groups and artists. In March 1998, Gerry Robinson was appointed to head the Arts Council. As the chair of the Granada Leisure Group, an entertainment and hotel consortium, Robinson initiated what many RSC administrators characterized as a radical reorganization and redefinition of Arts Council structure and policy. Scores of prominent theatre artists protested Robinson's perceived alignment with popular entertainment—and rejection of more traditional arts—by formally withdrawing from dealings with the council. In an article by Warren Hoge in the *New York Times* in June 1998, it was noted that contemporary British government leaders were more inclined to attend rock and pop awards ceremonies than theatre and opera. In the article, Barbican manager John Tusa complained that Blair and his colleagues were "much less attached in every sense—in their experience, in their knowledge, and in their beliefs—to whatever we're encumbered with, the Western history and culture that are our intellectual moorings."[9] The Labour government surprised many in the arts by continuing the Tory policy of reducing arts grants, forcing organizations to shut their doors or severely cut back production. In their rush to embrace high-tech and pop culture, Hoge noted in his article, government leaders largely abandoned support for the traditional arts.

In October 1998, Robinson unveiled a new approach towards arts aid. He shifted a considerable portion of funding decisions to regional arts boards, leaving only seven major institutions, six of which reside in London, to receive subsidy and oversight by the national Arts Council: the RSC, the Royal Opera, the Royal Ballet, the Royal National Theatre, the English National Opera, the South Bank Centre, and the Birmingham Royal Ballet. He also announced that he would pool the Arts Council budget and the National Lottery earnings, totaling close to £400 million, which would be available for both capital funding as well as revenue subsidy. Robinson's boss, Secretary of State for Culture Chris Smith, promised an increase in funding for the arts of about £125 million through 2001. Robinson, however, known for his rather provocative pronouncements to the media, warned that belt-tightening and scrupulous oversight by the organizations themselves were a prerequisite for funding. "There will be no blank cheques. In the new era no one should kid themselves that the Arts Council will be a soft touch."[10]

The RSC's Arts Council grant was frozen for five years in the late 1990s, which according to RSC Council chair Sir Geoffrey Cass, resulted in an erosion of 16 percent of its annual revenue grant in real terms.[11] In 1999, the RSC received a one-time additional Arts Council grant of about £600,000, a gesture that appeared to some as a signal that things were looking up. But the RSC still needed increased permanent funding, which the National Theatre was receiving and the RSC was not.

The competition with the National for funding primacy carries with it the burden of media attention, which can easily lead to public decrials. A January 1999 article by David Lister in the *Independent* entitled "RSC Goes to War Against the National" outlined the "simmering resentment" felt by some at the RSC. The article quoted Gerry Robinson, who had just announced the Art Council's decision to increase subvention for the National while maintaining the RSC's grant at the previous year's level. The sting of the funding freeze was exacerbated by the comparison Robinson drew between the two companies. "The RSC has problems. . . . [N]ot even an increase of 10 percent would have been enough to sort them out. It has taken on too much." By contrast, Robinson ventured, the National "has coped brilliantly with standstill funding for the past five years, and the quality of its work and success at attracting new audiences argued strongly for an increase of this kind." According to the article's author, David Lister, "An RSC insider added: 'It's not so much the differences in money that's the problem. It's the National being lauded like that.'"[12]

Nick Paladina, the financial controller, noted that although Robinson never publicly apologized for his statement, which struck some in the company as rather prideful in light of the reversal of the RSC's artistic fortunes in 1999, he did soften his approach. For fiscal year 2000–2001, the RSC finally received a 5 percent increase in its Arts Council grant, bringing it to £9.2 million. This figure represented about one-third of the total RSC budget of £28.5 million.

Perhaps this increase indicated a shift in the Arts Council's perception of the company. The council awarded the RSC a grant in 2000 to conduct a stabilization program to examine its own internal budgetary and production methodologies. According to Paladina, "This was the result of a kind of competitive application. We were told we would be viewed particularly favorably, part of an acknowledgment, I think, of the council's misunderstanding of our uniqueness and how wrong it had been to compare us with the London arts organizations."[13] The RSC agreed to investigate itself from stem to stern—its human resources department, workshop procedures, union agreements, artistic policy—and to hand in a report to the council at the end of it all, along with a request for additional funding. "At that point, a number of things can happen," said Paladina. "The council can do anything from saying, 'Yes, you're doing a fantastic job, here's extra money,' to 'No, you're getting the right amount of money, you're just trying to do too much, so sort yourselves out this way,' or anything in the middle. It's challenging, but a really good time to have a thorough sweep through the organization." One hope voiced by Paladina is that as a result of the program, the company would be able to determine a target ratio of unearned-to-earned income, which would provide the company with a financial polestar.

The RSC's other government funding source is the Corporation of the City of London, which contributed about £3 million to the RSC in 1998–1999, in both direct subsidy and management fees for RSC staff overseeing the Barbican facilities during the time the RSC is absent from London.

The RSC, like many not-for-profit theatres, depends on the generous sponsorship of corporations and businesses to make up the balance of their unearned income. Northumbrian Water Group, Royal Insurance, Unilever, British Gas West Midlands, AT&T, Honeywell, Jaguar, Royal Mail, Sumitomo Bank, Citroen, and others have all contributed to the RSC during recent years. The RSC's primary corporate sponsor is the international food and liquor conglomerate Allied Domecq, which will have contributed more than £1 million annually through 2001, when the seven-year agreement is due to end. This sponsorship subsidizes work in Stratford and London as well as on tour and allows the RSC to undertake some ambitious projects, but it also yields tangible benefits to the conglomerate beyond the prestige afforded by its association with the RSC. In an article in February 2000, Tony Thorncroft of the *Financial Times* wrote:

> The largest, most integrated arts sponsorship of recent years has been the relationship between the Royal Shakespeare Company and Allied Domecq. . . .
>
> This led to the RSC directors and actors training Allied Domecq managers, improving their creative and communicative skills. . . .
>
> It worked so well that management at all levels became involved in the workshops, which also embraced relations between secretaries and senior staff. In return, Allied Domecq helped the RSC to reorganise its box office and exploit its trademark, especially overseas.[14]

It takes months of strategic planning by staff members in a number of departments to create a seasonal budget. The RSC's fiscal year begins at the end of March, and while it presently falls roughly at the start of the Stratford Summer Festival, the budget must be devised well before the planners have collected many significant details concerning shows later in the season. Nick Paladina explained, "When we do a budget for the season starting in April, we know exactly what we're going to be doing from April to October or November, and then for the second half of the year, we're making really big guesses. We may know what the productions are, but it's going to be pretty vague. [For winter 2000–2001] fortunately, we did have quite a lot of certainty about what's happening in Stratford, but there will be a number of things we don't know details of yet, and we're going to have to be pretty strict that these stay within the financial parameters in which we work."[15]

Months before the RSC season begins, the general manager and the financial controller set out drafts for budget lines for the annual costs that they can most easily predict, such as front-of-house services, administration, production workshop costs, and publicity. The financial controller pencils in the likely level of earned income, with advice from the general manager and the head of marketing. They take into account the previous year's income as well as the assumed ticket price increases for the following year. When these budgetary modules are established, lines for actors and production costs are figured by simply subtracting known operating costs from estimated income.

Similarly, at this time, the artistic directorate and producers are planning the season with considerable input from the financial staff. This can take months, during which they will test the season's selections against various financial criteria. As the budget must be drafted before the season begins, generic production budgets—based on estimated income, previous years' costs for similar shows, and inflation—are initially established for each theatre; specific budgets for each show are then hammered out by the production controller and staff as specific titles are announced. The budget is then presented to the Governors' Finance and General Purposes Committee, although by this time it is essentially a fait accompli, as the season has already been announced.

When the RSC renovates the RST or builds another theatre in Stratford or does both, the expenses will largely be covered by lottery funding—or such is the desire of the RSC. In 2000, the company was awarded a grant of £755,000 by the Arts Council to study the options available for expansion and redevelopment. The lottery earmarked up to £50 million for the entire redevelopment project, but the RSC must also contribute matching funds, and the Arts Council might decide to subsidize a considerably smaller amount. Much depends upon the results of the study, which the RSC expects to conclude in September 2001. At that time, they will make another application to the Lottery Board—money from the lottery that supports arts organizations is administered by the Arts Council—to fund the design phase. When that is completed, according to Paladina, "We ask for the really big money to start building things and knocking things down."

In 1998–1999, the last year for which figures were available, the RSC operated on a budget of close to £29 million. The figures in the accompanying table indicate the percentages of various sources of income and types of expenditure.

Production budgets have seen little increase since the mid-1990s, which has resulted in less money available for materials. The producers and production managers establish strict guidelines for production budgets, although, as is the practice at most theatres, a contingency of about 10 percent is allocated for each show. Shows that are constructed in Stratford workshops (including all RST shows, some Swan and Other Place shows, occasional transfers to London, and the rare Barbican original production) appear at first glance to cost less than those built in London, which use outside contract shops and require a budget that includes labor as well as materials. Salaries for the crews in Stratford workshops appear on a separate staff-budget line, so these costs are not reflected in the production budget for shows constructed there.

A production budget for a Summer Festival show in the RST currently totals about £70,000, of which more than half is spent on sets and costumes. In the Swan, where the administration urges directors and designers to emphasize costumes and props rather than sets, a typical budget is about £30,000, with the lion's share apportioned for costumes and props. The Other Place shows receive about £8,000, with the emphasis again on costumes and props.

Fees for directors and designers, as well as salaries for actors, are consistent with those paid by larger not-for-profit theatres. The scale of fees is dependent on the theatre in which a director or designer works and ranges, for a director, from £12,500 for a show in the RST to £9,500 in The Other Place. Set and costume designers usually make

1998–1999 Sources of Income and Expenditure

Income or Expenditure	Percentage of Total
Income	
Self-Generated Revenue	
Box office income	41.86
Other operating income (includes income from all productions of *Les Misérables,* sale of rights, management fee for Barbican, etc.)	8.00
Sponsorship and donations	8.39
Net income from transfers and other ancillary income	3.77
Subtotal	62.02
Other Income	
Arts Council Subsidy	32.11
Corporation of London	5.78
Others	0.12
Operating deficit for the period	0.40
Increase in other unrestricted funds	(0.43)
Total	100.00
Expenditure	
Cost of Artistic Output	
Artists' fees, salaries and expenses	31.30
Production materials	5.87
Production workshop operations	8.30
Stage and technical operations (includes crew salaries)	20.83
Subtotal	66.30
Cost of General Facilities	
Theatre operations (front of house, cleaning, box office staff, touring costs, etc.)	11.22
Premises	8.03
Marketing	6.47
Management and administration	4.12
Other costs	3.86
Total	100.00

Source: Data from Royal Shakespeare Company, *Annual Report and Accounts: 123rd Report of the Council, 1998/99,* 14.

more than lighting or sound designers. A designer who oversees both sets and costumes in the RST will make about £11,000, while a lighting designer makes about £3,000. Actors' salaries are not keyed to a specific theatre, for most of the company will appear in more than one space in a season; their salaries range from £290 to £740 per week.

In the early summer of 2000, Paladina pointed to the shifts in the RSC's artistic mission over the last few years as the prime factor that affects the RSC's financial condition.

> As far as the realignment we've done and the knocks we've had from the press, I think we've had to look at those and say we are trying to achieve some very difficult things and have to move in steps towards a pragmatic artistic vision. That means coping with the changes in actors' attitudes and requirements to reduce the amount of time they are out of London and are tied to us but at the same time reacting to the realities of the audience. So, the fact that we have an aging audience, that we were not getting in young people to the extent we should, and making sure the spread of work we do encompasses all that means that we have to make big changes to things that people have gotten very used to. They were used to the fact that we did only Shakespeare on the main stage, so when we did *The Lion, the Witch and the Wardrobe,* they don't see the school children coming out of the morning matinee absolutely bursting with joy, they don't feel the house shaking when the curtain goes down because they're all stamping their feet and clapping and shouting. All they see is us "turning our back" on what we're supposed to be here for. But we're not just Shakespeare, we're theatre, and I think we need to be more confident in that vision.
>
> And that ties in with the stabilization program, to recognize that we are going to have to do that sort of thing, while finding a way to keep the actors' contracts short but also giving them the opportunity to come back to us year after year or to do a two- or three-year stint with us.
>
> Also, what we'll do is reduce our dependency on government subsidy. And that might be a reality were it not for our capital campaign for the new theatre. What we would like to do is raise serious endowments, which would generate income and reduce our dependency. That effort is now being put into raising the same sums of money but to go into bricks and mortar. So, I think we will have to be on the other side of redevelopment, perhaps ten years down the line,

before that can be done. What we have to do is explain our dependency on government funding and why that is of so much benefit to the nation. And unfortunately, that's where you fall back on economic arguments rather than the more important cultural and psychological arguments, but it's the economic ones that win the day.

Education and Marketing

Stand by and mark the manner of his teaching.
—Hortensio, *The Taming of the Shrew*

All the better, we shall be the more marketable.
—Celia, *As You Like It*

*T*he RSC's education department is responsible for implementing the broad spectrum of outreach programs that figures so prominently in the company's commitment to bringing theatre to the community and the nation. To render the company's work accessible to students and teachers, the department conducts workshops, events, and classes in Stratford, London, Newcastle, Plymouth, and on tour. In 1997–1998, the department involved more than twenty thousand students and teachers at five hundred schools and education centers in Great Britain.

Wendy Greenhill, head of the department for most of the 1990s, arrived at the RSC in January 1991. A Warwickshire native, she was a passionate admirer of the works of Peter Hall, John Barton, and Trevor

Nunn. "I grew up with the sound of Shakespeare really beating through my mind and head," she recalled.[1] A Cambridge graduate, she studied Shakespeare as both a scholar and an actor. She taught teenagers, trained as a director, became an Equity member, and then focused on arts education. After a "checkered career in which I taught literature and theatre in an arts college, in fear and trembling, I applied for the head of education at the RSC," a position that opened when Tony Hill, her predecessor, became producer at The Other Place. Greenhill characterized her work as head of the education department as "a fantastic opportunity to do interesting things on a national and increasingly an international scale that I think are worthwhile. If I were an ordinary mainstream teacher, I would have very little freedom now, and I can't think of a comparable job that would offer me this creativity." Upon her arrival, she initiated KIT (Kickstart, Insight, and Teachers' courses). The program introduced schoolchildren and teenagers to the challenge of viewing Shakespeare onstage as well as to the process of theatrical interpretation and production, and it offered teachers workshops such as "The Language of Shakespeare" and "The Language of Jonson."

To make the repertoire of the RSC accessible to audiences, especially younger ones, staff members run workshops and develop innovative, interactive programs intended to enhance the audience's knowledge and appreciation of the texts and the productions. As Greenhill put it, "It's not about people on seats but about people with alert minds and receptive sensibilities on seats." Frequent excursions to schools for day workshops led by department staffers in tandem with actors, musicians, directors, stage managers, and other company members create great enthusiasm and excitement among students. "It makes the students feel like they know the play and have a link to the RSC, so when they go see the show, they feel like an honored guest." When the RSC tours a region, it sets up week-long workshops for teachers and often mounts its own educational minifestival. Annually, the RSC runs training days for teachers in all areas of Britain and also oversees the Prince of Wales Shakespeare School, a summer project funded by Prince Charles that provides an intensive training program for sixty educators from around Britain.

When students attend productions in Stratford, the Barbican,

Newcastle, Plymouth, and on tour in Wales, department members hold preperformance talks, often pressing into service Adrian Noble or the production's director and cast members. This is especially valuable for those groups that have not benefited from an education staffer's visit to the home school. The department also holds these talks for general matinee audiences on designated weekends.

Does Shakespeare need explication? Are these productions incapable of speaking for themselves as works of art? "I'm open to directors saying, 'No, I don't want you to work on my play, I directed it, it's very good, I don't want any mediation,'" answered Greenhill. "But nobody's said that yet. Schools and groups are constantly asking us for help. Now that Shakespeare is part of the national curriculum, teachers are desperate for as much nurturing and stimulus and training as possible."

The department generates an impressive array of educational materials. In 1998, it published a handsome study guide to accompany Channel 4's two-part television documentary *Behind the Scenes at the RSC*. It also produces a young people's newspaper, *Billboard*, featuring focus pieces on company members and other, more idiosyncratic articles on topics of particular interest to younger audiences, such as the use of stage blood. And it publishes production profiles, which are slim volumes that expose the reader to the world of the play, the vision of the director, and the rehearsal process. Greenhill elaborated:

> With the production profiles, I try to define us in terms of what we're *not*, as it's almost easier than defining what we *are*. We are *not* a poor imitation of a university drama department, we're *not* simply a teacher-training establishment, we're *not* in a straightforward way teachers. We *are* members of a theatre company. We are a hybrid. When it comes to publications, there are endless interesting books of critical insight into the plays, so it would be foolish to write a book about the play. What we can do is write about *our* production and the choices we explore, by interviewing the director, designers, composer, the voice department, key actors, talking about the design and the concept, so these are very specific to *this* production. We're always looking at interpretations, choices, layers of meaning. We're trying to get across the point that a show is new each time it's worked on.
>
> It's not about table work, about talking too much. We try to get the students on their feet, much like a cast in the beginning stages of

rehearsal, to explore the text themselves. You have to experience the play in terms of voice, breath, movement. When it comes to text, it can be intimidating, the language can be dense, so we try not to be analytical or intellectual. We start with a very high-energy approach on extremely simple bits of language, highly emotional insults, extravagant protestations of love, to build up people's confidence at the beginning of the workshops. This way, they've spoken some Shakespeare, they've communicated with it, it generates energy, it releases tension, and it makes people understand that the meaning is multifaceted, emotional, interactive.

It's true that occasionally there is a production that is very difficult to work on, usually because we don't find it coherent to the extent that other productions are. No matter how hard we try, some productions are less rewarding. Because we're a target, a big national institution, some teachers and students take tremendous pleasure in hitting that target. So, we don't talk only about our productions; we try to keep the discussions open and not pin everything on our shows.

With so many plays in the repertoire at one time, the department is admittedly unable to prepare materials and disseminate information about every production with equal attention to detail. Greenhill acknowledged that not all plays generate audience enthusiasm to the same degree, and the department is usually aware of those plays that will require their greatest attention. "Outside of the Shakespeare canon, almost anything we do will find *some* people who are interested. We'll do quite a lot of work on Chekhov, since some of his plays are included in an A-level theatre studies text. We can always expect to do a lot of work on Ben Jonson. The whole Renaissance canon is going to find in the whole of Britain quite a lot of interest. If you're doing a Marlowe play, you know you'll probably be working with universities. If you're doing *Romeo and Juliet* or *Macbeth,* you know you'll be working with thirteen-year-olds, since these are introductory texts."

It is a formidable task to spread the word about the services of the staff around the nation, according to Greenhill. While the department's services are advertised in the playbill, and education officers in regional school boards are contacted, teacher word-of-mouth results in a considerable payoff. In the past, the department sent out mass mailings to every school district in the nation, but they were unable to cope with the large number of responses. Now, mailings are sent to advertise only the Prince of Wales school, and although only sixty teachers are selected, the mailing serves as a reminder of the department's existence to all teachers in the nation.

In 1992, with the help of a donation of £100,000 from the Sainsbury's supermarket chain, the education department launched the ambitious Antigones Project as an educational adjunct to Adrian Noble's staging of the Oedipus trilogy, *The Thebans*. Each of six regions in the United Kingdom sponsored a program in which a professional director and playwright collaborated with teenagers in workshop situations to develop a production based on Sophocles' *Antigone*. Greenhill described the venture, emblematic of the RSC's aggressive campaign to bring theatre to the nation.

> My idea was to see how far the archetypes of Greek theatre could speak to people today and what the young people would do once they'd been exposed to those archetypal stories. *Antigone* seemed ideal since it's about protest and young people differentiating themselves from their elders and the conventions of their society.
>
> I applied to Sainsbury's for the grant in 1991, and we won the award and did the project in '92. We set up companies in Scotland, Cornwall, Darlington in the northeast, a tough part of Birmingham, Cheshire, and the East End of London. In London, we chose a borough where we knew there was a strong arts education center and good people, appropriate local managers who would circulate information at colleges, help select a group of students, publicize it, find the place to do it, liaise with the schools so we could give school classes on the Greeks, that sort of thing. Each area provided something. In Cornwall, a local theatre helped with design and space; in Cheshire, a local teacher was seconded to help run the program. A local manager from each county's education department was provided, and the RSC supplied a director and writer, looking for compatibility of ideology and style, and when possible, a regional link as well. In Cornwall, both the director and writer were Cornish. The participants ranged in age from sixteen to twenty-five, from people taking A-levels to college students. Most of them were people who might go to drama school, but by no means were they all academic high-flyers. There was a broad spectrum of types.
>
> The projects started in spring and cooked until autumn. Lots of workshops were held. The groups used *Antigone* as a stimulus in their own work. The exploration ended in July, and the writers went away for two months to develop scripts. It was very cheeky of me to say to a writer, "You've got two months, we want a script by September. I

don't care if you get blocked, you've got to do it," but they all managed it, and by September there were working scripts. The groups met
individually with the writers and directors over weekends and
workshopped and rewrote. In October, the six groups came together
for two weeks of workshops at a youth hostel in Penzance. They
worked like mad, and in the case of the Cornish group produced a
fabulous piece of theatre with immense wit and style. They took
Antigone and transferred it to the Cornish nationalist movement and
called the play *Gonienta,* an anagram. In Birmingham, the story became that of a young girl who committed suicide because she was at
loggerheads with her parents' values, based on a story in the newspaper. In London, they looked at how media takes up real human
tragedy and trivializes it, really at the media hype around the *Antigone*
story and making a film about it. In Scotland, they based it on a Celtic
legend. If you didn't know they were using *Antigone,* you wouldn't
have seen it in the plays, necessarily; they were using it as a stimulus
for their own investigations.

In November, they came to Stratford, all of them high as kites,
buzzing with creativity and passion, and we had a short festival, two
days at The Other Place, performing to a public audience. It was real
theatre, which you don't always see even on the most elegant, professional stages. We saw people with something very supple and strong
to say, who were passionately committed to saying it, and who,
through the skill of their directors, were exhibiting very high levels
of performance skills in every way.

Unfortunately for Greenhill, the opportunities to mount exciting
special projects such as this were not as frequent as she would have
preferred. The demands of running the department's essential projects
were so great that resources were rarely available to create long-term
projects like the Antigones.

In 1999, Adrian Noble expressed his interest in expanding the educational possibilities offered by the RSC. "We will have demonstra-
tions, lectures and many more show-related events. I would like, as
part of our rebuild, to have an education centre in Stratford. Imagine one you could spend a day in: in the morning do a voice session
with Cicely Berry, see *Romeo and Juliet* in the afternoon, then pull
down from the digital archive four versions of *Romeo and Juliet.* . . .
The tip of the iceberg is the performance. At the moment we have
no education centre; we hire a church hall. It's pathetic."[2] If plans

proceed as anticipated and money is allocated by the National Lottery to erect another theatre in Stratford, The Other Place may indeed become the center Noble envisions.

The base expenses of the education department are funded from the RSC budget and the Arts Council; sometimes schools are charged a small fee to help defray costs. Corporate partners also play a significant role in underwriting departmental activities. In 1996, Allied Domecq sponsored an education staffer to travel to the United States with the tour of Noble's production of *A Midsummer Night's Dream.*

Marketing the RSC is a prodigious task, as more than two dozen productions annually must be profiled, advertised, and sold to both the RSC's core audience as well as casual theatregoers. Although the RSC logo cannot compete with the ubiquitous Phantom's mask, the marketing department channels its resources and its £1.5 million budget into campaigns designed to ensure that the company's productions are seen throughout the nation.

Stephen Browning oversaw the operations of the marketing, press, and publicity department for a number of years. An Oxford graduate, Browning worked in arts management at the Oxford Playhouse and the Greenwich Theatre, organized the Hong Kong International Film Festival, and served as tour organizer for the English Touring Opera, all prior to joining the RSC in 1980.

The department operates press offices in London and Stratford; marketing teams for all its resident and touring companies; a publications division that produces posters, programs, and for-sale items; a graphics studio; and a membership and information office that keeps the fifty thousand national and international members and associate members of the RSC apprised of company events and schedules.[3] The department also oversees the Stratford box office (the Barbican theatres' are run by the Barbican Centre). In the mid 1990s, as the RSC began to explore the possibilities of expanding its national presence, Browning established a handful of regional offices around the United Kingdom.

> I felt as a national company that we needed to grow in a number of regional bases and had a lot to learn about building that relationship on a local level. We set up an office in Oxford, which has been enormously successful. It allowed us to lock into the resident audience for

both London and Stratford, Oxford being strategically placed between the two, and to look at both the undergraduate and visiting
student audience there. . . . We've been able to tap into the educational network as well, setting up programs using our education department and working with the schools and the university, finding
out what they were looking for—technical expertise, assistance with
prop and costume rentals—whatever we could do to help. We've set
up an office in Cambridge now, too, and are looking for other loca-
tions. By office, of course, I mean some individual with a phone in
his kitchen, so it's not an enormous investment.

The most significant development in the latter days of Browning's
tenure was the shortening of the London season and the expansion of
the company's national presence, which caused a sensational brouhaha
in the media and government offices. Browning viewed the RSC's decision as a watershed of similar significance to Peter Hall's move to the
Aldwych thirty-five years before. Soon after the decision was announced,
Browning staunchly defended it from a marketing perspective.

The increase in touring will be absolutely smack in the middle of
where we saw our strategy going. It's an intensification of our process, underlined by the shorter London season. Yes, it's curtailed, but
in fact all the Stratford productions will still be transferred there, and
we'll still add a few new ones in London, so theatregoers are in fact
not going to miss much compared to what they've been seeing. Given
that we'll have a finite period in London now, we'll be able to underline the importance of the season there and really put a lot of resources behind it. It's obviously going to be key to us to maintain a
link with that audience in the summer when the Barbican is dark. If
we can create an ongoing relationship with our touring base, we can
have a fairly seamless sense of constant activity. As soon as people feel
that because the RSC's not operating in London we have somehow
ceased to exist, then of course we're going to lose contact with our
audience. Given, though, that the central London audience makes
up only about half of our Barbican audience, there is another 50
percent who we need to maintain an ongoing relationship with.

Most of those people live in the Home Counties, around London,
but it really is a national audience. If you look at what we'll be doing
in Stratford, London, Newcastle, Plymouth, and with two or three
national tours, there is going to be such activity nationwide that I
think we can ensure that there won't be a perception that we've less-
ened our impact.[4]

Browning noted that the national media's response to the announcement of the seasonal change was overwhelmingly sour. The general consensus was that the decision was motivated by financial considerations—the costs at the Barbican were too high, and the shows were not reaping sufficient income—but Browning denied that money was a prime motivating factor.

> I think this reflects the way that the arts press tend to seize on stories. It's been a great shame that the metropolitan viewpoint that obviously prevails within many of our national papers has not allowed those commentators to look at the enormous benefits that this new change will have to a national audience. And after all, we *are* a national company, we should be seen by the nation, since we're effectively funded by the nation. To therefore assume that we should stay in one or two places and that we've fulfilled our duty as a national company, we believe is wrong. On the other side of the coin, there is great support from the regions, from a large number of cities who are very keen for the RSC to perform there, and what is crucial is enormous support from theatregoers, which, after all, it is all about.

Surprisingly, there was a relatively restrained outcry from London audiences. Before the 1996 season, Adrian Noble sent a letter to all members of the RSC explaining the changes, which was followed by an in-depth interview in the RSC magazine as well as smaller pieces in the playbills. Browning opined that audiences considered the move a positive one and actually embraced the decision to make the RSC more accessible to the nation. Since no comprehensive, hard data exist on the sentiments of RSC audiences to the shift in scheduling, it is impossible to ascertain their true response to the maneuver.

Although the company was potentially faced with accommodating its usual, large London audience in a season half the length of its original duration, the marketing staff considered themselves fortunate that they did not have the sizable task of overhauling an audience subscription plan. Although many institutional arts organizations do utilize subscriptions in order to establish a reliable core audience, the RSC does not, as Browning pointed out.

> We tried one in 1991 in both London and Stratford. The initial response was very good. Many of our existing members were very enthusiastic about the idea. We then repeated it in a slightly modified scheme in '92 and also did a lot of research into the people who

booked a subscription in '91 but did not book one in '92. Our research clearly indicated that those members of the audience booked
as many seats in '92 off subscription as they did on subscription. Our
conclusion was that our core audience was picking up on the subscription but would have come anyway. So, in effect, we were losing money.

I actually question whether subscriptions are the route to a wider
audience in London. The National has used it in the past but does
not now, nor does the Royal Opera House, although the English
National Opera does. That's not to say that some schemes haven't
been successful in generating a large amount of income up front and
insuring the loyalty of that existing group of subscribers, members,
and supporters. But what I don't think it does in the UK is find that
wider audience. I don't believe that people who come on an occasional
basis will be prepared to make that type of commitment, nor will they
be really prepared to stump up that kind of money up front, even
when they can see the financial advantage. The key audience is just
outside that core group that will, and we continue to work on them,
but I'm not sure subscriptions are the right way.

In developing the most effective strategies to increase that key audience, Browning decided to move away from spending a considerable portion of his budget on mass advertising campaigns, print ads,
and posters in the Underground and on buses and to focus funds
instead on direct marketing. He observed that new computerized box
office systems, equipped with advanced data retrieval capabilities, have
offered the marketing department greater sophistication in determining the best ways to sell the RSC. Browning felt that with a substantial budget it is feasible for a mass advertising campaign to be effective, but he decided that it is of greater value for the RSC to build
relationships with individual members of the audience.

Our problem is that we're launching twenty-odd productions a year,
and it's very difficult to ensure that in any ad strategy you are really
able to create a constant presence for all those productions. And we
found that, as far as we can gauge, some of that advertising is not as
effective as it used to be. The marketplace is so crowded, and we're
competing with so many other theatres, that it's difficult to ensure
that our voice will be heard. We felt that it's better to put our resources
elsewhere. One of the problems with this is that our acting company
understandably wishes to be seen in a very visual way and finds di-

rect marketing difficult to comprehend. But we have decided that print work—our season brochure and repertoire information—will be the pillar of our marketing.

We've looked at new ways to present schedules to show what is happening every day in Stratford, London, and on tour. And as our activities around the UK grow, that kind of publication will grow in importance. Audience research indicates that print delivers over 50 percent of our audience. So, we need to find ways to put across, in print, the complexity of our message. Repertoire is a difficult thing to put across. The details are very complex. That's why ads on buses in the West End and the Tube are fine, in a West End context, if you've got one show or one idea to sell, and it may even be the absolutely right way to sell the London season, at least to show that it's happening. But we need one message, not twenty-five or thirty, to be able to do that effectively.

Although the department puts great faith in direct marketing, it does employ traditional visual methods to advertise its productions. However, the publicity staff realizes that the medium and the message must reflect the times in which they are offered. Barbican theatre manager Peter Cadley recalled the strategy employed by the late Andrew Canham, Browning's associate, to market the actor Toby Stephens, playing Coriolanus at the Barbican in 1995: "The play didn't do well in Stratford; it played maybe 50 to 60 percent there, and that wouldn't be good for a London show. Andrew took Toby to a photo studio but didn't do the conventional shot of him, the pretty shot, which would have made sense since all the girls love Toby. Instead, he splattered him in red paint, covered him in blood, and there was the poster: 'Natural Born Killer. *Coriolanus*. RSC. Barbican.' Whacked it up in Tube stations and on poster sites, and we sold out every single show. Kids who had spotted the poster came to see the show and left saying, 'Well, I didn't understand a word, but he was good looking!' It was fantastic, suddenly the Barbican was all abuzz."[5]

In 1998, the Barbican's fall advertising campaign involved plastering the Tubes with a poster featuring a photo from *The School for Scandal* prominently displaying considerable eighteenth-century cleavage, headlined "It's a Scandal!" It had the same kind of eye-catching dynamism as the *Coriolanus* poster.

One of the primary responsibilities of the marketing team is to identify the demographic profile of audiences in Stratford, London, and other key cities such as Newcastle and Plymouth. The core audiences in both London and Stratford comprise theatregoers who often travel between the two cities to see most or all of the productions. Beyond that core, however, differences exist. By virtue of Stratford's reputation as a tourist destination, many theatregoers there are from overseas, although Browning noted, "It is interesting that we've been able to bang on the head that myth that Stratford is filled only with Japanese and Americans to the exclusion of the British, and that's not the case. Across a year, the audience is about 85 percent British."[6] He concedes, however, that many theatregoers in Stratford are vacationers from around the United Kingdom who see a show because they happen to be visiting Stratford for the day and not because of a burning desire to attend the RSC. But the midlands district itself has produced a fiercely loyal home audience within a radius of one hundred miles from Stratford, and each of the three theatres in the town has its own partisan enthusiasts.

Barbican theatre manager Peter Cadley questioned the marketing department's assertion that Barbican audiences are composed mainly of Londoners and residents of neighboring counties, as well as the administration's decision to curtail the London season. He stressed that he and his front-of-house staff interact daily with the audiences, allowing them ample opportunity to assess the audience's makeup. The marketing department's use of questionnaires to determine audience demographics is not, he contended, the most efficient tool for doing so. "Tourists do come, but they just don't fill out questionnaires. If you're on holiday from New York or Paris, and someone leaves a form on your seat, you're not going to fill it in. It's the regulars who fill them in. And a lot of foreign tourists do the grand tour in the summer, and their plans don't include Stratford. They used to come to the Barbican, but now they can go to the Globe instead if they want to see Shakespeare."[7]

The late Andrew Canham pointed out that in London, with more than fifty mainstream and one hundred fifty fringe theatres to choose from, visitors are not the captive audience they are in Stratford. "London is Europe's most competitive theatre marketplace. We are operating in an extremely difficult environment," he observed.[8] Stephen

Browning seemed to agree: "Reviews mean far more in London than in Stratford. I've seen cases in Stratford where we've had poor reviews—fortunately rarely, but it does happen—and we've seen hardly a hiccup at the box office. Had we had the same reviews in London, it would have been disastrous."[9] In London, given the competition and the complexities of the repertoire schedule, the RSC must create what Browning calls "the must-see event. And it is getting harder and harder to do so. Perhaps it's the higher prices everyone is charging and the fact that there are so many shows to choose from." Browning was reluctant to articulate a specific formula for a successful season, offering that there is no mixture of plays, genres, or styles that will guarantee the largest audiences.

> I don't think there's an ideal scenario. Obviously, there has to be a mix of comedies, tragedies, histories, and a mix, too, of the perceived "well-known" Shakespeare plays with those of his that, quite rightly, are done rarely. There needs to be new work, too, and that's terribly important for us. And there should be both popular classics and the Jacobean and Restoration plays we've revived that, unless we do them, no one will. It's ideal to support your lesser-known work by ensuring that you've got large numbers coming to see the better-known pieces. It's also important to encourage audiences to experiment across our theatres. Large numbers of our audiences still tend to go to just one theatre. That's why the more we can excite them about that other work we do while they're here, the better.

The RSC is not immune to media assaults, and in 1997 and 1998, the RSC was subjected to lashings from journalists and theatre critics. The prevailing sentiment was that the RSC had been hobbled by shortening the London season, failing to attract a significant number of stars, and losing its artistic vigor. Poor reviews for several productions exacerbated an already poor box office turnout, and the critics seized on this as proof that the RSC was foundering. The company found these accusations painful. Katie Mitchell, the former director of The Other Place, explained one way in which the company responded.

> We had big box office problems right across the board in all three Stratford theatres in 1997, which was very difficult for the performers. And The Other Place is more acute, because you could play for twelve people on some nights, and that is very hard. The season there

was geared towards young people, sixteen-to-thirty-year-olds—two of the plays were chosen exclusively for them—but there wasn't enough marketing money to tell those people that these plays were for them. They did particularly badly.

So, we called in the marketing department—I think this was a first in RSC history—and had a roundtable with the actors to convince management that what actors have to contribute, once the bile has come out, can be of incredible value and use. And that led to the actors in each cast writing their own box office copy, so when anyone rang up the box office, the staff would have a copy of what the actors wrote describing it. We also looked to the visual arts as possible marketing tools in The Other Place, because the visual arts in this country are one of the most dynamic and sophisticated mediums and popular with young people. For instance, we did an installation where we took out the seats for a week, and an artist came in and did an amazing thing with a moving wall that talked, revealing a rectangle of grass, based on the theme of *The Mysteries*.[10]

Mitchell is disturbed by the enormous power the press enjoys in shaping public opinion. She echoed the sentiment, voiced by other company members, that the RSC needs to respond to media attacks by following through on those policies that it sincerely believes are best, rather than reflexively reconsidering its aesthetic and marketing judgment.

When we held that meeting with the actors and marketing, there was quite an interesting moment when one of the actors from the cast of *Roberto Zucco,* which was a big critical success but had been doing low houses, said, "What I don't understand is how a critic can say that this is a brilliant premiere, brilliantly acted and directed and designed. Who are they talking about when they attack the RSC?" It had just dawned on him that there was something else, other than what he was involved in, that was being attacked. You can only answer that question—is it valid what the critics are saying or not?—not by looking at any reports, or marketing, or by-products. You can only sit in a seat in the house, watch every show, and make your own assessment of what you thought it was saying aesthetically, politically, spiritually. The company is only the sum total of its productions in any given year, however much it might, like any organization, want to create an image of something to sell.

I think there is some sort of reductive, sensationalist bitchiness that goes on about the RSC. The critics are right to provoke the company, that's their function, as long as they're doing it to provoke the company and not just sell their newspapers.

But a string of stronger productions ensued, and by early 2000, *The Lion, the Witch and the Wardrobe, Richard III, The Winter's Tale, Don Carlos, Antony and Cleopatra,* and other successful works in both Stratford and London had earned substantial revenue and attracted new audiences. As a direct result of the shortened season in London and the split season in Stratford, stars such as Robert Lindsay, Antony Sher, Eileen Atkins, Michael Gambon, Nigel Hawthorne, and Alan Bates were again able to perform at the RSC. For the time being, at least, the RSC once more enjoyed the good graces of the media.

The Production Process

The play's the thing . . .
—Hamlet, *Hamlet*

Casting the Company

*T*he process of assembling a company for the RSC, always trouble-
some, has grown increasingly problematic in recent years. In the RSC's
salad days, when its reputation was new and dazzling and when film
and TV offers were fewer, actors were eager to sign on for long terms
at relatively modest pay in exchange for the exciting opportunity of
performing with the company. But as noted previously, Peter Hall's
initial vision of a long-term commitment from actors proved implau-
sible. What evolved—a sixty-week contract through the first year at
Stratford and Newcastle, with an option to renew for London—became for some time the working paradigm for hiring a company of
perhaps seventy-five actors each year. That eventually grew into the
current contractual offers of six to twelve months. The shorter contracts are especially attractive to actors with healthy film, television,

and West End careers, which offer more lucrative opportunities. The not-for-profit RSC pays modest weekly salaries—as do all institutional theatres—ranging from about £300 to £750.

The casting department, located in London and headed by Maggie Lunn, consists of a few hardy souls who conduct countless interviews and auditions and view performances of every stripe in the West End and the fringe theatres, at rep companies around the country, and at all the major training schools as well as on screen. They must familiarize themselves with virtually every casting decision made throughout the nation. According to executive producer Lynda Farran, "It takes a lot of patience and time, and the casting director needs a lot of diplomatic skills. The casting department have to be very knowledgeable, right across the board, to get the very best of the young actors, but also to make sure we get those who are just on the verge of playing the leading roles."[1]

In nonrepertory situations, the casting process, although time-consuming and frequently frustrating, is fairly straightforward. A casting director holds auditions, either by an open casting call that any actor who meets certain criteria—such as Equity membership—may attend, or more frequently, by an appointment made through the actor's agent. But it is a much more complicated process at the RSC. Alison Chard, Lunn's predecessor as the head of casting, explained:

> We're casting a company of perhaps seventy-five actors that we hope will stay together for more than a year. That's difficult enough in itself, finding *that* many talented actors who can handle the classics and modern work and are willing to commit for such a long period. Additionally, though, we need to see a bit beyond their talent to ascertain whether or not they'll fit into the particular company we're trying to mold. It's not so much a question of what roles they can play—although that's certainly our foremost consideration—as much as their ability to develop and sustain a company spirit. We ask a lot from these people over their time here, and whilst there are never any guarantees, we want a certain assurance that everyone can get along and work on company guidelines and principles.[2]

Generally, the RSC seeks to cast a company in a ratio of three men to one woman, reflecting the mixture of roles available in a typical season. Although Shakespearean plays have relatively few women's roles, the work of later playwrights tends to offer more opportunities for women. Actors cast in the Stratford Summer Festival are most frequently contracted for a "line of parts." Typically, the entire season has not been set at the time that actors sign their contracts, so they are contracted only for known roles with the proviso that they will be cast as needed in subsequent productions. Those actors with some experience and bargaining clout will often request a contractual clause that allows them to negotiate future casting assignments with the company, although their salaries usually remain unaffected by these decisions.

Some of the younger company members are cast in a number of smaller roles, occasionally with no lines. These members may be contracted "as cast" for the entire season, with no guarantee of any specific casting when they sign on. For these journeymen, the chance to join the RSC far outweighs the opportunity to play better parts at other theatres. The company provides what is essentially a second, professional phase in their training, since most of these actors have recently graduated from one of the better acting programs, such as the Royal Academy of Dramatic Arts, the London Academy of Music and Dramatic Arts, the Central School of Speech and Drama, or the Guildhall School of Music and Drama. Chard said of them, "This is the next logical phase in their development. We're very eager to develop our own, homegrown talent, and this is the logical place to begin. The work on the plays, plus the classes we offer, form a very effective, advanced, professional training ground." For these actors, who will receive perhaps three small roles, the plum in the season may be the understudy assignment for a major role, and the casting staff, the directors, and the producers frequently attend understudy rehearsals to monitor their development.

Occasionally, more established company members will take a turn at understudying. It is part of the "company" ethos. Charles Flower, founder of the Memorial Theatre, was heavily influenced by the Duke of Saxe-Meiningen, one of the first modern directors. His Meininger Players inaugurated a radical approach to ensemble acting in the late nineteenth century that invigorated and inspired theatre producers and directors in Europe and America. The duke's guiding precept was that company spirit was primary in making exceptional theatre, and even leading actors understudied and appeared as extras during the season. While not carrying the practice to such extremes, the RSC is built on similar principles. Chard agreed that the company spirit is "everything" but allowed that it is often difficult to foster.

> Stratford is like a college campus, very claustrophobic. The town appreciates the theatre's existence for its survival but really isn't too keen on having all these *actors* around! The actors, in turn, are forced into this hermetically sealed, pressure-cooker environment for months on end. When the company return to London the following year, they disperse physically and go back to their normal lives, so there's less of a company feel in London. This, too, has its positive points—it's a much less hypercharged atmosphere. Some actors adore Stratford—they think it's lovely and charming—whilst some absolutely loathe it—they think it's incestuous and inbred. And it takes only a few miserable people to destroy the company spirit and the chemistry that's so crucial to making the season work.

The audition process at the RSC involves much painstaking preparation. The casting staff does not employ the open call policy, for they would be overwhelmed by several hundred actors. Instead, the department sets appointments with perhaps two hundred actors annually. Each auditioning actor must be approved by an RSC director or member of the casting staff who has previously seen that actor's work in a production. All actors must be willing to accept a line of parts. In return, the RSC acknowledges that it is difficult for an actor to freeze a career for an extended period, especially while in Stratford, and tries to accommodate them with time off from rehearsals to undertake occasional television, film, or radio work. Former artistic director Terry Hands was quoted as saying that the long commitment can be costly in other ways for an actor. "You can't believe you've lost another actor because he's got a family and a mortgage and he can't afford a home in London and a home in Stratford. One of those homes should be paid for."[3]

The casting department's greatest challenge occurs when Stratford casting commences. Chard described the problem: "Ideally, all the directors for the season should be in the same room at the same time, watching every audition, as they're going to have to hammer out roles amongst them. But the directors' availability is a nightmare, as they're often working on other projects at the same time. Yes, the casting staff serve as quality control, so we're pretty confident that the directors are seeing a good crop of likely actors. Still, if they're not all there together, it's very hard for them, and for Adrian, the producers, and us to make final decisions. This often means that actors will audition several times so that everyone involved can see them."[4]

Once the directors decide upon likely candidates for the roles in their shows, they enter into protracted negotiations to convince their colleagues, for example, that a certain actress who is ideal as Titania in *A Midsummer Night's Dream* is also perfect as Marjorie in *The Country Wife* and as Nora in *A Doll's House*. Chard said, "My greatest problem is getting three or four directors to agree to casting an actor in a line of parts. It's tough to marry various directors' methods and creative processes with a given actor."

According to director Katie Mitchell, the casting process is a draining, hectic time. "At this point, you're competing with as many as twelve directors—if everyone directing a show that season is casting at the outset—and any one actor can be cast in perhaps only three plays. Therefore, there's tremendous competition amongst directors. Each director is best off familiarizing herself in advance with all the plays in the season, so you can do a good job of convincing a colleague or two that an actor whom *you* want for your play is perfect for a given role in *theirs*. The casting staff are terrific in helping us sort all this out."[5]

Ultimately, it is left up to Adrian Noble, Michael Attenborough, and Lynda Farran to fit together all the pieces of this intricate puzzle. Farran explained the work from her perspective as executive producer.

> We sit with all the directors—and there might be up to a dozen of them—and the producers and the casting staff and all together work on assembling a company of some seventy-five actors for Stratford. Hopefully, most of the directors are present for most of the process, but it takes us several months, actually, and each actor has to agree to the line of parts offered. So, there has to be common ground for at least three directors in that room who are not directing in the same slot. It's quite a lengthy and difficult process. Arm-twisting occurs all the time. There has to be a degree of flexibility and compromise, and it sort of works out that directors do deals with one another. "Okay, I'll go with him, but you've got to go with her if I'm going to go with him, because I'm passionate about her"—that sort of thing.

The further complication is that when you finally agree on a line of parts, an actor may say they want only two of the three roles and say, "Find me something else." So, it's a never-ending process, and it applies right across the board. And very few actors accept our first offer. Everyone's always trying to upgrade their line of parts. So, that's a delicate process, and obviously directors' tastes are very different.

But having cracked the casting process, with great relief, we're often in rehearsals without a full cast. We open five productions within three weeks, so you can be in rehearsals with a Romeo but no Juliet. It's quite complicated, but we always find a way around these things.[6]

In the next chapter, actors discuss their views on the casting process.

The Physical Production—An Overview

Each of the five RSC theatres presents special challenges to the designers who work in them, but the RSC's repertory system presents additional obstacles. Lighting designers face the restrictions imposed by working with a seasonal rep plot in which only a portion of the rig is available for use as "specials"—instruments that can be refocused, recolored, or otherwise tinkered with for a specific show. Set designers must resist the temptation to create scenery so large or unwieldy that it cannot easily be shifted during the restrictive time frame of a performance turnaround, and they must also consider the domino effect of scenic storage on other shows in the repertoire. Costume designers face fewer specific constraints, because their work does not usually have significant impact on the other shows—other than the time it takes to construct costumes for a number of large-cast productions—but the repertory process at the RSC creates many problems in the scheduling of actors' costume fittings.

The design process commences as an intimate dialogue between director and designers, but it quickly evolves into a matter of concern for much of the staff, from the artistic director to the carpenters at the scenic workshops. Designing and constructing shows to perform in repertory and on tour as well as to transfer to other theatres adds layers of complexity to the already time-consuming and intricate process of creating the physical production. Lynda Farran explained the work from her supervisory role as producer.

The director, designers, producer, and usually the production manager for the given theatre are involved from the beginning. That's in order to make a financial comment upon it but to look at the work, too, and make a judgment. I make every attempt to support the work. At that point, of course, if you're looking at something that's just physically too big or cumbersome, and you know you're never going to get the engineering together, then you have to have tough discussions. But that's part of the work in process.

There are times, though, when things just come out of hand or scale, when the interpretation is something you think might not be appropriate, and in that case, I think one would involve Adrian at that point. But generally I act as his eyes and ears. You have to make relationships with all the different director-designer teams, so that they give you the right to be part of the process. Then they carry on with their designs, and the designs go to the preliminary state where they're looked at in more detail by the production managers and the workshop heads. At that point, the production managers handle the budgets for the shows, but we monitor them, and if there are any problems on the way, as there always are, because we can never afford what we finally come up with, it's the producer who has to make the final decision, who has to have the difficult conversation with the director about scaling things down. That's the really tricky part of it, because, of course, there really is only one idea. By the time you've got to the final design stage, it's not possible to rethink it, so you're usually talking about how you can compromise that one idea, not how to throw it out.

We have had times where designers have had to throw out whole designs or go through four or five different processes to get to a design that works. That's rather an anxious time. And if a director and designer feel absolutely, passionately that this work has just got to be seen, whatever the cost and difficulties, well, they can talk to Adrian. But that happens very rarely, because Adrian is also part of the process, since we produce his work as well, and he too has to cut doors and windows and flats and flying pieces. And that's the only reason it works, because he is part of the process, and other directors then say, "Well, if Adrian is prepared to do it, then I have to do it." So, that's the way we manage to get the production budgets and scale of production under control. The producer keeps a wary eye on it.[7]

Tony Hill, a former producer at The Other Place, identified problems specific to the design process in that theatre. Although every RSC space has its own spatial idiosyncrasies, The Other Place, with its smaller run crews and lack of technological support, places limitations on the design process. Its intended purpose as a flexible theatre in

which experimentation is encouraged can create problems for directors and designers with a large-canvas vision.

> What often happens at The Other Place is that director-designer
> teams there view the work as a tryout for the larger spaces, and this
> creates immediate problems. The space is a black box, and we try to
> remind them of that, but often the subtext from a designer is "I don't
> give a damn what they say, it's not going to stop me from pushing
> like hell to get the set I want. It's not my problem that they have a
> two-man crew and a small budget; let them deal with that."
>
> On the other hand, if we present too many parameters at the out-
> set and say, "It's a black box, we have a small budget, you can have
> this but can't have that," then the directors and designers could turn
> around and say, "Well, *you* do the show, then." So, it's about finding
> a balance. I don't have a personal problem with extravagance and glitz
> and glamour—I'm really happy for someone to produce a stunning
> set and costume design—but what I have to do is get them sold on
> the idea in harsh, pragmatic financial terms that they can have a stun-
> ning set and costumes, but they aren't going to have any money left
> over for props. And it's not just a financial thing. It's about convinc-
> ing a designer that there is something extraordinary about a well-lit
> costume in a black box. It's about finding directors and designers who
> are secure enough in what they want that they don't feel they have
> something to prove in terms of "I can cram an awful lot of hardware
> into this space." Some teams come in here, they want power lifts,
> curtain tracks, flexible rostra, hermetically sealed see-through boxes
> into which they can inject colored smoke and have plasma displays!—
> and there's a point where you have to say, "Whoa! It sounds great for
> when you do the show in Lincoln Center, but this is *not* the house
> for that."[8]

Regardless of the theatre space, Hill acknowledged, most directors
have an identifiable approach to the design process, a signature of sorts.

> Katie Mitchell is the kind of director who doesn't feel she has to
> prove herself with every show. She wants, instead, to honor the play,
> and even if her demands seem absurd at first, they'll be because she
> has posited them on the basis of what she believes is required for that
> piece of work in this space, not based on some kind of intellectual
> baggage about what one *ought* to do in order to be regarded as a se-
> rious director.
>
> Another director will approach things differently. Michael Atten-
> borough, for example—I've never seen his sets look abstract or in-

terpretive, he strives for a degree of realism in all his work, it seems, and his sets are more representational. No problem—he will argue brutally, fiercely for the money and resources he needs to do it. But it's informed by that same sort of fundamentally commonsensical approach to what he's doing, the need to honor the work as he sees it. Mike would be the first to say, "This show, whether I'm directing it or not, needs *this* kind of resource. If we're doing a costume piece, and it has to be set in this period, don't tell me you've got *x*-thousand pounds budget, because this is what we need. If we can't do it right, we shouldn't do the show, we shouldn't be trying to cram it in."

The problem of bringing an artistic vision to life within the parameters of a specific budget and available technology is a common one faced by most institutional theatres, which do not have the deeper pockets of commercial producers. Financial and personnel resources can only be cut into a limited number of slices, and it is somewhat easier for artists to respect the existence of the whole pie when they are working on several plays in one season. On many occasions, however, a director or designer may be contracted for only one play in a particular theatre in a given season, and the resulting "one-off" attitude can create severe pressures for those whose responsibility it is to allocate funds and labor.

Production managers work alongside the producers and designers, ensuring that designs will work in the spaces for the allocated budgets. Once the set designs are approved by the show's producer and production manager, a model is built, sometimes by the designer's personal assistant and occasionally by the RSC's staff assistant designer. The head of the scenic workshop, Alan Bartlett, then examines it along with the design engineer, Bill Stoyle, to work out the fundamental mechanics. Simon Bowler, the head of technical services, also enters the process at this point to discuss mechanics, speed of scene shifts, control, and safety. After a series of revisions, the designs are handed over to the scene shops.

Scenic and costume designer Robert Jones, who is profiled later in this chapter, explains the steps in this early phase of the process from the designer's perspective.

> What happens is you get to the point in discussions over a half-inch white model, with Geoff Locker and Alan Bartlett and the design assistant, where we identify the problems at an early enough stage so

we don't waste too much time going down a route we then can't achieve. They will say, as they did to me on *The Merchant of Venice,* "If you made the tower half a meter shorter, we could move it off-stage and store it under the fly floor; at this height, we'll have to chop it off and rig the top part with a sling, and that will add half an hour to the turnover." At the time, you think, "Oh, I *want* it to be half a meter taller," but ultimately it's fine. It's that sort of thing where they make a designer aware of constrictions, but they try to take a backseat to the artistic process, not getting involved in that in any way. Geoff is brilliant at that, he's aware of what a designer is trying to do while at the same time is eminently practical, without letting the practicalities get in the way of the final image onstage. People often tend to just say, "Well we have to make it smaller," and you say, "*No*, it's about the overall image." If I can't afford to do the complete image, I'd rather start again than chip away, because there's an element of compromise in everything we do. If you *really* start to compromise on a design, it looks like it, and I would rather start with the bare bones and make it look stylish, rather than chop away. That's why it's important to have that early-to-mid-design meeting where they can say, "Whoa, it's too expensive," or, "It's too big," or, "It's physically impossible," or, "Yes, carry on," which is what makes you most happy.[9]

Scenic designers must fit their shows to work within a basic set of spatial limitations—largely influenced by storage considerations—established by each theatre's production manager. However, it is contrary to most artists' intrinsic temperaments to work easily within imposed strictures, and the RSC has had to develop guidelines to help designers do so. The following is an excerpt from Adrian Noble's directive to all Stratford designers, issued at the start of the 1992 season. His appeal to the company spirit was essentially an edict for designers to adhere to established practices.

Over the past few years we've followed a policy of having as few design rules as possible for our Stratford seasons: we've tried to impose on each creative team the least possible number of limitations as they have developed their production ideas.

But this year we've reached a watershed when, to be honest, the policy has become self-injurious and self-defeating.

The weight and volume of our sets has accumulated throughout the season until they have become so onerous that they have actually jeopardised our repertoire performance schedule. We've no longer been able to accommodate the sets within the four walls of the theatre, and they have spilled over into trailers parked outside. This has made changeovers so burdensome that we're having great difficulty in doing justice to each production as it comes back on stage.

I'm convinced that the health of our work next season requires that we re-discover a way of coordinating our scenic needs so that it will once again become possible for a whole season of work to be stored in the backstage areas (while still leaving the necessary working space for performances) and so that we can regain the certainty that our productions will be given the fast, safe and faithful turnaround that the repertoire demands.[10]

The ballooning size of productions was one reason for the current policy of having Summer Festival productions in the RST share many more basic scenic elements than in the past. The 1992 Stratford guidelines exhorted designers to take into account the substantial differences between the RST, Newcastle, Plymouth, and the Barbican, because most Stratford shows will eventually play in all four cities, and funds are not available for conceptual reworking. It reminded designers that in Stratford the stage crews must be able to change sets within the two-hour time span between matinee and evening performance. In the Barbican theatres, where there is no changeover on matinee days, a more generous four hours were allotted: one hour to strike the scenery, two hours to set the new show, and one hour for refocusing lighting. Barbican design guidelines are as specific to the needs of those theatres as are Stratford's.

Space for flying scenery is highly coveted at the RST. With the needs of four or five productions as well as the considerable number of overstage lighting instruments to take into account, Geoff Locker has divided the RST fly grid into a handful of zones, in which each show is allowed to use perhaps one batten. But Locker does allow some flexibility with designers as plans evolve. Designer Robert Jones points out that the first shows to load in are the luckiest. In the Winter Season, when perhaps only two shows perform in the RST, there are usually no conflicts, according to Jones, who designed *The Winter's Tale* for the inaugural Winter Season in 1998, a show that shared the theatre with Anthony Ward's design for *The Lion, the Witch and the Wardrobe:* "For these two shows, the only two in the repertoire, Anthony Ward and I have the whole stage space to share for ourselves, as normally there are four or five shows in there. I've used the whole stage depth from the front to back wall, and Anthony is using the whole grid. I'm not flying anything, so his set is above all my scenery. Anthony and I talked a lot as we were designing and were able to accommodate each other. And that's rare. When I did *Merchant,* there were only four flying bars left at that point in the season, and you could only use a certain width and depth. But it was great on *The Winter's Tale.*"[11]

Barbican production manager Simon Ash spends considerable time figuring out ways to fit transfers and new shows into his theatre. Although offstage storage space in the capacious wings of the Barbican Theatre is rarely the problem it is at the RST, there is still the challenge of adapting shows to fit the peculiar shape of the Barbican stage. Ash himself draws up many of the working plans for sets transferring to the Barbican, as the Stratford design studio generally focuses on Stratford shows. Sometimes, all Ash receives from a designer is a model and a basic ground plan; it is up to Ash to produce a full set of plans that can be sent to either the Stratford workshops or, more frequently, London contract workshops. Ash allows about a four-week lead time to develop plans and models for a transfer, as the shops generally need about two weeks to rebuild a show for London. The additional period allows just enough time to review technical and budgetary considerations and to cost out the show. "Transfers are never as easy as they might be," says Ash, "because directors and designers are always looking for the opportunity to correct the mistakes they *think* they made in Stratford."[12]

Shows transferring from the Swan to the Pit must undergo a considerable transformation before they are ready to be loaded in to the smaller theatre. The design guidelines remind designers, "It is hoped that these were considered at the original design stage as the lower transfer budgets will impose financial constraints on these alterations. Please particularly bear in mind the fact that it is not possible to re-create the Swan trap and cellar in the Pit." Designers are also warned that all floors must be level if the public will walk over them: "Lumpy floors have been refused in the past."[13] Designers are also strongly encouraged to refrain from removing seats to accommodate the set. In earlier days, the Pit seats were unnumbered. As numbered seating is now used, the removal of seats can cause problems if the box office has begun selling tickets prior to the design deadline.

Although the RSC production staff has produced more written guidelines than are common in most other theatres, without such regulations—which, of course, are broken or adapted as often as necessary—the RSC would falter and collapse under the weight of a brutal production schedule. As designer Robert Jones noted, "There is an eighteen-week design deadline, so you have to design the set before you go into rehearsals. Because the RSC is a machine, doing maybe fifteen or more new productions a year, if you don't get your show slotted into that conveyor belt, it doesn't get built, it gets behind, and then it can't change very much. And that is sad."[14]

The season repertory lighting plot is designed for each theatre by its master electrician and is hung for the entire season prior to the first show's load-in. This allows lighting designers the chance to hand in their plots at a later date than in most theatres. The first lighting designer to work in any theatre in a season will have greater influence over the layout of the plot than subsequent designers.

The sets and props for many of the shows are built and painted in spacious RSC workshops a few miles from the theatres, in an industrial park off Timothy's Bridge Road. There, a corps of some thirty draftsmen, carpenters, machinists, painters, and prop artisans brings a production to life. Given the number of shows produced in a season, the workshops are unable to build them all, and some designs are contracted out to other workshops throughout England. Most RST productions and some of those from the Swan and The Other Place are built in Stratford, while Barbican productions are almost exclusively constructed in contract houses.

The Timothy's Bridge Road workshop opened in 1991. Previously, the work had been carried out in a shop in the old town converted from an old stocking factory and given to the RSC in 1947. The area was growing increasingly residential, however, and the company sought larger and more isolated facilities, a decision that pleased most personnel. But William Lockwood, long the head of the props department, voiced concerns about the move and the new workshop, however airy and spacious it is.

> We're very isolated from the theatre, and it's hard to get back and forth. People tend to use faxes, and you lose the personal contact. If you're wanted on the stage, you can't just pop down and grab the prop and work on it; it can take a half hour to make the trip around. It's

difficult especially in getting actors out here for face and body casting. And it's all a bit cold and impersonal here. The RSC owns the building and has made an offer for the next plot of land. We hope to build an extension, as one side of this building could be removed for those purposes.

It is useful, I will admit, being close to the paint shop, as they were in the old library opposite the theatre, which is now used for boots and armory. It's easier now than transferring things to the paints workshop up the road, bucking the traffic. But if we build anything higher than three meters, we have to build it in sections or we can't get it out of here. We have a spray room, but anything bigger than six feet has to be worked on in sections. With the floor space we have, when we do three or four productions in here at once, everything just piles up, and there is no way to store it. In the old building, there was a vast concrete area behind, where we could lay items out. And here, if we try to distress items using flame, it sets off alarms, so you have to do it outside. If it's raining, you have to stand outside with umbrellas, and it's all very difficult.[15]

Still, the workshops produce a vast array of scenery and props of exceedingly high quality throughout the year. Frank McGuire, a former senior draftsman, explained the process from his perspective.

If a show is opening in Stratford in early November, we expect to see a design in mid-September. But we don't always see a full set by then. We usually get a dialogue between the director and designer going first, and everyone is putting in their two cents—lighting, props, and so on. We normally build a show in about six weeks from receiving a final design. It's about thirteen weeks or so from first designs to fitting up the set in the theatre prior to tech rehearsals, but sometimes it happens in as little as six weeks time.

Once the show is being loaded in, it becomes quite intensive. We all want to oversee the things we've drawn, so we'll go down with the boys who built it and watch it go in, just to steer it in the right direction. The head carpenter at the RST comes down here a few weeks before fit-up to see what we're doing and have some production meetings.[16]

Not all scene shops are created equal. Although most professional shops are staffed with competent carpenters, painters, and other craftspeople, the RSC shops are known for the exceedingly high quality of their work. Designer Robert Jones commented on their exceptional skill.

Their finished product is phenomenal. They care so very much. I have had really bad experiences with commercial workshops, where what tends to happen is that they often underbid because they want the work. They'll do it for a cheaper price, and the work quite often is not up to standard, but at the RSC all the labor budgets are separate from materials budgets—these guys are there all the time, so they take great pride in their work, and it's beautiful. Some commercial shops just bash it out, and I walk in to the theatre and have to redo this and redo that. They've met the deadline, but they haven't done the job. You walk in and look at it and say, "But that's not what I wanted," and they say, "Well, we did it for the money," and you say, "No, you *didn't*, since that's not what I wanted." They take shortcuts. Alan Bartlett doesn't allow that. I had a great conversation with him the other day, discussing my set for *The Winter's Tale*, when he asked, "You know the panels on the walls? We're building them as true panels as they would've been; do you want square pegs or round pegs?" Now, no one will see it, but it's an important detail, it is important to *him*, and he was right in the end—after it was painted, you *could* see the pegs. I thought it was tremendous, since it was extra work that didn't need to be done, but he knew that it was a little finishing point that would zing out and look good, and I would like it. I really value that. The scenery looks as good from behind as it does from the front, the steelwork and timber and mitering, everything is immaculate, front and back. I don't like scrappy work, I hate scenery that looks good from the front but bad from the back. If it looks bad in the back, it's all going to fall apart. It's important.[17]

Stage Managing the Production

The stage management staff forms a production's logistical nucleus, amassing, analyzing, synthesizing, and disseminating all information pertinent to a production's development and maintenance. The stage manager is the director's right hand and the production's coordinator, liaison—and often, voice of reason—whose informed opinions are crucial in guiding a show smoothly through the production process. The stage managers are the only artists involved with every aspect of a production, often beginning work weeks before the play is cast and completing their duties when the show closes. The director's responsibility is most often discharged on opening night, and she or he may return only occasionally, if at all, to give some maintenance notes to the performers. A talented stage manager can make the most grueling production process seem relatively painless for the director, designers, and actors; a poor one can seriously hamper a show's artistic health and security. The director provides the central, guiding artistic vision, but the stage manager implements it and creates a supportive environment in which to realize that vision.

The stage management staff—comprising a stage manager, deputy stage manager, and assistant stage manager—schedules rehearsals, costume fittings, voice, combat, music, and choreography work, and every other aspect of the actors' professional day. They are in constant consultation with the designers and workshops about every aspect of the sets, props, costumes, lighting, and sound. They compile the prompt book—the production bible—that includes shorthand notations of all the details critical to the development and maintenance of the show. Each character's every move and gesture, all scene shifts, costume changes, light and sound cues, and often the director's artistic intentions are transcribed. Stage managers oversee the difficult transition from the rehearsal hall to the theatre and conduct the technical rehearsals—that brief, hectic period before previews in which the staff and cast work out every nuance of the production's physical life onstage. The stage management team supervises each performance, cueing, or *calling,* the show nightly, and maintains the production's artistic integrity throughout the run. It is a demanding and stress-filled job, and the RSC stage managers are additionally challenged by the needs of several plays rehearsing and performing simultaneously.

Sonja Dosanjh and Charles Evans, the Stratford and London company managers who oversee the stage managers, assign a different team of stage managers for each new production, rather than keeping teams together for the whole season. Dosanjh said: "It's a much healthier system when we can shake things up and put together new teams for each show. Otherwise, things could get quite uncomfortable if a team were to develop problems, and they're stuck together throughout the day and night. Also, in this fashion we're able to craft a new team for the particular needs of a given production. Many of our staff have been here for a number of years, and some might work better on a particular type or genre of play, or some may have a particularly good—or poor—relationship with a director. This way, we're able to do our best to ensure that the most efficient team is assembled for a given show."[18]

The stage manager, or SM, has overall responsibility for the show and undertakes the considerable task of generating the reams of necessary paperwork: the daily rehearsal schedules; the daily rehearsal reports, which are notes distributed to all areas and departments describing in detail the work accomplished each day, problems encountered, and specific requests from the director and others regarding design and technical issues; and the myriad plots and charts that trace the flow of scenery, costumes, props, and effects. The deputy stage manager, or DSM, is most frequently in the thick of things at rehearsal, transcribing the blocking and rehearsal notes, ensuring that breaks are taken according to Equity rules—sometimes eliciting an unkind response from a frustrated director in the midst of a creative spurt—prompting the actors from the script, and overseeing the smooth running of the rehearsal hall. The assistant stage manager, or ASM, is the workhorse of the team. This individual obtains or makes the rehearsal props, sets up the rehearsal room daily, looks after the actors' immediate rehearsal needs, and ensures that all backstage elements are properly coordinated.

In technical rehearsals and in performances, it is the DSM who cues the show. With the input of the director and the designers, the DSM determines the placement of every scene shift, lighting, sound, and effects cue in the show and then cues the operators and stagehands, both verbally over a headset and with the use of a bank of cue lights at the stage manager's console. It requires considerable skill and talent to watch the show (in some theatres, the view of the stage is obstructed, and the DSM must watch on a video monitor), follow the cues in the prompt book, listen on the headset to the simultaneous conversations of electricians, sound operators, deck carpenters, flymen, the musical director, and the other stage managers, and still call every cue (of which there may be several hundred) at precisely the right moment. One cue called a beat too early or one cue light thrown out of sequence can quickly turn what should have appeared to the audience as a flawless shift from one scene to the next into an artistic train wreck. At best, it looks less than magical; at worst, someone can be seriously injured.

The ASM runs the backstage area, checks on the setting of props, double-checks that scenery is ready to be shifted, takes a head count of actors prior to entrances, and performs similar tasks. In technical rehearsals, the SM is usually found onstage or hovering in the wings, conferring with the director, designers, the DSM, and crews about scene shifts, schedules, and other important issues. During performances, the SM follows along in the script at a console backstage, alerting actors to upcoming entrances and the crew to scene shifts, generally monitoring the flow of the production, and troubleshooting the inevitable problems that occur at every performance.

An example of the stage manager's daily logistical chores is the coordination of the actors' rehearsal schedules. Each director receives a certain block of priority rehearsal time during the day, during which all required actors can be called. For the remainder of the day, the director is allowed to work with actors still available—those not called for other rehearsals, understudy rehearsals, costume fittings, or matinees. At the end of each day, the stage managers for all shows meet to hammer out an equitable rehearsal schedule for the following day. This process is most difficult during rehearsals for the first two slots, when each actor might be cast in two shows. Once the season is under way, it generally grows easier, as slots do not usually overlap their rehearsal periods, and an actor can perform in only one show per slot.

Stratford stage managers, as a rule, remain in Stratford when the season closes. London stage managers usually join the shows in Newcastle and accompany them to the Barbican and often to Plymouth. However, deputy and assistant stage managers from Stratford normally stay with their productions for the full performance cycle in all four cities. Michael Dembowicz, who has been a stage manager with the RSC for more than twenty years, noted that stage managers will move around to accommodate the needs of the show but believes that it is in the best interest of the RSC for them to remain in Stratford and London and allow the deputies and assistants to shuttle back and forth.

> SMs should be "house SMs," as we know what is best for the house and are intimately familiar with our theatres here. If they brought London SMs here and vice versa, there'd be no continuity in the houses. But we do what we need to. For example, if a show goes out on a world tour, the administration will favor giving it to a London SM, as he will have been with the show more recently. But I did the 1994 international tour of *The Winter's Tale,* because the London SM

was a family man and didn't want to be away for so long, and the next logical person was me. I wanted to turn it down—I wanted to bring *Macbeth*, with Derek Jacobi, up from London, as I had with Ken Branagh in *Hamlet*. But the word on *Macbeth* wasn't very good, and it didn't seem as if it would go anywhere after Stratford, so I chose to do the tour instead.[19]

Assistant directors are hired for the season to work with directors during rehearsals and to oversee productions after they open. Given the company ethos, it is more common for RSC directors to revisit productions during the run than for directors at other theatres, especially when a show needs to be revamped for transfer to Newcastle or London. As Dembowicz noted, "It's good for company morale, and it looks good for Newcastle. If we just sent the assistant directors, over the years God knows what practices would develop. But sometimes directors just can't go because their schedules don't allow."

Technical Rehearsals

Theatres do not earn money when they are dark. The RSC's relentless production schedule and the need to maintain box office momentum on shows already running allow relatively little time for the technical process. To minimize the effects on the box office, the RSC schedules "techs" at the same time for all shows opening in one slot.

In a typical schedule at the RST—which may vary somewhat from show to show—the crews report at nine o'clock on Sunday morning— always a dark day, with no performances—and strike and store the set from the previous night's show. That play and any others already running in the theatre will rejoin the repertoire in two or three weeks, after the new production has teched, previewed, and opened. The set crew then commences the load-in—or fit-up—of the new set. At a certain point in the load-in, when sufficient scenery is onstage, the electrics crew begins to focus the lights, although the set crew will likely still be working. This generally occurs on Monday morning.

Depending upon progress made in focusing the lighting, actors will report for tech either Monday evening or Tuesday morning, but as the first few hours are usually spent in a final flurry of preparation for the actors taking the stage, tech does not usually get under way until a few hours after the official call time. Tech continues through three sessions daily on Tuesday and Wednesday and generally ends on Thursday afternoon. The first dress rehearsal might then take place on Thursday night, but often the tech is not yet finished; in this case, the first—and only—dress rehearsal takes place Friday afternoon. The show performs its first preview on Friday night. It can be rough going, but the crew is experienced at working quickly through techs and they know intimately the idiosyncrasies of their theatre. Teching this quickly allows only enough time to roughly approximate the lighting cues, and scene shifts may still appear rather ungainly. This is normal for the RSC, and the usual expectation is that the production fully jells by opening night.

There are two previews on Saturday, so no rehearsals are scheduled, and Sunday is dark again. The process resumes on Monday morning; during the day, the actors work selected scenes with full technical support, allowing the director and designers the opportunity to hone or change moments or entire scenes. Another preview is given that evening, and the process continues in the same vein until opening, which is usually held midweek. Opening nights of the two or three plays in a slot are staggered at least one night apart to enable the press and staff to attend all of them. Each night, after technical rehearsals and previews end, the artistic and production teams meet, often in the greenroom, to review production notes, discuss problems, hammer out the next day's schedule and the allocation of stage time for the various crews, and pick apart every moment that seemed problematic—often over endless cigarettes, cups of coffee, or cans of beer.

At theatres around the world, the complaint is frequently voiced that the time allotted for the tech and dress rehearsals—especially on shows with some degree of technical complexity—never seems adequate. At the RSC, however, tradition and fiscal exigencies require the production teams to accomplish a lot of difficult, precise work—work that needs to be performed slowly and deliberately—in a very short period of time. Executive producer Lynda Farran agrees that the technical process can be exceptionally stressful: "There's always the financial issue. Every lost performance is so many thousands of pounds, so there is a huge pressure to get the show on in a short period of downtime for the theatre. In the larger houses, the RST and Barbican, it's an ongoing debate. Sometimes it all goes fine, but often it's hot and heavy and uncomfortable down there when people feel they don't have time to do the work. We spend seven to ten weeks rehearsing, and then they've got three days, and the set doesn't work, and we're pressurizing like crazy to get it up. It's certainly true that lately the scale of production has become more complex, and the new technology has meant a more complicated technical time."[20]

Lighting designer and former RST electrician Chris Parry evaluated the tech process from the unusual perspective of having worked on both sides of the proscenium arch.

> I think they're too ambitious. They try to accomplish too much in terms of design, given the schedule they have each year. It's always been bad, but it actually seems to have gotten worse over the years. The scale of shows is such that they can't be loaded in quickly enough. There's no time for anyone to consider any decisions—everything is a mad rush to performance. And I get the lion's share of my work done in tech, as the only time I can really light the show is when the actors are onstage and in costume. All I can do is write rough cues into the board. I think the RSC would be wise to scale back a bit, so that more attention can be paid to quality during the process. But there's no time to do it. The director wants a cue here, a cue there, another cue here, and each cue is the result of levels changing in hundreds of lamps. That all takes time, and it's slow and painstaking, I know, but that's the only way to do it. It's during previews that I'm doing the real work, which is perhaps unfair to the audiences who see those previews. I spend each preview in the back of the house talking to the electrician running the board, making adjustments to the cues as we go through the play. It's far from ideal, and the poor preview audiences are seeing something very strange indeed.
>
> Still, you get to work with marvelously talented people on interesting, challenging, visually arresting productions of high quality in one of the world's most prestigious theatres. Who can argue with that?[21]

The Scenic and Costume Designer's Process

Robert Jones's elegant scenic and costume designs are admired frequently on stages at the RSC and elsewhere throughout the United Kingdom. A graduate of the Central School of Art, where he studied under veteran RSC designer John Gunter and Pamela Howard, Jones worked his way up the design ladder through a series of internships at repertory companies. "They offered a good grounding in washing out the paint buckets, making props, and assisting other designers."[22] After serving as the resident designer for the Nottingham, Newcastle, and West Yorkshire Playhouses, "the last of the big, new, out-of-London theatres, built in 1990, for which I was involved with the whole design process," he moved to London in 1992 and began working at the Royal Court Theatre, the Greenwich Theatre, the Chichester Festival, the Hampstead Theatre Club, and the Birmingham Repertory Theatre, as well as in the West End and at the RSC. His West End productions include revivals of *Black Comedy* and *The Real Inspector Hound, The Killing of Sister George,* and *The Prime of Miss Jean Brodie* and the musicals *Jolson* and *The Goodbye Girl.* At the RSC, he has designed sets and costumes for *Othello, The Winter's Tale, Pentecost, The Herbal Bed* (which played the West End and Broadway), *Henry VIII* (which toured to New York and Washington, DC), *Cyrano de Bergerac* (which toured the United Kingdom and played the West End), *Romeo and Juliet,* and *The Merchant of Venice* (for which he designed sets only). It is relatively common in the United Kingdom for one person to design both sets and costumes but much rarer in the United States. "When *Henry VIII* toured to the States, I got very good reviews for the sets, but the reviewer looked in the playbill and gave costume design credit to the costume supervisor, since they didn't understand that I did both. I like to design both, as it allows me to control the color palette." He designed his first production at the RSC in 1994.

> I had done a lot of new work at the Hampstead Theatre, a lot of new writing, and was very involved in the new theatre they were planning to build. Michael Attenborough was an ex-director at Hampstead and had seen a lot of my work, so we got to know one another. He was doing a play at the RSC called *Pentecost,* by David Edgar, and called me, saying, "I'd really like to work with you on this."
>
> It's a fantastic play but impossible to design. It involves the discovery of a supposed fourteenth century fresco in an old ruined church in Eastern Europe. It's in a bricked-up wall, and a restorer and some other characters have to remove the bricks to discover the fresco, and they have five lines in the script in which to do it. The audience sees this section of fresco revealed almost filmically, and then blackout. Next day, all the bricks have been removed, there's the fresco.

Blackout. Two days later, the whole fresco has been covered in mus-
lin in order to remove it from the wall. Scene change: another configuration of the fresco. Scene change: the whole thing explodes and
collapses in front of the audience. And this was all in The Other Place,
if you can imagine!

This led to fruitful collaborations with Attenborough as well as with
RSC associate director Gregory Doran, with whom Jones had worked
years before at the Nottingham Playhouse. Jones enjoys the balance
created by his relationships with the two. "Mike and I have mostly
worked in the smaller spaces, and it's very emotionally detailed work,
wonderful if the audience is four feet away; you get so involved in the
flicker of an eye or the flare of a nostril. It's terrific. Greg and I have
worked on big, more opulent projects like *Henry VIII* and *Cyrano*."

Jones tends to avoid naturalism in design. He examines architecture and abstracts it into a style appropriate to the work. "I like very
spare stages. A lot of my work is completely empty, perhaps just a floor
with a very beautiful piece of architecture or a back wall. I often use
very strong diagonals, creating areas that collide and cause a tension
on the set."

Jones began work in May 1998 on Gregory Doran's production of
The Winter's Tale that would open in mid-December in the RST. Jones
had until August to submit his final designs, at which point budgets
are finalized, models are built, and working drawings of the specific
scenic units are developed in preparation for construction.

Gregory and I had time to talk about the designs when we were both
in New York with *Henry VIII*. We talked on the plane over and back,
and then we worked for six weeks, which isn't a long time, but we
had no other distractions and were able to work solidly on it. We went
through about five different concepts. What constantly kept coming
back to me, though, was an image that I showed Greg on the first
day, of a very small room with a glowering sky above it. Greg responded quite strongly to it on the first day, but being a designer, as
we all do, we feel we can't do our first gut reaction, we feel we have
to go through the process of doing everything else. We often wind
up coming back to that first image, at least I often do, but I've got to
work through a number of ideas to see if there's something lurking
there that I've missed. And we came back to this photo and just kept
at it.

When we worked on the text together, reading through the play scene-by-scene, the image began to make sense. There are many references to the sky, to the elements, and it all began to work. I felt that it had to be a domestic space, somewhere they could actually live, but it had to appear and disappear, and that's where the technical aspects came in. We wanted to do a three-walled room, but then how do you get rid of it, how does it get there? And then we started looking at large rooms of the late-Victorian period, a lot of which were long galleries with windows and panels and lots of furniture, and it began to come together from those images. What I tend to do with most directors is to surround us with paintings, images, photographs, drawings and talk about it, and the same images start to appear.

For Jones and Doran, the late-Victorian period served the play well. In *The Winter's Tale*, the inciting action is the accusation of adultery made by Leontes, King of Sicilia, against his devoted wife, Hermione, and his best friend, Polixenes, King of Bohemia. Leontes's denouncement erupts, seemingly unprovoked, from deep within him. What would cause Leontes to make such an unfounded and devastating charge? "For me, the Victorian period was a highly moralistic one," said Jones, "where everyone was corseted and no flesh was shown. At the same time, sexually, they were incredibly hypocritical, with so many children born out of wedlock, sexual encounters behind closed doors, illicit drinking and dining clubs set up as normal dining spaces, with rooms at the side where the gentlemen would have sex with the hostesses. High moral values and sexual repression, but as soon as the door was closed, they were at it like rabbits. It seemed to fit for us, because Leontes begins to think, 'Is this what Hermione and Polixenes are up to? I know this goes on in my court, but I don't acknowledge or confront it.'"

Many directors and designers work through a play scene-by-scene, creating storyboards of the events and planning the progression of scenery and costumes. Jones described the action of *The Winter's Tale* as it unfolded in this production, from both scenic and costume perspectives.

We are setting it in a very real world, not a fairy tale or magical or pretty or sweet world, but a very harsh and very cold and very bleak world. We've gone right through the proscenium and built a tunnel, in very steep perspective up the rake, of six towers that are faced with panels. Each tower is motorized and can move on and offstage. At first glance, it could look like a long room. It's bleached timber, sandblasted rough, blue-gray, as is the floor, built with diminishing perspective and using the 1:15 stage rake. On either side of these towers, legs extend offstage, with clouds painted on them. Above them hangs a silk sky with clouds. It looks like a room floating in the sky, but it isn't.

The first image is of a completely empty stage, with all the company on it. They walk downstage, and then the walls close in, and we're in a very domestic, cozy world, away from all the elements. We wanted to emphasize that it's a family story with Leontes and Hermione and their son, Mamillius, and it's all very happy.

Suddenly, Leontes gets it into his head that his best friend is having an affair with his wife. We wanted to emphasize that it was both a royal situation and a domestic situation by the fact that they live in a building, in a room. The court is terribly rigid and formal and hierarchical. All the men are in high collars, the women are in corsets, there's no flesh on display at all, just faces and hands, late nineteenth and early twentieth century, it could be European, it's very nonspecific. As his sexual jealousy becomes more apparent, the court start doing certain small things. One of the ladies may cross the stage and suddenly raise a skirt, and we see a bright red stocking appear in a flash, or one of them may appear in a corset. We just get these flashes as he begins to think, "This is what my wife is doing!" and there is this sense of people lurking and going off into other rooms. As he begins to think this, the walls literally close in on him, and he ends up in a tiny corridor which is cross-lit, and it all begins to chase him down, with people walking in and out of the crosslight. We're working with a choreographer from a company called Kosh, and the work is all very physical. There are nightmare sequences in act 1 which develop as his jealousy gets bigger, as he gets more and more enraged, and we begin to see the courtiers in various stages of undress. At one point, they're all in their underwear, some are seminaked, and Leontes is in the middle of this, the walls are closing in on him—and then it's all suddenly back to normal.

This leads to the trial scene, where the silk in the sky begins to subtly undulate and turn into a tempest. The sky is the full width of the stage, and at the end of the trial, the sky essentially erupts. It covers the whole stage and is lit from above and from the sides. It constantly changes, deep blues and clouds, although it's really just white, it's all done by lighting effects, and at the end of the trial scene, the whole thing drops to the stage, covering the actors and the furniture.

Then it pulls up and collapses and flies up in the back, right up into the flies, and suddenly it's created a snow-drift valley, with wind howling, and we have the scene with Antigonus and the baby. Greg wanted the whole cloth to tell a story. The cloth turns into the bear, the bear rises out from a trap in the stage into the cloth, sort of the image of a polar bear. Antigonus is engulfed by the cloth and taken down, and that's the end of act 1.

We begin act 2 with Time, wearing the sky as his cloak, holding something as if he's swaddling a baby, telling us that sixteen years have passed. He tells us about Perdita, and as he's telling us this, he drops the cloth and Perdita emerges, age sixteen. So, the cloth has taken us through the act. It begins to rise up again, and the sheepshearers in Bohemia come in with tent poles and raise the canopy to become a big tent. In Bohemia, we actually use piles and piles of wool for the sheep festival, and the scene begins with a huge piece of machinery, flywheels and belts and all, and lots of wool, very rough, very sweaty, very dirty, and loads of bare flesh, naked torsos, bare arms and feet, skirts tucked into underwear. And the glowering sky in Sicilia turns into a beautiful blue sky in Bohemia. So, from the court and its buttoned up moral values, we end up in this very different Bohemia. At the end of Bohemia, of course, the whole thing reverts, the sky changes to a different color, and we have the whole statue scene and redemption. The sky hangs down, a sort of drape through which we can look, lit by candles. So, the sky tells a story again, taking us right through to the end.

As for costumes, you have to have a period in which you can show the hierarchy of the play visually on stage, and you have to see the multilayering in the household, the upstairs-downstairs thing. It made sense to have a true court as it existed in that world of the Victorians, either here or in Germany or Austria or Russia. People may allude to Nicholas and Alexandra when they see the costumes. It wasn't intentional, although there is that look of high tunics, sashes, frock coats and spats, big whiskers and mustaches, very controlled, and women in constructed dresses and corsets, but with modern, fitted sleeves. It appears a period piece, but it's not. It's our version of period. I didn't want to be slavish, it's not a film where every detail has to be right. It's all about silhouettes; we see the shape and register it, and it looks Victorian, and that's all that matters. That look tells us a story in itself.

The color palette of the costumes has its own contrasts. The first time we see any color is in Bohemia, and it's all vegetable dyes, mustards, heathers, greens, beetroot, very rich. In the court, it's all steel grays, blues, purples, cool, almost colorless.

When Jones designs costumes, he considers input from the actors
vital to his process. In most theatres, the relatively short rehearsal
period and the advance time needed by the shop to construct clothes
for a large-cast Shakespearean play cause the design deadline to fall
at a point well before the start of rehearsals. At the RSC, rehearsing
two cross-cast shows simultaneously yields a longer rehearsal span,
allowing the designer greater time to develop designs organically with
the actors and the director. *The Winter's Tale,* the second production
of the 1998 Winter Season, performed in repertory with *The Lion, the
Witch and the Wardrobe.* The exceptionally long rehearsal period for
the two shows, almost three months, provided Jones with the welcome
surprise of a relatively late deadline that fell four weeks after the start
of the rehearsal period.

> It's important, whenever possible, to have a dialogue with the actors
> about costumes. On this show, I had the luxury to look at the com-
> pany and the way they moved, let them have two weeks in the re-
> hearsal hall to work a bit, and then talk to them, do rough ideas, go
> away and do sketches, show them to the actors, get their input, and
> then go off and do the final drawings. There was an infusion of the-
> atrical adrenaline; they felt they contributed, so when they came
> around for fittings, it wasn't a surprise. They had time to absorb the
> text, work with the director, interact, react to my ideas and give feed-
> back. It was really successful.
>
> On *Henry VIII,* Jane Lapotaire, who played Catherine of Aragon,
> and I worked very closely. There is a particular scene in which Jane
> didn't want to look like she did in the rest of the play. We didn't de-
> sign that costume until about five weeks into rehearsals. She wanted
> to age very quickly but didn't want to wear makeup or gray her hair,
> so we did it physically, with the costume. She'd been wearing period
> shapes until that scene, and suddenly she appeared in a shapeless dress
> of a very fine jersey, with no bra or underwear, and she showed the
> whole of her body. She looked thin and gaunt, and when she sat down
> it all collapsed around her. That only came out of rehearsals, because
> we had gotten various pieces of fabric, draped them over Jane, played
> around with it. She physically helped as well in the way she molded
> herself. This give-and-take should be intrinsic to the process, but it's
> rarely the case.

Design deadlines generally fall very early in the rehearsal process,
if not before the commencement of rehearsals, which precludes the

organic evolution of the costume design within the rehearsal process. The RSC costume workshop works ceaselessly to produce the clothes for the many actors in a season's repertory, and later deadlines would create untenable conditions for the workshop. More money would not easily remedy the situation or make later deadlines possible, because the most competent stitchers, cutters, and drapers in Stratford are already working at the RSC, and the physical facilities are crammed with cutting tables, sewing machines, and other paraphernalia.

Each theatre possesses characteristics and dynamics that are highly individual and largely immutable. When designing either scenery or costumes, Jones must consider the impact of the theatre's size, ambiance, and sight lines on his creations. He evaluated the dynamics of the five RSC theatres from a designer's perspective.

We were just designing the transfer of *Merchant* from the RST to the Barbican for late 1998. The RST proscenium is narrow, as we know, but there's a large stage beyond, and a large stage in front, with a fairly wide auditorium. The Barbican has a wide auditorium with a wide proscenium as well, but if you take an RST set and put it on the Barbican stage, it looks like a deep well, particularly if it's a tall set, as there are acres of black masking on the sides [of the Barbican] to make the proscenium look the size of the RST's. What we've done with *Merchant* is clad the proscenium and taken it downstage, increasing the width of the set visually but not physically, just turned the corner of the proscenium with dressing. The acting space remains the same but looks wider, and proportionally, it all fits in the Barbican now, filling the space and embracing the auditorium. The auditorium does that in reverse, in a sense, as it embraces the stage and follows its shape.

The Pit is a whole other matter. It's so incompatible with any space in Stratford. On a ground plan, it looks compatible with the Swan and The Other Place, but the height, or lack of it, is a huge problem. You do a set in the Swan or The Other Place, and it goes into the Pit, and you lose two to three meters from the height. It's sort of degrading to the set in a way; you've got this image that looks imposing in the Swan, and in the Pit it looks like a letter box. That was one of the reasons *Henry VIII* didn't go into the Pit, because we used the full height of the Swan as well as the feel of the theatre and the height of the thrust. The Young Vic was therefore perfect. *Pentecost* was similar. It didn't go into the Pit because of the technical demands of the fresco needing a certain height and the feeling of being in a large, derelict church, which you don't get in the Pit, as it's a small, claustrophobic space. The claustrophobia works very well for some shows, like the recent *Romeo and Juliet* that originated in the Pit, because you were in the action, in the piazza, you felt you were in the fights and in the bedroom. I do like the Pit and its immediacy, but I just want to lift that ceiling!

My favorite space is the Swan, followed by The Other Place. I like the sense of occasion the Swan brings with it. A lot of people don't like the wood. Admittedly, I think the timber is slightly too pale, it is a "feel-good" theatre. It's quite hard to do dark, moody pieces there, but it's a wonderful platform, a theatre that concentrates on and enhances the costumes and props. Sets are not really important there. It brings the actor into focus, what they're wearing, handling, what they're sitting on. The set becomes almost a background. I don't think you can build huge sets in the Swan, you've got to acknowledge the building. You can't cover it up. *Deferential* is the wrong word, but I think you have to tip a nod to the architecture and say, "Okay, you're here, you're a very strong, dominant presence, and we're performing within you."

The Other Place, for that matter, you can disguise and make into whatever you like; it's a chameleon-like black box. The audiences are there with us, and if you close the doors, you enclose the audience, and they're complicit. In any proscenium theatre, the audience is looking *at* an image, and it's very hard to get beyond the proscenium. The main thing about The Other Place is getting everything down and center stage.

The Lighting Designer's Process

Chris Parry arrived at the RST in 1976 to take a position as a stage electrician and eventually rose to the position of deputy head of stage lighting. The heads of the lighting departments in the RSC theatres oversee the continued artistic integrity of the designs during the season, and when productions transfer or tour and the original lighting designer is unavailable, they are called upon to re-create the design in the new theatre. After this intensive seasoning, Parry began to design his own productions for the RSC. Although he is now a resident of the United States, this Tony and Olivier award-winning designer returns regularly to the RSC and to the National.

He counts two productions at the RSC among his proudest artistic achievements: Adrian Noble's 1988 production of *The Plantagenets* in the RST—a three-play reworking of the three parts of *Henry VI* combined with *Richard III*—with scenery and costumes by Bob Crowley and featuring Ralph Fiennes, Cherry Morris, Anton Lesser, Joanne Pearce, David Calder, Ken Bones, and Penny Downie; and Howard Davies's 1986 staging of Christopher Hampton's *Les Liaisons Dangereuses* in The Other Place, with scenery and costumes again by Bob Crowley and starring Alan Rickman, Lindsay Duncan, Fiona Shaw, and Juliet Stevenson.

For a lighting designer, one of the distinguishing features of working in a repertory situation is the use of a rep plot, drafted by the theatre's master electrician and hung prior to the tech of the first show of the season. Some designers prefer starting with a blank slate, that is, designing a complete plot from scratch. Parry, however, feels that the rep plot has distinct advantages.

> I like working with a rep plot. It feels like a lot of the basic spade work has been done for you; they've already figured out how to cover the stage from the front, back, and sides, all of which you're going to use at some point. It makes my work easier, as you don't have to reinvent the wheel. As far as the rest of the instruments you can use, you usually receive a list of available equipment, and it's usually not much. So, if you want to use a gobo wash of bare tree branches for a scene, you figure out that if you do it from a specific angle it will take ten lights, and then you must determine what ten instruments are still available. It usually comes down to asking, "Do I have ten of some type of unit that I can use, and if not, have I used them elsewhere, and can I then substitute some *other* instruments for those and make them work here instead?" The first phase of the design process, drafting the light plot, is about getting the ideas for the design on paper, like whether to use bare tree branches in one scene or shadow uplights on the edge of the stage in another or two red specials from above—then looking at the inventory of units and figuring out where to hang them and prioritizing instruments for use. It's a question of deciding which idea is most important and sometimes sacrificing some concepts because you don't have the instrumentation.[23]

At the RSC, as at other theatres, the lighting designer may well live in a different city and may have to communicate with the director, set and costume designer, and stage manager via phone, fax, or e-mail. The lighting designer drafts the light plot after analyzing the ground plan and photos of the set and depends on the daily rehearsal notes from the stage manager, which convey details about staging and effects. Usually arriving at the theatre a few days before tech, the lighting designer watches a couple of run-throughs in the rehearsal hall and then commences the critical phase of the design work with tech. Parry, however, lived in Stratford during the conceptual phase for many of the productions he designed at the RSC, because he maintained his electrics crew position for a number of years after beginning his independent design career. Being in Stratford afforded him the great advantage of attending rehearsals, chatting with the director and the designer in person, and watching the evolution of the scenery and costumes as he created his approach to the lighting.

For *The Plantagenets,* designer Bob Crowley devised storyboard drawings to help the artistic team follow the narrative over the more than thirty scenes in each of three separate plays. Crowley often indicated his ideas for lighting by using slashes of yellow watercolor on his drawings, not to indicate his preference for yellow light but as his method of showing Parry the angle of light he envisioned for that scene. The lighting designer found these helpful as he began to articulate his own design concept. "I like to see a storyboard and prefer it to just a model, which is what most designers use," Parry remarked. "Storyboards help me understand the designer's emotional feel for each scene. Ideally, at the end of the process, the sets, costumes, and lighting should all look as if they were designed by one person."[24]

Parry and Noble had relatively little discussion about lighting initially. "It's often difficult to pin directors down about lighting early on," Parry said, "as it's not as tangible as looking at a model or a swatch of material for a costume. It's much more difficult to picture the effects of three hundred lighting instruments in a scene. But you can have just a half-hour conversation with a director like Adrian, and you come away knowing exactly what you're going to do, because he's said enough to spark your imagination." Noble worked quickly through the play with Parry and Crowley. He articulated exactly where the scene occurred and described the emotional feel he was hoping to create. Parry elaborated on the process.

> Adrian started talking very precisely, something along the order of, "The first scene starts with the funeral of Henry V. We're in a Russian church, very cold, high ceilings, high windows, light streaming

in them, the coffin isolated; and upstage, outside of the great doors, are the villagers peering in, there's incense in the air, and it's smoky. Scene two: a band of marching men floating in space. Scene three: a garden in Paris in winter." He went through the play like that, giving a quick, pithy, atmospheric description. Sometimes, he would try to capture the emotion of the character. "This scene is about the downfall of Henry, everybody's against him, he's very isolated." For one battle scene, he mentioned that he wanted the look of the mustard gas used in the World War I trenches, so we had York isolated in a spotlight down center, making a speech, and upstage in this smoke drifting from stage left to right, they're dragging bodies across the stage. We tried using yellow-colored smoke, but it was too noxious, nobody could stand it, so we wound up using regular smoke effects and coloring it by shining yellow sidelight through it.

   With some directors, you can sit in a meeting for hours and walk out having no idea what they really envision. For some reason, directors like Adrian have a knack for talking about the play in very succinct terms that stick and conjure up pictures and images. I was never really stuck for an idea after coming out of that first storyboard meeting, which was surprising, since the show was so big. For one battle scene, he said, "It should feel like one of the movies of Akira Kurosawa," so I used saturated reds, blues, and yellows.

Some designers prerecord cues into the light board before the start of tech as a point of departure for crafting more finely honed cues during tech. For Parry, this is a pointless exercise, as he cannot see the actors in their costumes or connect emotionally to the dramatic moments he must light. The real challenge for Parry occurs during the tech process—despite the urgency of the proceedings at the RSC—when he fashions each lighting cue while the actors work through the production on stage.

   Lighting during tech forces me to work instinctually. I remember watching the coronation scene of *Henry VI* in the Ashcroft rehearsal room, which didn't look like a big deal—there was a musician at the piano playing a little tune, and the actors were all proceeding downstage, and I thought, "Okay, it looks kind of interesting." And when we got to the scene in tech, there was a huge orchestral sound, with drums and trumpets and timpani, a huge event suddenly, much more lavish with the music and the costumes, and I realized, "I have to do something that matches this!" And you do, you have to match the scale of the event, especially in Shakespeare. Music in his works plays a huge part in what I do, it influences the scale of what I do and is a big contributor to the emotional feel of the scene. If I had lit the scene ahead of time, without the band, I would have done something small, and when we got to tech, it wouldn't have worked.

Les Liaisons Dangereuses, directed by Howard Davies, presented Parry with a stark contrast from his work on *The Plantagenets,* where the grand sweep of events over three plays provided an enormous physical as well as emotional canvas on which to fashion his design. *Les Liaisons,* staged originally in The Other Place, is a single-set show, and that setting—the decaying interior of a French aristocrat's house just before the Revolution—is considerably more claustrophobic than the panoramic landscape of the Wars of the Roses.

The rear wall of Bob Crowley's set was constructed of wooden, accordion-pleated standing screens with built-in venetian blinds. Director Davies wanted to suggest specific times of day and changing seasons of the year throughout the play. The trick for Parry was to convey this to the audience, and he solved the problem by utilizing the blinds, through which he could focus a number of lights.

The first scene is at night on a warm, August evening, and Howard wanted the feel to be quite romantic. I used light coming through the blinds at a low, horizontal angle; it was a warm, sunset color, the shadows were a rich blue, and it felt very romantic. The next scene is at breakfast the following day, and how do you clue the audience in to that? The light came in through the shutters at a fairly steep angle and was a very pale, straw yellow, with not much blue to fill in the shadows. If you use blue, it starts to feel either romantic or nighttime, so you leave that out, and everything is much thinner, paler, watery sunlight. A scene at night in the bedroom used candlelight, shadows from the floor, some broken-up gobos for the actors to walk through. There's a scene in which Valmont comes in to rape Cecile, and he's carrying a candelabra, which he puts down on the bedside table and then crosses to her and stands over her. So, I put a light on the floor under the bedside table, so the light was coming up as if it came from the candelabra, but it was a much more of an up-lit angle, casting a shadow on the screens upstage, that made him look very menacing.

As the play progressed, we removed sunlight from the show, so as we got to autumn, the sunlight became very thin and watery, so by the end, it was icy cold, with no sunlight, even though we were still indoors. One of the stage managers remarked that it looked like Antarctica. And it also fit the language and relationships, as there's no love lost between Valmont and the Marquise; they've become harsh and brittle with each other. So, in the scenes just before the duel, there was nothing warm, just harsh blue, cold light coming through the blinds. For the duel, which happens in the wintry fields, the furniture was struck, and there was a huge amount of backlight but not coming through the blinds this time, and there were some leafless tree gobos shining on the front of the blinds. The last scene of the play is the one in which the three women are playing cards and discussing events, and Howard wanted them to look as ugly as possible, so I used very low-angled, horizontal, harsh, cold light slicing across the stage, with no front light at all, looking stark and uncompromising, with the body of Valmont lying downstage. It was a big journey through the play, told by lighting.

Parry's design was replicated later in the Pit and then at the Ambassadors Theatre in the West End. When it was transferred to the Music Box Theatre on Broadway, his design earned him his first of three Tony Award nominations.

Parry has never designed lighting in the Swan but would enjoy the opportunity to do so. He believes that the preeminence of the actor in this space and the lack of emphasis on scenery both increase the necessity of lighting to create atmosphere and shape the audience's perception of the event. Swan master electrician and lighting designer Wayne Dowdeswell cautioned that this theatre presents certain obstacles for the designer. "The greatest difficulty in lighting the Swan, apart from the usual problem of lighting an open stage, is caused by the very close proximity of audience to actor, who is raised by about two feet. When an actor stands at the edge, facing downstage, his heels virtually touching the front row, it is difficult to light his eyes without blinding the audience. We have not found an all-purpose solution for this."[25]

But Parry has worked in the other RSC theatres, and he discussed their aesthetics, design challenges, and physical limitations. Although most actors and directors are deterred by the RST's dimensions and dynamics, Parry finds it a viable space for his work.

I like the RST a lot. The size of the proscenium is on a human scale there; it's not as big as most prosceniums in the US. Actors don't seem dwarfed in the RST, the way they can behind a bigger proscenium arch. The first few years I worked there—as an electrician—I had never seen anything like it. The amount and scope of scenery seemed overwhelming to me. Now, though, it seems much more manageable. In the RST, the stalls and the dress circle have the best views, whilst the balcony has a horrible view, and from the rear of the balcony, you feel like you're in another county. I like designing there, it's a comfortable space, and the lighting rig hasn't changed much over the years, so I know how to work in there from season to season without many surprises.

The Other Place is warm, flexible, and inviting. There's an exceptional audience-actor relationship in that space that I find very appealing, and the design of the new building has been successful in creating a much more pleasant working environment.

I quite like the Pit, actually, although some designers loathe it. It's got real problems for a lighting designer, insofar as the air-conditioning duct work hangs dead center from the grid, and there's no way to put a light anywhere center stage. Still, the atmosphere is good in there. *Les Liaisons Dangereuses,* for example, never looked as good to me as it did in the Pit.

The Barbican is my least favorite space, by far. There are dreadful lighting positions, especially in the front of house. They're hard to get to and hard to maneuver around. The onstage positions are okay, but as you move farther upstage, and the grid narrows down, you have decreasing lengths of batten to hang from, and you're trying to backlight this huge space with few positions to work with. I also feel that the Barbican, perhaps because it took so long to be built from the day it was conceived, has been overdesigned. Too many people had a hand in it over too long a stretch, and that is reflected in the lack of coherence in the technical and design elements available. The space, to me, is neither fish nor fowl. It's not a proscenium theatre, really, nor is it a true thrust, and as a result, it seems stuck in no-man's-land. Every few years, a decision will be made to make the Barbican more like the RST, or vice versa, to facilitate transfers, either by bringing the Barbican legs in or building the RST thrust out, and neither decision works. I will admit, though, that the audience gets a terrific view of the stage from all seats.[26]

The Voice Coach's Process

Formal work on the actor's voice—expressiveness, connective function between the written text and the actor's body, sound and impact on the ear, articulation, and perception—has been, to a varying extent, a concomitant of the RSC's production process since the 1950s. The first efforts of coaches focused on part-time instruction in singing and vocal production; the current emphasis on vocal work, as a tool assisting actors and directors in developing a freedom with language, results from an evolution of actor training. The voice is no longer considered merely a physical instrument; it is now recognized as having a deeper, organic relationship to emotion and character development.

Andrew Wade is the head of voice at the RSC. He trained as both a teacher and an actor at the Rose Bruford School and was brought into the RSC in 1988 by the legendary Cicely Berry, now the voice director, whose seminal advances in identifying and developing the intrinsic bond between voice and acting have been lauded by artists around the world. The overworked voice staff at the RSC consists of Wade and his gifted associates; Berry, although still very much a part of the company, enjoys a position that now allows her to pursue a broader range of interests on an international level. Rather than articulating a specific dogma or approach, the voice coaches respond to the needs of the individual productions. "Our work is provoked, promoted, and determined by the challenge of the company and the personnel who are around, as opposed to some formula," said Wade.[27]

Cicely Berry, said Wade, was brought to the RSC by Trevor Nunn, who recognized that a number of factors—the state of actor training at the time, the perspective of actors working at the RSC, the demands of the theatre spaces, and the prevalent acting styles—created the need for serious and consistent vocal work. Berry had several areas to address: aiding the actors in relaxing when they spoke, helping them find the breath necessary for the larger spaces, discovering the range needed to respond to the demands of a role, and refining the actors' ability to, as Wade put it, "muscularly define sound." As her work evolved, so did the directors' enthusiasm and dependence on it, and it gradually became firmly enmeshed in the rehearsal process.

Wade's exploration with the company lies in "finding a freedom with the language." "How do we find a way for actors to connect to classical language and for an audience to connect to it? Voice work for me is very much part of the word. It's the central mission statement. We are concerned with the actor's voice, but I see it as part of the word, which is a slightly different focus. And I see the work very much as part of the process of the rehearsal period and the play in performance, as opposed to just training the actor's sound, purely." It is not enough that the actor speaks well; one must also act well. The two things are inextricably linked. "We are the Royal Shakespeare Company. The work has to be about Shakespeare and about finding ways for the actors—who may not be doing Shakespeare all the time—to actually feel they have the right and confidence to do it. And that's becoming harder."

One of the biggest challenges facing the voice department, and the RSC as a whole, is the changing nature of both the training and employment of actors in Britain. In a paper on the work of the voice department that Wade prepared for use in college and university acting classes, he wrote about having to contend with the results of contemporary approaches to theatre education.

> As we all know, an actor today is expected to be incredibly versatile. Consequently, drama schools are torn as to what aspect or for which type of theatre they are preparing their actors. The result is that voice work is having to cater for an actor who is possibly going to work in film, television, radio, theatre, schools, restaurants, outside and inside, with classical, text-based language, contemporary writing of all qualities, in forms of art such as musicals or theatre whose reference is the visual and the physical.
>
> The key word is flexibility today, a concept which all too often serves as a facade concealing the facts of economic reality. The chances of playing Shakespeare on a regular basis for professional actors are increasingly few and far between. Drama schools, while determined to offer their students the most complete type of training, have naturally the welfare of the students at heart. Realistically, television is now the largest employer and provider of first acting jobs. The tendency—whether openly declared or not—is therefore to lay the emphasis where the opportunities are.[28]

It is tempting to make an invidious comparison between the quality of classical acting today and in previous generations. However, theatre cultures and performer expectations are by nature largely evolutionary. Actors develop skills experientially and by exposure to role models. As contemporary actors are trained in the style of realistic acting acceptable in television and film, they increasingly resist developing big, resonant voices, fearing that they will sound "old-fashioned." Andrew Wade recalled one illustrative incident: "I did a workshop at a college, and after a session, one of the actors said, almost spontaneously, 'My God, I'm sounding like an RSC actor, which is the very thing I *don't* want!' He was finding a bigger sound and a connection to the language he'd never found before, but what he'd *heard* after that session was, 'I'm sounding very different, not what I'm used to, and I don't want that.' What he was really discovering was that language had an active place in his life, had a function of communicating and defining self that he hadn't felt before, but all he could hear was that he was sounding like something he hadn't heard before."[29]

The actor's challenge lies not only in developing both the technical and analytical skills needed to "speak the speech" properly; the greater task, as television and film have rendered contemporary theatregoers passive spectators, lies in exciting the audience to *want* to engage in active listening. Wade referred to Peter Brook's caution that if the theatre's seats are too comfortable, the audience will not willingly participate in the event; he compared that observation to his own specific challenge in training voice.

> There's obviously a right that you have to hear the actor, but that's a very complicated statement. It's not just about easily hearing. There's something about chasing an actor in terms of wanting to know what's going on that's infinitely more interesting in the end. But I feel we're becoming more of a consumer society, and we want it to be more like having a volume control in the theatre, easy for us to get. People want the same experience wherever they sit in the theatre. A hundred or more years ago, people would never have expected the same experience in the cheaper seats as in the expensive ones. I don't want to excuse the work if they're not, but they're never going to. It's going to be a different experience, but there's a given expectation, and perhaps theatres have provoked this, that you are going to have the same experience and be able to hear from every seat.

Wade remarked that this inability to hear is often attributed to a suspicion that the actor's volume is inadequate, when frequently other factors—the audience's inexperience with certain types of language, preconceived notions of the "proper" way of speaking classical text, lack of directorial focus—are at work. "I often hear audience members saying about actors, 'They were very good when they got into it, weren't they?' That may be true, but it's also the case of the audience getting into it. And that's a big challenge for us." For Wade, voice work is an integral component of performance, intrinsic to the larger goal of provoking a response from the audience. "Cicely Berry mentioned that it was not necessarily a compliment when someone said to her, 'I heard every word.' Not that they *shouldn't,* but what I really want people to say is that they were affected by a production, that they thought about it after they saw it, and I hope speaking is a part of that. I don't want them going away appreciating what a good voice coach I am because I got the actors to sound nice."

Wade has discovered that to most effectively serve the production, his first task is to forge an understanding with the director. Each director has a particular viewpoint about voice work, articulated or not, and Wade must discern the most appropriate methodology for each production. Some directors are more intuitive, some more analytical, and Wade must adapt to their styles to avoid, however unintentionally, creating a barrier between director and actor. "If a voice person is going to have a place in the theatre, we must not be a threat to the director, in terms of challenging his or her work. Finding a practical way to work on the language and the actor's sound actually is part of enhancing the work of the director, and that's the interesting challenge for me. For some, that would be a frustration, that somehow we aren't recognized, that perhaps the director doesn't allow us to do enough. Like in many roles in a performance, you're constantly learning your role afresh each time. At the moment, there is a healthy state, a body of directors who want to find a way to welcome input from the team, and we're part of that."

After assessing the needs of the production, Wade must then determine the needs of the individual actors. This phase of the process calls for tact, diplomacy, and empathy on his part as well as a profound respect for the fact that each actor works differently. "You must understand where the actors are at and remember that you're not there to change them. Nevertheless, just going through the basic voice work, what I think a warm-up is about, is not about teaching them new things necessarily but providing them with a framework to apply their own principles to. There are people who come here with a bad experience of voice work or those who have not had much, and it takes time for them, rightly so."

Working on so many plays simultaneously allows little time for what Wade views as the "luxury" of preparation. The continual process of rehearsal, performance, touring, and transfers that is life at the RSC obscures the natural arc of a production's life. One show opens while another is mired in midrehearsal doldrums. The voice coaches are always involved in the process during rehearsals and the run and rarely find a comfortable cushion of time in which to leisurely contemplate their next production. "I'm more prepared, I think, by having done the work over and over again. I'd love to say I have two or three weeks to study associated texts, find poetry I'd like to use with the actors, but that doesn't happen with the resources and scheduling we have." He must divide his focus, with some degree of equity, among several shows in varying phases of production. Speaking about projects he was currently working on, he offered an example of the scope of his oversight.

> *Troilus and Cressida* opens tonight at the Barbican, and the same cast is in *A Month in the Country* as well, so they go back into rehearsals next Monday. Both shows will open in Stratford in a few weeks time, along with *The Lion, the Witch and the Wardrobe* and *The Winter's Tale* in the RST. The *Troilus/Month* company will be performing in both the Swan and The Other Place, and they'll both go out on regional tour in early '99. And last week, after a very concentrated period of work, *Richard III* with Robert Lindsay opened, and then it is going out again, so one has to keep an ear and an eye on them. And we're coming to the final week of *School for Scandal,* which played Stratford and then the Barbican. So, you're juggling a lot, and there are also about seventy actors right now in Plymouth, about seven or eight shows there over a few weeks, and one is responsible for them—which is where my colleague is right now.
>
> The work, in essence and in principle, does *not* stop after opening night. The stark reality is that often my time and availability mean that one isn't able to continue in a way that we should at the RSC, but that has to do with resources. You must keep touching base with a cast or you'll lose what you develop. In principle, the work continues, and you like to be able to lead warm-ups in the spaces or just solo work, so people can say to you, "I've had a chance to play it for a few weeks, and I'm sticking on this speech, so can I come back to

the language work with some voice work around it?" The reason I want to work with a company that holds onto the repertoire system is that I have a different working relationship with the actors, which allows them to challenge their own work and grow.

That relationship includes both individual and group work with actors, lunch sessions devoted to studying verse, warm-ups held in different theatres, and community outreach projects. The staff also maintains contact with ear, nose, and throat specialists and voice therapists and offers talks on voice care for the actor. British Equity has ruled that a theatre cannot require a company warm-up before a production but must allow each actor instead the choice of preshow preparation, so attendance at warm-ups is voluntary. Wade attempts to hold them three times a week for all productions in performance. Given the demands on an actor's time prior to a performance—there are wig and wardrobe calls, fight rehearsals, physical warm-ups—Wade tries to "whip through" voice work in about fifteen minutes. Most often, the warm-ups are held in a rehearsal room, but when other productions are rehearsing, they are done on one of the theatre's stages.

> What's wonderful is you might get actors from different productions coming along. It's nice to get actors who may not even walk on the main stage in the season to actually do a warm-up there, and sometimes some actors only meet other actors at the warm-up, so just having a different dynamic can be healthy. But one mustn't get purist about voice warm-ups and start being paranoid; people don't come along to them sometimes because some actors prepare in different ways. I fundamentally believe the principle of the group warm-up is beyond voice work, and I mustn't judge the quality of the voice work in the performance on whether people showed for the warm-up. Sometimes that period between matinee and evening performance has to be about doing your washing, and wrongly or rightly, you're going to go mad if you actually stayed on. That sounds sacrilegious for the head of voice at the RSC, but I've got to keep it in perspective. I believe in the work, but I don't believe in whipping them all or putting a guilt trip on them to get them in there. You have to understand the actors and find a way that voice work meets with their particular needs and talents.

As stretched as he is by the demands of monitoring the vocal work of as many as one hundred fifty or more actors in more than two dozen productions around the United Kingdom, Wade thoroughly relishes his work. "I'm hugely lucky. I can't do this work anywhere else, as there isn't the span of work anywhere else. I hope there continues to be the leadership here that believes in the spoken word and believes in the actors' ability to resource that through voice work. It would be a great loss, beyond theatre, if we no longer have this work going on."

The Director's Process

Katie Mitchell possesses keen and passionate insight into the subtle alchemy of making theatre as well as an impressive self-awareness and a refreshing degree of humility. She is articulate, funny, and fiercely intelligent. Mitchell is in the vanguard of younger directors, many of whose careers first blossomed at the RSC, who are responsible for a large percentage of the impressive showings currently seen on British stages. She has directed several productions for both the RSC and the National Theatre, has made successful forays into directing opera and television, and has served as both the director of The Other Place and one of Adrian Noble's handpicked associate directors.

Educated at Oxford, Mitchell spent two years touring as an assistant director with the Paine's Plough Company, worked with her own group, Classics on a Shoestring, and directed at the King's Head Theatre, the Tron Theatre in Glasgow, Dublin's Abbey Theatre, and the Gate Theatre in Notting Hill. At the age of twenty-three, she applied to newly appointed RSC artistic director Adrian Noble for a position as an assistant. She spent one year in that capacity in Stratford and another in London during the RSC's season at the Almeida Theatre, assisting on *Much Ado About Nothing, The Man Who Came to Dinner,* and *King Lear* and directing *Stars in the Morning Sky.*

Her first main-stage directing assignment at the RSC, at the age of twenty-five, was Thomas Heywood's *A Woman Killed with Kindness* at The Other Place in 1991. This domestic tragedy, written in 1603, combines "greed, lust for land, a love triangle, and personal betrayal," said Mitchell with great delight.[30] The show received excellent press. The RSC seasonal brochure in 1992 quoted from the exceptional review it received in the *Observer*: "Katie Mitchell's memorable RSC debut . . . beautifully acted . . . a minor masterpiece." The following season, she staged S. Anski's classic, haunting drama of love and demonic possession, *The Dybbuk.* "It's a beautiful love story," said Mitchell, "better than *Romeo and Juliet.*" For eight months, Mitchell and the design and dramaturgy team researched the world of Eastern European Jewish *shtetl* life of centuries past, gaining access to a Hasidic community in north London and traveling to the Ukraine. This painstaking research process is characteristic of Mitchell's work with her collaborators during the preproduction phase. *The Dybbuk,* too, garnered enthusiastic reviews.

Adrian Noble allowed Mitchell to choose both plays, for which she was grateful. Many theatres select a repertoire and then hire directors to stage the plays. Noble, however, had made a commitment to the development of new directors, and implicit in that commitment was nurturing these directors' personal vision and predilections. "The RSC has been brilliant in allowing me to bring in outside designers and composers," she observed, referring to set and costume designer Vicki Mortimer and lighting designer Tina MacHugh, neither of whom had previously worked at the RSC.

In 1993, she was offered another production at The Other Place. "Adrian asked me to choose a well-known play with a small cast." She picked Ibsen's *Ghosts.* This choice represented a departure for Mitchell, whose preference is usually for plays in which she can forge an ensemble and explore aspects of ritual and choral work. However, Noble's dictum regarding cast size and the nature of that season's production schedule compelled her to examine the work of Ibsen.

She prefers to spend a considerable period researching, analyzing, and thinking about a play before she is ready to commit to directing it, but the RSC's time frame didn't allow for this. She characterized her decision to direct *Ghosts* as "compact and rushed, a slightly dishonest process. Initially, I didn't burn to direct this play." Still, the more time she spent with it, the greater her affinity grew. She received a grant to travel to Norway to research the play, and her stunning photos of Ibsen's landscape—shots of desolate, craggy, and foreboding fjords and mountains—formed the centerpiece of an evocative lobby display at The Other Place.

Mitchell initially found the RSC's rehearsal schedule difficult to negotiate. She preferred the rehearsal process at nonrepertory theatres, where the absence of double casting allows the director more hours each day with a full complement of actors. In *Ghosts,* Mrs. Alving and Pastor Manders have several long, difficult scenes together, and Mitchell was insistent that Jane Lapotaire and John Carlisle, cast in these roles, be available for full-time work with her and free from the demands of other rehearsals and performances. The casting committee acceded to her request, and they appeared in only *Ghosts* that season. "I have had to adjust my rehearsal techniques to RSC rules. I'm used to working long days, perhaps from ten in the morning to ten at night, but of course you can't do that at the RSC. I've learned new disciplines as a result: how to be economical with time, a willingness to learn from actors, the need to compromise and stay calm. On my first show here, I fought with the environment. My process was too much for the cast, given their split attention and focus due to other rehearsals, and didn't yield what I initially expected. I kept running into brick walls, so I adapted."

The production was relentless in its unraveling of Ibsen's study of hereditary debauchery and featured outstanding performances by Lapotaire and by Simon Russell Beale as Oswald. A rain curtain upstage physically reinforced Ibsen's sodden, suffocating world—devoid of vibrancy or color—in which incest, betrayal, and despair grow like mold. In the close, stifling confines of The Other Place, it was a powerful, wrenching production. Mel Gussow wrote in *American Theatre* magazine:

> The necessity of *Ghosts* suffuses every aspect of Mitchell's version, which is as close to a perfect production as one could imagine. In her hands, the play is an emotionally shattering experience. . . .
> In reviewing the last Broadway mounting of *Ghosts,* a 1982 production starring Liv Ullman, I said that we rarely felt the intensity and the metaphorical mist of unforgiving memory that pervades this blighted Nordic household. That is precisely what Mitchell and her actors convey at Stratford's intimate Other Place.[31]

Critical praise was heaped on the production, and it was nominated for several Olivier Awards. Mitchell, however, has an artist's hunger for developing greater skills and insight. A few years after the production closed, after enjoying more critical successes, she voiced her awareness—without a hint of gratuitous self-deprecation—that she was continuing to evolve as a director.

Ghosts was a big success with all sorts of nominations and praise, but something was wrong. I couldn't have articulated what at the time, as I was seduced by all the attention. Then a fantastic Russian teacher from Moscow, Professor Solyova, came to see it, and she is a leading authority on Stanislavsky. We went out to supper afterwards, and she said, "Yes, it is very interesting, you have a lot of skill with the mise-en-scène and the atmosphere, but (a) there is absolutely nothing going on between the actors, and (b) you only directed one of them," referring to Alex Gilbreath, who played Regina, someone I'd worked with before in the Fringe.

It was terrifying at first. I resisted it, but I went home and shamefully realized that she was right. A friend of mine had worked with the director Tarkovsky, and he's my great love, and I had to listen to her. And she said, "Katie, you misunderstood Stanislavsky. It's not about making it *like* life, it's about *making life onstage*." And the two things are completely different. You're not reconstructing something, but you're making something that lives in the moment.[32]

In the spring of 1994, Mitchell directed her first show at the National, a highly successful production of early-twentieth-century English realism, *Rutherford and Son*. That summer, she directed the RSC's tour of *Henry VI: The Battle for the Throne*. Mitchell believes that the cavernous Cerritos Center outside of Los Angeles was an absolutely ill-conceived choice of American venue for the production, which had premiered in the close quarters of The Other Place and had been staged for intimate spaces. By necessity, the cast of an international tour is filled with actors from outside the main company of the RSC, and this group comprised mostly young performers. Although the production displayed tantalizing glimmers of Mitchell's vision of a stark, war-torn landscape upon which the Byzantine complexities of fifteenth century intrigue and betrayal unfolded, the physical production and the performances lacked the stature to respond to the demands of the Cerritos Center. Mitchell remembered the opening night experience with a mixture of good humor and horror. "It looked like a little baby thing; these little actors couldn't possibly fill that space. It was agonizing. I had to sit next to Steve Martin on my right, Oliver Stone in front of me, and Prince Charles was there—and the show was *obviously* not going to work. It was a nightmare." Still, the production received strong notices in the American press.

In 1995, she staged Euripides' tragedy *The Phoenician Women* in The Other Place. This examination of the ravages of war allowed Mitchell to draw parallels between the mythic Theban civil war and the contemporary internecine Balkan conflicts. The production, though, avoided any obvious or literal allusions, as Mitchell preferred to let the audience make its own inferences. As is the case with many of her productions, theatrical ritual served as a touchstone for her approach. Audience members were handed sprigs of sage upon entering the space and sat on backless benches in an incense-infused theatre. The prominent design feature of Vicki Mortimer and Rae Smith's set was a black brick wall adorned with a few rough-hewn, ceramic sconces in which candles flickered mysteriously. The actors, all of whom portrayed both individual characters as well as members of the chorus, were clothed in stained, dusty, earth-toned robes evocative of some previous millennium yet carried valises and satchels on their backs, visually reinforcing with contemporary resonance their journey into exile. The cast danced and whirled and chanted the choral episodes, providing their own eerie musical accompaniment on improvised and primitive instruments. The performances were muscular and powerfully disturbing, creating a palpable sense of tragic inevitability. The production, again, was a critical and box office success.

Yet Mitchell decided to radically rework the production when it transferred to the Barbican. She had recently participated in a workshop conducted by former RSC director Peter Brook—widely regarded as one of the most influential experimental directors of the latter half of the twentieth century—and that experience generated a desire to craft the piece anew.

> I did a workshop outside of Paris, with other British and French directors and Brook's actors, on how you prepare the actor for rehearsals. We all did our various preparation exercises, and Brook took part. Can you imagine the horror of that? But he's not intimidating at all, he's a facilitator, and there is no good or bad or right or wrong, just something that's alive or not, and he's very generous. So, we did this for three days, and I realized that I didn't know how to direct, even though I had been getting away with it for seven years. I discovered that a lot of what I did to prepare the actors was about avoiding getting on with the work promptly, that a lot of exercises were gratu-

itous and meaningless and just generated energy without focusing the actor physically, vocally, intellectually, emotionally.

Subsequently, I've done a long workshop where there's a warming up of the body and voice, and then there are games, which have to be very specifically designed for that piece of work and the method that you're going to work on when you get the scene up on its feet, and it's basically Stanislavskian, this interaction. I had a lot to learn about the space between the actors and what actually occurs there.

All these revelations that I had been doing gratuitous work with the actors led me to basically taking *The Phoenician Women,* a piece of work that was phenomenally successful, and reworking it from point zero. In doing that, I met a lot of initial resistance from the actors, but I had to admit where my tricks lay, had to tell them that "I put in sound or atmospheric lighting because I don't trust you to change how we hear or give atmosphere. And I'm giving you these bowls to hold and these suitcases to wear because I don't believe that you can do vocally what bowls can do or that you can convince me that you've traveled unless you've got a descriptive item on your back." And they were shocked by that, but eventually, after a lot of work, they jumped on board, all but one, but he was neutralized by the rest of the group.

Mitchell delights in discussing the dynamics of making theatre, particularly working with actors. For her, a complete understanding and application of core Stanislavskian precepts of action and through-line are critical—for directors and actors—in developing a coherent production that lives in the moment. Her version of Chekhov's *Uncle Vanya,* staged for the RSC at the Young Vic in 1998, was her "experiment to really put a fourth wall down. And we got absolutely annihilated for it, had people shouting because the performers were talking so quietly. It was an experiment, but it appealed to a lot of theatre practitioners because they weren't being performed *at.* I'd love to do the play for an audience of ten. I think it's a classic stage directors go through."

Mitchell, whenever possible, seeks to create an ensemble in rehearsals, one in which trust—in the text, in the director, in the company, in the process—enables the actors to experiment freely and to contribute willingly. The dynamic of an ensemble is hard to quantify and often harder to create, given the fragility of actors' egos and the rigors of rehearsals and performances. It requires the director to constantly evaluate the process to ensure that the emotional and artistic environment remains supportive and nurturing. Some actors willingly tackle every challenge and adapt easily to a variety of rehearsal methods; others require prodding, coaxing, and reassuring; and a few will refuse—from fear, intransigence, or both—to fully commit. In an art in which personal transformation is achieved in no small way through the actor's willful vulnerability, exploring unfamiliar methodological territory can threaten the actor's often precarious equilibrium. The more accustomed the actor grows over time to working in a certain fashion, the more difficult it is to adapt to new ones. Mitchell finds that the older, more classically trained RSC actors—who might initially resist more experimental techniques—are able to give themselves over to new processes if the director provides the appropriate mechanism and a safe rehearsal environment. She cites the experience of working with David Ryall, an older member of the company of *The Mysteries*.

David played God—a very hard role to play, as you can imagine! But he found the child in himself, gave into the process like a little boy. It was absolutely beautiful, he hadn't played like that in years, and it started a bit of a creative resurgence in him. Offset against that were the defense mechanisms he'd built up over the years, and every now and then they would come back in, but he was always able to get his child back. It's complicated, doing that type of ensemble work. But I'd hate to be ageist, hate to say you could only do that work with certain-aged performers.

It's all about ego. A Slovenian director, a friend of mine, said, "If your ego is stronger than theirs, you can get them to do it; if not, you can't." It's not about being autocratic, it's about will. If you can convince them, and if the exercise is valid—and that's very important, you can't have anything gratuitous—you can get them there. Many of my experiences with older male actors have been terror to begin with, followed by revelation and surprise. There is an amazing willingness, often, when they realize the director is there to make the whole piece clear and make them do their best work. I think you can get fantastic work from actors, but it takes a long time, because they've been bruised and wounded, often quite badly.

A true ensemble should be small, she pointed out, if any serious, long-term theatrical investigation is to be undertaken. "Six to ten actors is a viable ensemble, if you're going to be attentive to everyone's growth and development and if you're going to have to constantly reinvent a shared purpose, which is an egalitarian one that everyone puts themselves behind. Seventy actors is impossible; you have to be told what your purpose is, you can't birth your purpose or how you work, you can't explore on that scale."

That inability to continue the kind of exploration she craves weighed heavily in her decision—made after a painful deliberation—to resign her positions as an associate director and the director of The Other Place in 1998. "It was seven years of my life, 70 percent of my work." But the unwieldy size of the acting company, the impact of unceasing production work on both actors and directors, and the demands of administrative responsibilities forced Mitchell to reconsider the production process at the RSC and her role within it.

> Sometimes, actors barely see the directors after press night, and it's four months into the run with no feedback. What are they supposed to do? How can they run, without completely mangling their shows? And I suppose that's the way I got into conflict with the RSC. They want development, experimentation, growth, but until the directors themselves put their time behind that, it's never going to reach the audience. I think it's cultural, the way it works out. In a lot of cases, the directors were just working, particularly the associates, who are working like dogs at the moment, so they simply weren't available. In other cases, it's about your personal view. I think the job stops on the last night, and a lot of people think it stops on the first night. I've said this openly to Adrian Noble, that I don't think you can have an ensemble of seventy. For me, it's a full-time job, housekeeping fifteen over two years, and sometimes I can't deliver even that, and I'm quite attentive. It's about what you think *ensemble* means. For me, the company is slightly unclear about what that means for the practical health and growth of each individual actor and for every single show.
>
> I still believe in the work. I just don't think I'm built to run theatres, for a start. It's hard for me to justify time spent on anything other than the work, so if I'm asked to do a tremendous amount of administration, I dwindle, the artist in me is like a caged animal. I started to do less work over time, did like a third fewer shows than I would have, while running The Other Place. More importantly, as an associate, I didn't see a way to help the company focus itself. I wasn't constructive any longer, and I feared becoming destructive and cynical as a member of that team.

Mitchell continues at the RSC as an adviser to The Other Place, which allows her much greater freedom to work on her own projects. Her immediate plans after her resignation included staging a new play with Italian actors at the famed Piccolo Teatro in Milan, a show at the Young Vic, Ted Hughes's two-part version of Aeschylus's *The Oresteia* at the National, and operas at the Welsh National and the Scottish National operas. "I love being paid to hear people sing daily; it's an amazing luxury!"

Mitchell generally prefers small spaces for her theatrical work. In examining the challenges of directing in the RSC theatres, she finds the Swan impressive but noted, "It's a bouncy, vibrant space, and it's not really in keeping with my darker vision. The RST and the Barbican are too daunting. How do you make a play work there?" The Other Place was at first problematic, insofar as it had bad sight lines. "How do you give the audience upstairs the same experience as those downstairs?" As a result, Mitchell oversaw the removal of the balcony section, but she still believes that the theatre lacks the appropriate atmosphere. She prefers the slightly older Pit, a theatre she feels has more character. "The audience is thrust right into the work, and I like that." The audience—packed tightly in the steeply raked, cramped theatre—can grow hostile, making the actors work harder to win them over. Mitchell feels this makes the experience of seeing plays there more vital and immediate.

Acting at the RSC

I'll prove a busy actor in their play.
—Rosalind, *As You Like It*

*A*ctors are attracted to performing at the RSC for any number of reasons. It has history and reputation solidly in its corner and has served as a proving ground for many of Britain's foremost actors. The challenges of performing a repertoire of classics and new plays provide a bracing exercise for most actors, who admit that the demands of such a season help hone their skills in ways that straight runs cannot. Actors also observe that the opportunity to shift gears radically from one day to the next while performing different plays in a range of theatres provides an effective means of staying fresh and alert over a long run, which is considerably more difficult when playing the same role eight times a week.

At the RSC, its members frequently state, the company ethos is all-pervasive. The RSC hires dozens of actors annually to participate in its resident seasons and tours and seeks to engender an artistically productive atmosphere within the company by offering workshops and classes and by cross-casting among plays and theatre spaces. But a company of actors is not perforce an ensemble, for which the guiding artistic precepts of longevity and stability and a common performance methodology and vocabulary are critical ingredients. At the RSC, several factors conspire against the creation of a true ensemble: the divergent approaches of the corps of directors, the disparate methodologies of the actors, the sheer size of the company, and the significant turnover of performers annually. For a given production at the RSC, a director might choose to employ an ensemble approach that combines exercises and improvisations in a more democratic rehearsal process, but the RSC as a whole is too large and unwieldy to ever be considered a true ensemble. Ensemble theatres, in fact, are extremely rare in the world of contemporary professional performance, because lucrative film and television contracts lure actors away from such commitments.

But the lack of a true ensemble does not deter some of the finest actors in the United Kingdom and abroad from auditioning annually for the company. Below, four actors describe their perceptions of life, process, and product at the RSC.

Simon Russell Beale

Simon Russell Beale—an enormously versatile, chameleon-like actor possessing great range and power—proved to be one of the RSC's greatest assets in the first half of the 1990s. He is in constant demand by directors and a great favorite of audiences throughout the United Kingdom. He was honored for his exceptional artistic contribution to the company by being named an Associate Actor of the RSC,[1] was seen in featured roles in the films *Orlando* and *Persuasion,* and has appeared in several heralded productions at the National, where he was lavishly praised on both sides of the Atlantic for his performance as Iago in *Othello.*

Russell Beale's roles with the RSC have ranged from the demonic—Richard III—to the ethereal—Ariel in *The Tempest*—in one season, although he first made a name for himself, he noted, by perfecting the art of playing Restoration fops. The critic Mel Gussow, writing in *American Theatre,* said, "Beale's Ariel is the opposite of an airy sprite. One could hardly imagine him perching on Prospero's shoulders." Despite the actor's size, Gussow wrote, "His appearance has, if anything, nurtured his virtuosity in such widely divergent roles as Konstantin in *The Sea Gull,* the title role in Marlowe's *Edward II,* [and] the son in *Ghosts.*"[2] Other roles he has tackled for the RSC include the Young Shepherd in *The Winter's Tale,* Ed Know'ell in *Every Man in His Humour,* Oliver in *The Art of Success,* Fawcett in *The Fair Maid of the West,* Kulygin in *The Storm,* Nick in *Speculators,* Clincher Senior in *The Constant Couple,* Sir Fopling Flutter in *The Man of Mode,* Lord Are in *Restoration,* Henry McNeil in *Some Americans Abroad,* and Edgar in *King Lear.*

Russell Beale, born in Malaysia and educated at Cambridge and the Guildhall School, did not make it into the RSC on his first try. "I might have made it in strictly on an 'as-cast' basis, but the casting director urged me to go out and do larger roles elsewhere."[3] This additional experience made him a more attractive commodity at subsequent auditions. After performing in William Gaskill's production of *Women Beware Women* at the Royal Court, he was invited into the RSC.

The soft-spoken actor, by turns incisive and droll, is a great supporter of the company in which he has spent much of his professional life. Although many actors criticized the two-year commitment the RSC previously required, Russell Beale—active in the company before the season reconfiguration and subsequent shorter contract options—counted that as one of the great benefits of performing there. "I have no great lust to be a film or television star. The intellectual stimulation of working at the RSC is much more exciting and gratifying to me. I have to admit, though, that initially the idea of spending a year in Stratford and being 'away from it all' in London was daunting." He did acknowledge that though a contract with the RSC was a prestigious feather in an actor's cap, the prolonged absence from London caused many actors to fear that casting directors would forget about their existence.

This fear of working away from the heart of theatrical activity in London is a critical consideration for many actors in deciding whether to join the RSC. All actors, even the most successful, have endured dry periods, and this feast-or-famine cycle creates some ambivalence regarding long-term commitments. Some actors sign on for the initial commitment in Stratford and then, for a variety of reasons—exhaustion, better job offers, displeasure with the demands of repertory—choose not to re-sign for the Barbican. Russell Beale, however, viewed this as a mistake. "You'd be a fool not to do London. That's where everything's happening." Although critics, agents, directors, and producers regularly make the trip to Stratford, the Barbican season offers the actors a chance to enjoy the spotlight of London, seek additional work, and live at home with family and friends.

The primary attraction the RSC held for Russell Beale was the chance to work on great plays in the demanding, rigorous environment of repertory. After several seasons with the company, he spent almost a year on the road with the regional and international tour of Sam Mendes's celebrated production of *Richard III,* which had originated in The Other Place in the summer of 1992. The production returned to open the Swan in the spring of 1993; after the straight run closed (it played opposite Branagh's *Hamlet*), the indefatigable actor was featured as Edgar in Adrian Noble's production of *King Lear,* starring the late Robert Stephens. The physically and emotionally demanding role—in the Mad Tom scenes, Russell Beale wore little more than a diaper-like costume and spent much time wallowing in dirt— was followed a few months later by his powerfully understated performance as Oswald in Katie Mitchell's bleakly tragic production of Ibsen's *Ghosts.* Three such roles in rapid succession, two of which were performed in rep while rehearsing Ariel in *The Tempest,* opposite Alec McCowen's Prospero, might easily exhaust another actor. Russell Beale, though, enjoyed it immensely. "Granted, after playing Richard for so long on a straight run, I was somewhat out of shape for the demands of rep. It's difficult for the muscles to get back into the grind. Then I performed Edgar while rehearsing Oswald. These are difficult roles, but I had no stamina, no regimen to keep it up. Soon you begin to adapt, though, to feel your way back into the demands and routines of rep, and you make the necessary adjustments. You can't blow yourself out during rehearsal, knowing you have a three-and-a-half-hour performance that night."

Actors cope with the demands of performance at the RSC in different ways. Some read, some take long strolls along the banks of the Avon, some putter in their small gardens, and some exercise. After performances, many unwind over a pint or two and a bite to eat at the Dirty Duck pub across the street from the Swan. When simultaneously rehearsing and performing, actors have precious little time to do anything other than work, and according to Russell Beale, tend to run on adrenaline. "But the toughest period is actually late in the season, when you've opened the last play and you're *not rehearsing* anymore—just performing. It's then your energy drops, and you must be careful. Performances can slack off, and one can become careless. I find that at this point in the season, it's the intellectual stimulation of performing this variety of roles that keeps me going."

Russell Beale observed that another challenge of working at the RSC is performing in as many as three radically different theatre spaces within the course of the week. Each theatre confronts the actor with a distinct set of obstacles to vocal projection, focus, and actor-performer dynamics. Russell Beale prefers the Swan.

> It's the perfect space for me. It helps my strengths—enunciation, rapid speech, a certain type of performance virtuosity I have—and challenges my weaknesses. I have a tendency to show off a bit, and the Swan requires you to hold your head up to reach the upper galleries. You have to be careful not to exceed the intimacy of the theatre. It's an extremely adaptable and comfortable space for audiences.
>
> The RST, however, is more difficult, more challenging. I realized, about four weeks into the run of playing Edgar, that one doesn't have to push so much in the RST. That only shows up the weakness of not having a great voice.

Russell Beale noted that despite its enormous backstage, the Barbican is more intimate than the RST and thus "a great house." He characterized the Pit as "okay, but anonymous," and observed that The Other Place affords an actor "a chance to have a place to mumble, which is important. I was really surprised to see that a big, aggressive play like *Richard III* played so well there."

His work as Oswald in *Ghosts,* first at The Other Place and later at the Pit, received critical accolades. Russell Beale was quietly passionate and created great audience empathy as the feckless son of a domineering mother. His final, terrifying disintegration was all the more impressive due to his refusal to indulge in grand gnashing of teeth, in keeping with director Katie Mitchell's concept. The actor remarked that hers was "a very cool production of *Ghosts.* Katie was very careful to ensure that no one in the show touched anyone else. It's a play about people who don't know each other."

For Russell Beale, it was advantageous to rotate between his roles as Edgar and Oswald. Many directors, when staging a Shakespearean production, admonish the company to keep the pace up to sustain the dramatic action that is found in the verse. In *Ghosts,* however, a play whose psychological realism is streaked with symbolism, this matter of pacing was not an issue. "There's no subtext in Shakespeare, but it's intrinsic in Ibsen. This requires a different pace every night. Thankfully, Katie is not a 'pace merchant,' and we're allowed to find it anew at each performance."

His wish list for subsequent roles included Malvolio, Galileo, and especially Hamlet, although he admitted with a laugh, "I probably won't get to play him at the RSC." Perhaps not, but in 2000, Russell Beale played the role to great acclaim at the National.

Kate Duchêne

Kate Duchêne appeared as both Queen Elizabeth and Prince Edward with her old schoolmate, Simon Russell Beale, in the 1992 tour of *Richard III.* That production served as her entree to the RSC. The following year, the tall, graceful actress appeared as Jessica in David Thacker's contemporary staging of *The Merchant of Venice* in the RST, as one of three women of the pared-down chorus in Steven Pimlott's austere *Murder in the Cathedral,* and as Alithea in Max Stafford-Clark's bawdy version of *The Country Wife,* both in the Swan. In 1995, she appeared twice in the Swan, in the ensemble of Michael Bogdanov's controversial two-part staging of Goethe's *Faust,* and as Varya in Adrian Noble's comic yet affecting production of *The Cherry Orchard,* which later enjoyed a successful run in the West End. In 1997, Duchêne took over the role of Susannah Shakespeare in the West End transfer of *The Herbal Bed,* an RSC production directed by Michael Attenborough. Other work included roles at the National and the Almeida and appearances in film and television.

Duchêne, an actress possessed of a strong sense of humor, an infectious laugh, and a refreshingly candid inclination towards self-appraisal, described her background.

> I never trained in theatre! I studied modern languages at Cambridge, did Footlights and Mummers [theatre clubs] there, and always wanted to be an actress, at least since I was fourteen. My parents had begged me, "Please don't. Go and get a degree!"—my parents are both jour-

nalists, and my dad is an economist and a professor, too; taught at Berkeley for a bit—so I got a degree and never regretted that. My French grandmother died just as I left university and left me five hundred pounds, and I thought, "Well, I'll use that to try and get a job as an actor." Looking back, I don't know how I did it, how I had the *chutzpah*. I answered an advert in the *Stage* for a company that tours England by canal, performing in pubs, called Mickron, and I got the job and an Equity card. It was like a dream.[4]

As Katie Mitchell described previously, the audition process at the RSC is a formidable one for directors faced with the task of assembling a cast compatible with the needs of several colleagues. Duchêne acknowledged that the casting process is no less daunting for actors who are cognizant that they must fit into the artistic vision of not just one but several directors. She described auditioning for the 1993 season while performing in the tour of *Richard III*:

> I had auditioned in London while doing *Richard* and then flew to Tokyo to perform the play there. I had been offered a few roles but had turned them down, because there wasn't enough meat in them. These roles would have to sustain me over two years—which, of course, is changing now—but the only way I accept parts is if I read them and I really want to say the lines. That's all that really makes sense to me in the end, in terms of accepting something. You have to have enough to sustain you—literally, food—over that time, so I turned the offer down. But I did let on that if I could play a certain part, Alithea in *The Country Wife*, then I would accept the other two, Jessica in *Merchant* and the chorus in *Murder*.
>
> So, there I was in Tokyo, taking a bath at 4:00 in the morning, and suddenly there was some beeping. "How funny, there's a phone in the bath," I thought—and there was Max Stafford-Clark on the phone, whom I didn't know, but who I knew was a great manipulator. I mean, he must have known it was 4 AM in Japan! And he was saying, "You've got to accept this line of parts or else you'll lose it!" He was trying to get me to accept a different role in *Country Wife*. It was so funny to be rung up at such an hour, and I just said, "No, I really want to play Alithea," and I put the phone down and thought, "That's it, then, they don't want me, fine" and went off for the weekend. When I came back, they called me again and offered me Alithea, so I have no idea what went on behind the scenes. Max, whom I quite got to like when we worked together, later claimed he couldn't remember my audition, which is such a typical thing to say. Why, then,

did he offer me a leading role—just because I said I wanted it? I actually think it's best *not* to think too much about how actors get jobs.

Sam Mendes once told me about the casting process at the RSC, that there are big blackboards with lists, sort of like a terrible market, with directors going, "Well, if you have her, could I have him, I *want* him, you see, so all right, I'll have her in this if I can have him in that, but then you'll have to have *him* . . ." Potentially, I suppose, you could end up with a company full of people nobody really wants, with all sorts of middle-of-the-ground compromises, a lot of people playing unsuitable parts. I mean, it's very funny, it would make a hysterical sketch! To an actor, this is so potentially depressing that you don't ever think about it, since there's no point, no solution. I've just come to the conclusion that my new way of operating is to say what I would like to the people I should tell it and then forget about it and see what happens.

At the time of this conversation, in December 1995, Jennifer Ehle, who had recently received exuberant reviews for her television portrayal of Elizabeth Bennett in *Pride and Prejudice,* was considering leaving the company and a prized role in the Restoration comedy *The Relapse,* playing in the Swan. As Duchêne debated her own interest in replacing Ehle and considered whether she would be effective in the role, she reflected on the evolution of her growing competence and confidence as an actress: "Today, I just mentioned to Ian Judge, the director, my interest in taking over for Jennifer. He might say it's not a good idea, and if so, that's fine. But the other thing that happened to me recently is that I now feel that what I do, I do well, and sometimes you get it wrong and sometimes you don't. If they don't want you, that's fine, so once you feel a certain security in that, it's freeing. When it goes right, it's like flying, you know it's going right, and you don't quite know why. That is something they can't take away, even if you're rejected, which you constantly are. I suppose that's what happens in all walks of life, self-respect gets corroded."

Duchêne, when asked to articulate her own approach to acting, responded with a smile and a considered answer. She allowed that many actors relish the prospect of discussing their craft but that she finds it a rather elusive topic.

It's curious, talking about acting, to think, "What is it that I actually *do?*" I have a friend, Phyllida, who is a marvelous singer, and that's something she can do, it's right *there*. But I've never really felt I have something like that. I suppose the nearest thing I feel to that is that I feel more relaxed onstage now, and that's important, but it's not the same thing. Phyllida knows she can sing, but with acting, nobody knows. Is it having a loud voice? Hah! I always thought it would be wonderful to be a violinist or a painter or a singer and say, "This is what I do," because with acting, you can't do that. I suppose you could *read loudly*, but there's nothing definable that you can say you do. And actors talking about acting can sound just awful, sound so pretentious sometimes, and I cringe. I mean, I know what they're talking about, and they sometimes are talking about important things, but it's so inarticulate and wanky-sounding, all about "going into yourself" and blah-blah-blah.

Most people just don't recognize the fact that all this is work. It can be fun sometimes, but it's *not* easy. And it can seem silly, to nonactors, the exercises and work we do, especially in rehearsals. And if you're in a bad rehearsal process, you can do all this work and not know why, and then nothing happens as a result. I'm interested in the rehearsal process and what our work is, in part because it's so difficult to define.

The rehearsal period is a time of imprecise, intuitive movement towards, at least at the start, an often indistinct goal for both director and actor. When the process succeeds, rehearsals can generate sparks of brilliant insight and crystal clarity along the path to performance. Duchêne is intrigued by the adaptive abilities of actors, who must contend with a panoply of styles and genres while always seeking the core, human truths that root their characters in the world of the play. She acknowledged that actors, who are at their most vulnerable during the trial and error of rehearsals, attack the process armed with a variety of methods.

I know some actors do a lot of preparation and homework on the script prior to and during the rehearsal process. Frankly, I've only recently been introduced to the notion of homework, which is pretty funny, since I do have an academic background, but because of that I associate homework with a different kind of work, a different set of disciplines. Right now we're rehearsing a workshop production of *Woyzeck,* and I've got some scenes I have to look at outside the rehearsal room. I'm banging my head against a couple, and I have to do them tomorrow. I've got a little knot of tension in my stomach about it, because I don't really feel that I know where to start, and it makes me nervous to have to work on something on my own, on a piece of text, because I don't feel like I have the proper tools to do it.

In fact, I do, but I have to do some proper emotional thinking, which is straining. I suppose I worry that I won't reach the answer, because fundamentally I really think you can only get the answer by working with the other people you're doing the scene with. So, it's a slightly false thing you're setting up for yourself, trying to make these decisions in the abstract. And yet you know that you've got some sort of block, and you have to be terribly relaxed or lucky or alert or awake or brave or in the right mood to chuck away something you may have thought was fundamental that is not working, to find something new. And you have to be very on the ball to do that, and sometimes, in some moods—if you're tired, or whatever—it doesn't happen, and then you have to look at it yourself and work out what it is you're *not* doing, to take it back to the rehearsal room. There's always the fear of failure. And the fear of failure on my own is always greater than the fear of failure in the rehearsal room. But I know I have to do *something* on my own, and the tools are not easy to find. It's not as if you're learning a language where you can say, "Right, I'm going to conquer this, I'm going to read this and learn twenty words a day." It's not like that, it's something you have to look at in yourself and look at in the script. It's an emotional thing.

I've never been used to doing any work outside the rehearsal room. It's only recently I've started doing any. I don't learn my lines outside the rehearsal room. It sounds like I do nothing on my own, and that's not true!—I pace about, underline my lines, pace about, go for walks, sort of talk to myself. Sometimes I look at other people's scripts, and they've got writing all over them, and I get very jealous, trying to read what they've written. I *want* to write things!

If Duchêne is an autodidact in the rehearsal process, it has not diminished the power of her performances. She is in control onstage, alternately strong and vulnerable, and appears relaxed and comfortable as she performs. That relaxation, according to Duchêne, is critical to her performance process.

One night during *The Cherry Orchard,* I suddenly realized that for me, relaxation is what being professional is about. I didn't worry at all about the fact that there were a lot of people looking at me. But I don't yet have that feeling in front of the camera. Sometimes onstage, I get so relaxed I get nervous about it, nervous that I'm not really performing at all, just *being.* Working in front of a camera, I get a slight intake of breath, and I never get that in the theatre. The theatre is my workplace, and I don't believe I ever used to think it would be like that. It means I can actually work without strain. I feel easier on myself about a performance that just isn't very good.

I've only done some bits and pieces of camera work. I do enjoy it. The first thing I did was an evil chambermaid on an episode of *Miss Marple*, and I was being interviewed by the police. In actuality, I was talking to a lamp shade and holding a piece of polystyrene under my chin to reflect the light. It was strange and exciting, and I remember thinking, "This *is* interesting, talking to a lamp shade, holding a piece of polystyrene." You're just left completely on your own with your imagination, and I rather like that and the challenge that it's all shot out of sequence.

Onstage, Duchêne has worked with a number of RSC directors, including David Thacker, Adrian Noble, Michael Bogdanov, Max Stafford-Clark, and Steven Pimlott, but is unable to perceive a particular style or stamp that is common among them. Each, according to her, is unique, with an idiosyncratic approach to the work. Max Stafford-Clark, for example, with whom she worked on *The Country Wife*, is well known for his painstaking labors with the actors in early rehearsals to *action* every line of dialogue. This process, based on precepts of Konstantin Stanislavsky—in which actors and director discuss the active, transitive verb, the specific action the character employs to reach a goal or objective in the moment—provides the entire cast with a dynamic framework for rehearsals.

Adrian Noble, who directed Duchêne in *The Cherry Orchard* along with Alec McCowen, Penelope Wilton, and David Troughton, employed his own versions of Stanislavskian exercises to help the cast discover their characters and the world of the play. The process Duchêne described helps debunk any notion that the British actor's mastery of skills and style is compensation for a lack of rigorous emotional investigation.

Adrian put two chairs in a corner of the rehearsal room. We walked around the room as our characters—doing it all together so no one was watching—and Adrian said, "This is a door between these two chairs, and when you feel like it, come through the door into a room you loved as a child." For most of the cast, it was a room in Ranevskaya's house, the house in which the play takes place. For my character, Varya, it was a room that the first act is set in, the nursery. I had built up this image of Varya coming to the house for the first time, maybe at age eight: she's the child of Ranevskaya's husband's lover in the village who died, and Madame Ranevskaya said, with her characteristic reckless generosity, "Well, bring the girl to the house." So, I was a little girl, coming to the house, only really feeling safe in the nursery, because you can see the orchard from there, and it's safe and warm by the fire, and Grisha, the little boy who died before the play starts, is there. That was the room I came into. You don't always know the room you're going to come into when you come through that door; you just walk around like a child and make the discovery. We did the same exercise with a room we hated, and for me it was the ballroom, because it could be very intimidating and frightening.

And we did these exercises, very relaxed, all in our heads, and you could sometimes see something in the way people behaved when they came into the room, but sometimes you couldn't see anything. But then we'd talk about it, just say where we'd been, describe where it was and why, and people could get very emotional about it, because sometimes it would bring up stuff from their own past. Slowly, collectively, you began to build a picture of the house as well, and other people's idea of the house, and then you'd bring into the exercise the whole district and other people's ideas of the house. The house is the emotional power of the play, as we all know what it's like to feel safe or unsafe in a physical place and have that emotional bond with a place, with a house, with a memory of a place. Maybe it's about dispossession, about a class being wrenched away from that past. I admire Adrian for latching on to the house as an emotional trigger, not just as a logical one in talking about characters' histories. I think that's why this is a good production, because in these exercises an idea of the house is built into what people are playing. In a sense, we're all in the same house, to the extent that everyone's imagination can conjure the same house.

We did another exercise where Adrian put a sheet on the floor and told us, "Find something under the sheet, something that meant something to your character." It was very funny to watch. I remember David Troughton, playing Lopakhin, crawling up to it and peeking under it, and you didn't know what he found there, but it was very funny. I was very confused about what to find, and it's not a logical process, but you know when it's not right, and I thought, "Well, maybe a bible or a crucifix or something," but it all seemed very boring. I couldn't think of anything, but then suddenly, when I lifted up the sheet, I found a rocking horse. I'd sort of thought about it before, but not quite, and then when I got onto the set, there was a rocking horse in the room, so it made sense. These emotional triggers work, because they're all about *your* past as the character. And by doing those exercises, you start asking the questions that matter. I am not good about writing loads of personal character history, so these exercises were a way into my own past as Varya.

One other exercise that really helped was one in which Adrian had us stand about the room and then told us, "Go to the person you talk to the most in the play." So, I thought about that—it's kind of hard, initially, to figure out, "Well, whom *do* I talk to most in the play?" I ended up going to Lucy Whybrow, who plays Anya, which is interesting, and again, just that decision makes you think, "Oh, yeah, that's why she's so important to me, why she's my angel." It's not just because she's a lovely young girl but because she's the one I communicate with. Of course, *she* went off to Trofimov, so the groups that emerged were very interesting. Varya was on her own, as was Carlotta, and Ranevskaya was surrounded. Then Adrian said, "Go to the person you *think* about most," which, again, was difficult. You know you're making important decisions. For me, it could've been Ranevskaya, but it wasn't in the end, it was Lopakhin. And so I went over to him, and of course, he went over to Ranevskaya. In the end, you've got another set of groups, different groups, and these, in the end, show patterns in the play, and it was a very good working process.

This exercise contributed to the development of one of the most heartbreaking moments in the play, in which Varya (Duchêne) and Lopakhin (Troughton) come very close to expressing deep feelings for one another but—for a multitude of psychological factors—do not. At the moment of critical action—at which Varya and Lopakhin teeter precariously on the brink of heartfelt revelation—the characters' fears and insecurities hold sway, and they stumble backwards into the safe embrace of their familiar, lonely lives.

Duchêne could not identify a strong, stylistic through-line that links the performances of actors at the RSC. She ventured that if any sort of RSC style exists, it is associated with acting in the RST.

> I think it may come, from the actor's point of view, from the RST being very, very hard to play in. You have to play out and loud and forward. It's not intimate at all, but I don't think it's a question of directorial style. When we did *Merchant* there, a lot of the stuff we had done in the rehearsal hall, which was very good, just didn't show once we got onto the main stage. That's not because it's a big stage, because in some big theatres, like the Barbican or the Olivier at the National, tiny things can show up. It feels to me that in the RST you

can't ever see anything that's small or intimate, which means you can't really understand relationships between people very easily. The performance then becomes rather showy, rather presentational in a way. There seems to be no direct communication between actors and audience there.

Frankly, of all the houses, I like the Swan the best. And I do like The Other Place. Third would be the main house at the Barbican. But as much as I like the Swan, it's quite difficult to play, because it's intimate, and you want it to be low and realistic, but you've got people quite high up in the galleries and behind you. That's tougher than it can appear at first sight. In *The Cherry Orchard*, our focus is quite low, as Adrian wanted to experiment with that, and I always worry that people in the higher galleries won't get it. But I love the Swan, with people all around, and there's also the wood; it feels light, it feels like the energy goes up—a positive energy that the RST doesn't have, I'm afraid.

Duchêne was enthusiastic about the RSC's decision to expand its touring itinerary throughout the United Kingdom. She felt that a periodic shuffle of a company's routine could produce bountiful results and believed that Noble's decision to curtail the London residence and emphasize touring would eventually lead to increased flexibility in producing. She feared, though, that the RSC's greater presence in the regions might lead the Arts Council to reduce funding to smaller resident theatres in those areas.

That would be appalling, and I would hate that if it happened. From the RSC's point of view—and that is all Adrian can really be concerned about, I suppose; he's not responsible for the nation's arts policy—it can only be a fantastic thing. That is, again, assuming that we could tour more and the Arts Council continues to fund the rep theatres. I love touring. But it's very tiring, you're constantly on the move, living out of a suitcase. They look after you well when you tour with the RSC, so at least you can afford to go to a small hotel and have a shower. It's very exciting, though, to perform, and the theatres or other spaces we work in are always packed, people rightly want to see it. When we toured *Richard III*, we made theatre in gymnasiums, and that's great.

Duchêne has high regard for the audiences who see RSC shows, both on tour and in Stratford. She cited several people she knows, enthusiastic RSC supporters, who see the same production several times in the season to observe its evolution.

I don't think audiences are passive in Stratford at all; I think they're very involved, sometimes startlingly so, since they'll sometimes know more about the last production of *The Tempest* than you certainly do, and you're supposed to be in it. They've seen five different actors playing Lear. There are a lot of knowledgeable people seeing plays here. And you get masses of schoolkids who aren't like that but who might be very enthusiastic.

I suppose what happens on tour is that it's more intense, in that people aren't used to seeing this particular company all the time, or aren't used to seeing theatre in their own town, and the event is very exciting for them and for us. Going to see a good production in your own town, just down the road, there's a sort of intensity about it, a newness that you don't get in Stratford.

In one respect, life in Stratford does not differ greatly from life on tour for the many RSC actors whose permanent residences are in London. Although a contract for Stratford affords them the opportunity to unpack for several months at one go, while touring is constantly peripatetic, the actors are still away from home, friends, and often family. Like most of the actors in the company, Duchêne makes her home in London. When she is in residence in Stratford, the RSC finds accommodations for her, usually in one of the company-owned townhouses they let out to the actors. She discussed the sense of being a displaced person that life in a regional theatre can engender.

I have a flat in London, and I usually rent it out if I'm away. So, when I do go home for a day off, it doesn't feel like my place anymore. I tend to move lock, stock, and barrel when I come here. I feel like I'm in a very nice little capsule that's gone and been plunked down somewhere. You're sort of divorced from your real life for the moment, and yet it *is* your real life. I suppose that implies a bit of a rift. I know some people actually prefer to live year-round in Stratford, but I don't.

I have had relationships while here with people in London, and it's very difficult to spend most of your time off bumming up and down the motorway. You have only one day off in the end, and it's very intense to do that. Up here, it becomes a club, you're living and eating and working and drinking with the same people, so it can become a bit excluding to partners as well. They come up here and find they have nothing to do. It's a notoriously difficult place to keep relationships going.

I don't actually do a lot in the little spare time I have here. I go for walks. There's a gym down the road, and I go there a lot. Some actors go up the road to a multiscreen theatre to see films. Apart from that, there's the Duck—the actors' pub—and a few restaurants. I always have masses of stuff I want to read, letters to write to keep in touch with people in London, but in reality, there's so little time off, and I just bundle around.

At the National, things are different. First off, you're in London, and I like that; I like the South Bank and the fact that you can walk along the river. I also like the fact that it's less intense than it is here. At the National, you get a sense of company with the people in your show, but there are always people around whom you don't know, who are in different plays. You come and go, things finish while you're starting, other things come in when you're in the middle, it's constant turnover. Here, you spend all your time with the same people. And even at the Barbican, where you have your normal home life, you're still working with the same company all the time. There's much more of a strong company feeling at the RSC, but it can have its limitations. People can get fed up with each other, or it goes on too long, or people wonder, "What new is happening out there?"

One of the things that can happen here is that you lose sight of the fact that working at the RSC is somewhat special. I suppose there's sort of a professional danger of that happening, because it becomes pedestrian, it becomes normal, and there's a danger of it becoming *too* normal. You forget you're in something potentially very exciting. Yet all actors know, even the most apparently jaded actors, that they're there because they love it. There's a danger in a big institution like this to forget that. You're paid for acting, you're in a place with very good facilities, good rehearsal rooms, playing—sometimes—in plays you love.

In addition to performances for main-stage productions, the RSC offers its cast members other opportunities for professional development. Duchêne was grateful for the RSC's efforts to provide excellent vocal coaching and workshop performances, such as the production of Georg Büchner's *Woyzeck* at The Other Place for which she was rehearsing. These opportunities help to keep actors flexible and fit, but they add to the already busy Stratford schedule of main-stage rehearsals and performances.

I never trained formally for theatre, so much of what I've learned about voice I learned here and at the National. They have such marvelous people here, Cicely Berry and Andrew Wade and others. I don't often go to the weekly vocal warm-ups, at least not when I'm in rehearsals and performing. When there's a voice warm-up at six o'clock, and you're already running around trying to have dinner and prepare for the performance, there's not enough time to live a life. But I do avail myself, and one of the things I most like is that sometimes, if you've got a problem, you can go and have individual sessions. I like that the best, since you know when you're getting tense and when you're breathing or in the wrong register or whatever. And other people will do things on an ad hoc basis. Zubin Varla, one of the actors in the company, was holding yoga classes, which were quite good. And of course, with workshops like *Woyzeck,* you're working all the time on different things. Doing *The Cherry Orchard* and rehearsing *Woyzeck* is quite wonderful, because they're such different plays, *Woyzeck* being so angry and snappish, with so much overt anger. We're working on the play in a completely different fashion than we did on *The Cherry Orchard,* which is appropriate. It's important to remain flexible and remember that there's no one set way of working.

When asked to articulate what she found most appealing about working in the theatre, Duchêne smiled and shared her thoughts about the transitory and evanescent qualities of her art: "My father once said to me that in his opinion, theatre is *not* art, because too many people are involved. But to me, that's one of the strengths. It's a human, plastic art form, one that relies on what goes on between people, and one that will always, by necessity, be ephemeral. I've always loved the fact that theatre *finishes.* I love watching them take down the set for the last time or smashing it up, preferably. Because then it's gone, you don't have a record, you had to be there, it's in the moment, and I think somehow that reflects life. It's about life and death. I suppose that is one element left in theatre that is like ritual. The fact that it finishes, that it dies, is somehow part of the creative process."

David Troughton

An impassioned and pugnacious actor onstage, David Troughton can appear alternately terrifying and comically benign, trustworthy and deceitful—all in the same play. One of the leading actors in the company in the 1995–1996 season, Troughton was seen playing the title role in Steven Pimlott's production of *Richard III* in the RST as well as Lopakhin in Adrian Noble's production of *The Cherry Orchard* and Fitzdottrel in Ben Jonson's *The Devil Is an Ass,* directed by Matthew Warchus, both in the Swan. Troughton, an Associate Actor of the RSC, is the London-born son of Patrick Troughton, the second actor to play Dr. Who on the popular British television series of the same name, and he is the father of young Sam Troughton, who appeared in the RSC's 2000 production of *The Taming of the Shrew*. David Troughton first worked with the RSC in 1982 and has since appeared as Ross in *Macbeth*, Conrade in *Much Ado About Nothing*, Aslak in *Peer Gynt*, Bottom in *A Midsummer Night's Dream*, Hector in *Troilus and Cressida*, Kent in *King Lear*, the title roles in *The Venetian Twins*, Caliban in *The Tempest*, and Bolingbroke in the cycle *This England—The Histories*. His résumé is replete with roles at the National and at repertory theatres throughout England. He has been seen in many television dramas and films such as *Our Mutual Friend, Poirot, All the King's Men, Sharpe's Rifles, Midsomer Murders*, and *Dance with a Stranger*.

Troughton is an ardent populist, demanding that theatre be made accessible to those who want to see it and deriding Thatcherite policies that reduced support to not-for-profit theatre in the United Kingdom. "It was all about making money. If you don't make money, you're nothing, and that's what we have got to eradicate from this country. Since Thatcher, all the news is about the stock market, nothing else, and all the programs on television are like *Dallas*, about getting rich."[5] Troughton is committed to sharing his art with as many as the auditorium can hold.

Although he enjoys working in film and television, Troughton naturally gravitates to theatre. The opportunity to play three such rich and divergent roles as Richard, Fitzdottrel, and Lopakhin in one season was an offer he could not pass up, despite the punishing rehearsal and performance schedule.

> It's really difficult doing these three plays in a week and also doing normal things like going to the Safeway, so I have to pace myself during the week. Certain weeks are real nightmares if you've got three *Cherry Orchards*, two *Devils*, a day off Friday, and then two *Richards* on Saturday. That's the worst—it's like looking at the Himalayas and asking, "I've got to go up *there* again?" But why not? A lot of people get exhausted doing their job, and I'm not complaining. Opera singers have five weeks off between three shows—all right, they use their voice more than we do, maybe—but tell me they do what we do, rehearsing from ten till five-thirty and then doing a show in the evening. I suppose it's my fault—I accepted three major parts. But I like do-

ing all three, and every part is an investment for the future; you'll always learn something. At least, I didn't rehearse any two at the same time this year. I learned, after my first season here, not to do that, rehearsing the first two shows of the season so you don't get a night off until June. Right now, I've done three years without a break, two full seasons in a row, and I have to admit it is beginning to tire a bit.

But at least it's in rep. A change is as good as a rest. I mean, eight in a row of any of these three plays!—it's good to come in every day and do something different. Like my father, I don't like doing things for a long time. I like challenges, trying something new. Before this season, I had never done Chekhov or played a part as big as Richard, and I always find Jonson difficult.

If Troughton was exhausted by the demands of his work in Stratford, he had the daily consolation and support of his family, because he makes his home in the town. Although a Londoner by birth, he moved to Stratford in the early 1990s, when he and his family fell in love with the area. "But I live here, so I don't get the subsistence pay. When actors come up from London, there's a big organization to get them properties that the RSC owns, places to live for the season, but when we go down to London, there's nothing, and that's something I'd like to change. In London, I stay with my mum, sister, brother-in-law, and two nephews!"

Like other members of the company, Troughton was excited by the prospects of expanding the RSC's national role. The recently announced residence in Plymouth and the increased touring both had great appeal for him. This common response within the company seems largely to have been ignored by the media when decrying the RSC for effecting such a drastic measure.

I think Adrian is right to make the decision. He is trying to forge his own style, trying to get the RSC out into Britain. The only national theatre in this country right now is *not* on the South Bank, it's *television*. The only theatre people see is in their living rooms. What we've got to do is say, "It's much more exciting if you come to the theatre."

One of the reasons I think Adrian wants to get out of London for six months is that he perceives—I know I do—that it is so elitist there. Adrian wants to get out of London and bring theatre to the people. In London, the audiences are usually the same. I don't think you're going to introduce too many new people to theatre at the Barbican, because people can't be bothered to get there, it's not like being in the West End, where you used to be able to see "RSC at the Aldwych" adverts from a bus and think, "Oh, I'd like to see that." No one knows where the Barbican is, and you have to get an audience wanting to come, you can't just get people off the street.

Troughton acknowledged that convincing an audience to attend the theatre is only the first step. For many occasional theatregoers raised on a diet of television and film, the transformation into active participants in a live event can be intimidating. Educating younger audiences about the special relationship between actor and audience is to be encouraged, said Troughton, but it is still difficult for the performer to overcome the subconscious belief of many viewers that they are just staring at a large, three-dimensional screen.

> I really feel for the audience. If you're watching television, you're passive, but in the theatre, you've got to work hard, sometimes as hard as the actor, and that's difficult, since we're so used to just watching the box. In theatre, you've got to be active, move your head, listen, look, and then things can really start happening. And when it does, it's great, especially when you're young. In *Richard*, at the end, when we don't have any battles, at 11 AM in a matinee filled with school kids, you can hear a pin drop, because they want to know what's happening, what is going to happen next. That is the art of storytelling—as Graham Greene said, "what is on the next page"—and if you can make people get involved like that, they'll want to know, they'll be quiet, they'll be in it with you. In this play, for me, it's very important. The audience *is* me, my alter ego, my successful self that turns into my conscience, which kills me. So, their reactions during an evening are very important.

Troughton's Richard III was described in the *Independent* as "a semi-official court clown . . . a cross between Rigoletto and a love-deprived psychopath."[6] Unlike Antony Sher—whose book, *Year of the King,* provided an insightful and detailed observation of the evolution of his portrayal of Richard for the RSC's 1983 production—Troughton did not use a "bottled spider" image as his creative point of reference for developing the character. A more potent and viable conceit for him was a court jester. "The image came slowly out of lots of things we don't actually do anymore in the production. But I still carry my jester's stick with me in production and try to play to the audience so that they become my conscience, which is more active and involving. I'm a bit of an extreme actor; I like going out on limbs, putting my head on a block. I like saying, 'This is how I'm doing it, you can like it or hate it, but at least it's watchable.' In another production, maybe I'd have Richard as an emcee or a stage manager, setting up the scenes, introducing characters, totally in control, and then throughout the play lose it, metaphorically."

He pointed out that some actors and directors spend years studying the complexities of speaking Shakespearean verse. Peter Hall, for example, is known for having developed a precisely articulated approach to verse speaking that, according to some critics, results in cool, measured, rational performances. Troughton, however, is not particularly concerned with slavishly adhering to these rules.

> I learned how to speak verse by trial and error. You learn all about beats and iambics and caesuras and all that, but I learned that what I love is trying to get the character from the way he speaks, the words he uses. It's more valuable to me, too, to figure out what Shakespeare tells us he is doing rather than undertaking a lot of research about what sort of bloke the character really was and *then* trying to fit that into what Shakespeare wrote.
>
> The idea of the jester came about because Richard uses a lot of internal rhymes. He's a metaphorical jester, and no one suspects him. He talks in proverbs, and the only metaphors he has for love are in courtroom parlance: "Be the attorney of my love." He's not a romantic man except when he talks about his father, and then his language totally changes, and there you have a clue that his father mattered to him. And rhythms are important, too. Lines like "'Tis death to me to be at enmity"; why is it rhythmical? I chose to bring out the internal rhyme when I say it and use that as part of his performance.

Actors who have been trained primarily in techniques deriving from the Stanislavsky system—which evolved from the Russian actor-director-teacher's search for a methodology that afforded actors a disciplined, repeatable approach to a performance grounded in theatrical truth—frequently spend considerable time outside of rehearsal hours working on their scripts. They do not just memorize lines but often write detailed notes investigating a character's history, motivation, emotions, and previous actions, which assist them in organically connecting to the life of the character. Troughton, however, offered his own ideas about acting process, and while aware that some actors

pursue this work on their own, he admitted to a degree of incredu-
lity. "God, that's far from acting! I mean, anyone can be brilliant in
the bathroom, but that's not my way. I like it happening in rehearsals, listening to people, seeing what they give me, what I give to them.
And I like working script in hand—I don't like coming in with lines
down cold—although for Richard, I did make the effort to get it up
and about in three weeks, since we had only seven, and two of those
were gone with matinee and evening shows for other plays. With the
deformity, I couldn't hold my script properly, so I tried to get off the
book for that, since it's a massive part."

The physical production of *Richard III* in the RST was likewise
overwhelming and imposing. Tobias Hoheisel's set was all walls, looming balconies, tightly enclosed rooms—a bleak, bleached landscape
in which nothing flourished except intrigue and betrayal. Troughton,
though, believes that large, technically complex sets are not essential
to the success of a play, especially Shakespeare, "where you're invited
to use your imagination." Troughton preferred the Spartan, understated set for *The Cherry Orchard* designed for the Swan by Richard
Hudson. "There's not a samovar in sight, and it helps us to get more
involved in the story, to use our imagination as to where we are, and
in theatre we don't let people use their imagination enough."

Troughton observed a trend at the RSC towards bigger and more
complex sets, especially in the RST. He bemoaned the fact that, as in
most theatres, designs must be finished and turned over to the workshops for construction before the production has been developed in
rehearsals. This, he felt, shoehorns the actors and the director into a
specific physical world that may no longer be appropriate for the production by the time the play opens. He also reiterated the pervasive belief
that the RSC's short technical rehearsal schedule allows little time for
the organic integration of actors, sets, costumes, lights, and music.

> We need more time onstage to get it right. Things change when you're
> onstage. When you have only two and a half days, or with *Richard,*
> one and a half, because the set wasn't finished, it's impossible. It's not
> good, and you're compromising all the time. And the sets keep go-
> ing wrong, which is no one's fault, but the pieces of equipment and
> the computers that run them keep going down, and you think, "Why
> do you need *computers* in the theatre?" When someone draws a cur-
> tain or runs the light board, you want a *person* doing it, so the stage

manager can say, "Ah, the actors are going at a different pace tonight, so let's take it a bit more slowly." So much of the new technology is just unnecessary.

Troughton holds equally strong opinions about the performance dynamics of the different theatres in which he performs at the RSC. In the RST, he said, the dimensions of the auditorium and the distance to the back rows inhibit an actor from adequately gauging audience reaction and can alienate spectators from the immediacy of Shakespeare.

> In the main house, in *Richard,* I have to pretend to talk to people in the audience, since I can't see them past the first few rows. Well, that's all right, that's acting, but in the Swan you can actually see them, and that's why I'd like to do *Macbeth* in there. The Swan is definitely my favorite of the RSC theatres. Between the RST and the Barbican, there's not much to choose. The Barbican is plusher and feels more three-dimensional; it's wider, while the RST is deeper and narrower. In the RST, it's easier, vocally, on the actor, while the Barbican is very difficult. Everyone else says it's not, but I think it is. Around row M is a dead pit, the sound just whisks above the audience. In a comedy, you hear a double laugh sometimes, coming back at you onstage; it's as tangible as that. The Pit is okay, and I haven't worked yet in the new Other Place. The old one, the tin shed, was lovely.
>
> I don't think we've discovered everything yet about the Swan. The first year, there was hardly a set in there. The second year, designers came in and said, "That big hole in the back, we've got to fill it in, that's where I can put my set." That's a mistake. That's why *The Cherry Orchard* is great in there. One of the best acting positions in the Swan is that back wall. You can see everyone, and they can see you, and in *The Cherry Orchard,* we play all the way back. Everyone thinks the point between the two big pillars, farther downstage, is the best, but it's not. Everywhere can be good in the Swan, if you get the focus right and play as if it's in the round. If you're standing with your back to someone for ten seconds, you've got to shift your weight, that's all you have to do. Then various people can see you, another thirty or forty. It's a technique I don't think we've yet addressed properly.
>
> It's dangerous, however, to think of it as a small space, as there are nearly five hundred people in it. Although it's small, lengthwise, it's extremely tall, but that is what gives it its wonderful charm. You can talk to people up there and down here. As long as they can hear you talking to them, they think, "Wow, he's talking to us, this is wonder-

ful!" But you have to be quite large in there. Pure emotion doesn't carry. You can't cry during a performance and think, "Come on, I'm rather good tonight, I've got real tears"—but row D can't see it. You've got to *show* that you've got tears, and that's a theatrical technique, not one from television. The back of the gallery maybe can't see your face, they have to see something else, movement, reactions, and although one could say, "Well, that's hammy, it's overacting," you've got to physicalize emotions in the theatre. Young actors, brought up on television and film, think it's okay to just stand there. Well, it *is* okay, but only if the audience can see what's going on.

Troughton, like most actors, enjoys a variety of directorial approaches and explains what he finds particularly appealing in collaborating with two of the RSC's prolific directors, Sam Mendes and Steven Pimlott, exemplars of contrasting working styles.

Mendes is brilliant at casting. A director's job is getting a group of people together who are good and who will get on, and he's very good at that. He's good at making things happen. He loves cricket, which I love, and he's like a cricket captain. He manages very well, treats everyone differently, he's very quick at picking up how they like to work, because every actor does work differently. I like his simplicity, his clarity. If he wants something, it's for a reason, not just for an effect.

Pimlott is rather like me. He throws a bucket of paint at a blank canvas and sees what will happen. That's great, I love working like that. I'm not a great builder of blocks. I like going everywhere at once and then picking bits out and saying, "Oh, that's quite good," and then sort of molding the clay and building each character note.

Outspoken and analytical, Troughton himself might make a good director. He resisted the idea, however. "I've never directed, never would. You never get a day off. I couldn't do all that, no. I say lines and pretend to be someone else. I can't pretend to be everyone else and tell them where to go and what to do."

Robert Bowman

In 1996, the RSC's production of *The Comedy of Errors,* directed by Tim Supple, played The Other Place for several months and then departed for the road. After dates in Britain, Europe, India, and Mexico, the tour ended in May 1997 with a sold-out one-week run in San Francisco. For Robert Bowman, who appeared as Antipholus of Syra-

cuse in this unusually haunting production that married the mystical, mournful, and farcical elements of the play with understated grace
and harmony, this final date of the tour represented a homecoming of
sorts. Bowman—whose performance, as the visiting merchant fever-
ishly seeking clues to his devastating loss of identity, anchored the
strangely moving and lyrical production—is an American, a native of
Washington state. On closing night in San Francisco, his parents and
family, along with the rest of the transfixed audience, quietly wept in
empathy as they witnessed the final, harmonious, awe-inspiring reconciliation of the characters—a moment quite unexpected in a play that
is usually offered up as a knock-'em-down farce. Robert Hurwitt, of the
San Francisco Examiner, praised the production and Bowman's work:

> Director Tim Supple sees it as . . . a serious meditation on issues of
> identity in a world of overheated commerce—with comic overtones,
> to be sure. It's an idea that could be deadly or inspired. In Supple's
> sharply performed, stripped-down, musically driven production, it's
> a provocatively intriguing delight. . . .
>
>   Robert Bowman's Antipholus of Syracuse . . . is the keystone of
> this approach. Easygoing and casually curious at first, he's an every-
> man caught in increasingly absurd entanglements. His long pauses
> as he confronts the confusions of having unknowingly entered his
> brother's world . . . convey every possible explanation, from madness
> to witchcraft to being made the butt of some joke.[7]

Bowman—agile, trim, and engaging—appeared previously at the
RSC in *Twelfth Night,* as Sebastian, and in *The Wives' Excuse* and *The
Broken Heart.* And at the National, he originated the role of the son
in Stephen Daldry's highly acclaimed production of *An Inspector Calls*
and appeared in subsequent productions, including Katie Mitchell's
1999 production of *The Oresteia.* Offstage, Bowman speaks in a dis-
tinctive English accent that reflects the more than fifteen years spent
in Britain and Ireland, but certain words receive an unmistakably
American pronunciation.

> In high school, I came across a teacher, Marjorie Davenport, who
> offered to work with us on some Shakespearean scenes and speeches.
> I was fascinated, and she told me that the best place to study would
> be London—I think she was a bit of an Anglophile—and I took her
> at her word. I hadn't yet applied to college, and it all kind of hap-

pened in one day, really. I just decided I was going to be an actor and would train in London. Luckily, I didn't think too much about it. If I had, I would've put myself off. So, I did some auditions in England and was recalled and got into the Guildhall School, right next door to the Barbican. I had a year off before I went, where I worked to pay my fees.

Towards the end of the program, I got married to a girl who was in school with me. She was Irish and had a year left to finish. She didn't know this at the time, but she wasn't a legal resident in England, and for me to stay on, she had to be considered a resident. I had to go back to either America or to Dublin, so I went to Dublin and hung out until she finished. In a way, it was quite a good thing, in retrospect, although at the time, it was very hard to do, as I'd been offered three jobs leaving drama school, one of which was playing Hamlet at the Actors Touring Company.

At that time, getting your Equity card was quite a hassle, and all three jobs came with a card, so it was a real blow. But I went to Dublin. By the end of six months, I had attached myself to a small fringe company, got some work with them, and then got a year contract at the Abbey Theatre. They offered me more work after the year was up, but I thought, "If I don't get back to England, I'll wind up more Irish than the Irish." I went back and started working at some of the regional reps, in Leeds and York.

I met [director] Stephen Daldry in York, and we did *An Inspector Calls* there for the first time. Then I moved down to London and worked at the Gate, did some shows with the Cambridge Theatre Company, and then the National's run of *An Inspector Calls*. As successful as that was, I left when it moved to the West End. I was tired—it had been a long run at the National and such a demanding play to work on—and I didn't want to do it every night. It had been nice, but it was time to leave.[8]

Bowman then met director Tim Supple, who was about to stage productions of *Oedipus, Antigone,* and *Seven Against Thebes.* Supple was experimenting with a highly physical and heightened style of acting, according to Bowman, with performers stomping and banging on pieces of wood. Bowman and three other actors, disenchanted with what they viewed at the time as an unfocused production process, left the production in the middle of rehearsals. He was then cast for the first time at the RSC. "When I first came over to study, my idea

was eventually to work with the RSC, because it had such a great reputation. I'd seen the actors on video—Derek Jacobi, Ian McKellen—
and I admired them, thought it was brilliant. It seemed like a great
place to work, the last of the companies with an ensemble that size.
Most people, I think, hanker to work there. It's a bit like climbing a
high peak. So, about eight years after I finished my training, I finally
worked there. I'd sort of completed what I'd set out to do, and that
felt good."

Bowman had been working professionally for a relatively brief time,
but it was long enough for him to discover that the theatre world in
England is remarkably small and that previous, precipitous actions
might have a subsequent deleterious effect on one's career. Bowman
was lucky in this regard.

> After Tim Supple and I had that "interesting" interlude with the
> Greek plays, we ran into each other at the RSC. It was a bit strange
> at first, but we always got on well before that, so soon we were chat-
> ting away. He rang up a few months later and asked if I wanted to
> go on a tour to New Zealand, Australia, and Hong Kong with some
> Grimm tales, a production they had done at the Young Vic. I said I
> was interested, and we had a chat and cleared the air about the pre-
> vious work and had a go and really enjoyed working together. Then
> he told me that *Comedy of Errors* was coming up and wanted to know
> if I was interested. And since the show was going on tour and wouldn't
> be part of the rep—although it would play The Other Place—I didn't
> have to go through the whole audition ordeal again, especially as
> Maggie Lunn, the new casting director, knew my work, and I had
> worked with Tim before.
>
> My first audition for the RSC, however, when I did three shows
> in a season, was different. I met Ian Judge first, did a speech from
> *Romeo and Juliet,* and then I met Max Stafford-Clark and then
> Michael Boyd. I had to read for each of them individually, but luck-
> ily they decided there was a line of parts for me, so it worked out.

Bowman relished working with Supple on the production of *The
Comedy of Errors.* The director and cast rehearsed eight and nine hours
a day for six weeks as they thoroughly investigated the text before
putting it on its feet. Some actors, used to the increasingly short rehearsal times that many theatres' budgets frequently dictate, might
consider this rehearsal period unusually protracted. There is a ten-

dency—common among actors in both Britain and the United States—
to adopt a "get it up, get it on, get it over" attitude towards production, but Bowman embraced Supple's process.

> Tim is very story based. We sat around telling stories for the first
> couple of weeks and doing a few other things. We didn't get stuck
> blocking right away, so everyone focused on the story that we were
> trying to tell, and we just asked questions about it. We came to a point
> where we didn't assume that just because it's called *The Comedy of
> Errors* we had to make it a comedy. Tim is confident enough to be
> uncertain about things in rehearsal. He uses yoga to wake you up and
> make you a bit fitter, and we'd play games to get the energy up, espe-
> cially after lunch. And then he started moving into some Stanis-
> lavskian things as well, but we actually saw more of that when he'd
> rehearse with us in brush-up work after we opened.
> I like that work. I think you can apply certain Stanislavskian pre-
> cepts to any piece, pretty much, but you still have to adhere to cer-
> tain rules about language. I find it gets you away from generalized
> spouting and makes your choices specific. And that helps, in a strange
> way, to get you in touch with the language. We would decide what
> our actions were, and that was a great tool.

Although Bowman had no exposure to this system while at the
Guildhall School, he subsequently studied with a Russian acting
teacher who, in turn, had been a student of one of Stanislavsky's pu-
pils at the Moscow Art Theatre. Bowman found great artistic nourishment in this approach. While some directors never discuss certain
basic Stanislavskian terms like *action* or *objective* during rehearsals,
Bowman discovered that he could employ them anyway, especially
when he worked on the text on his own time, outside of the rehearsal
hall. "Some actors don't like to work that way, but so much depends
on how the director sets it up. It's important to have the director and
actor suss out, in the audition room, what someone is willing to do,
and hopefully you get a number of like-minded people that way. Ian
Judge wouldn't use any of this stuff, nor would Michael Boyd, but Max
Stafford-Clark uses actions. As an actor, you have to be quite flexible.
That's why I like to do the work at home; you don't have to hold up
rehearsal and ask, 'What's my objective?' You have to figure it out on
your own and make it as believable as possible, and that really helps.
It's a useful tool."

For Bowman, the most difficult aspect of cracking the role of Antipholus was understanding and identifying with the character's willing belief in witchcraft and the possibility that demonic powers were at work in Ephesus. Several people mistake him for another man—who, it turns out, is his twin brother from whom he was separated at birth and whose existence is unknown to him—and Antipholus quickly ascribes this identity shift to dark forces. It was not easy, at first, for Bowman to integrate Antipholus's immediate and wholehearted response with the character's through-line as he first perceived it.

> Being able to believe in that, to make it real, was a challenge. I think that's why most productions go for the comedy instead; there's an unreality about all the witchcraft and loss of identity and confusion, so it's simpler to play for the laughs. When you first start working on it, you ask, "Why doesn't he think that there could be someone else who looks like him; why does he go right away to witchcraft?" And when you first start working on it, there are big leaps of the imagination you must make, though those leaps are much smaller for me right now. For me, tracking his journey in the play, keeping it focused, finding what he's feeling throughout the whole play, that was the main challenge. When you play different spaces in different countries and get different reactions from audiences, it can be a bit hard to hold onto.
>
> The one thing we worried about over the length of the tour is about losing the stakes of the play. The fact is that despite the humor we have in the show, it's a very moving, disturbing production. The first few months we did it, our emotional commitment to it was such that we knew the audiences were feeling something, but as it went on, and we played bigger spaces, we'd lose touch with the audience, so it's good to know that it still works. The age-old thing you think is, "If I'm not feeling it, it isn't working," and I think that it doesn't always mean that. If we get the situations right and play what we feel at the moment, some people will be moved by it. That's what we wanted, a whole experience, not just the laughs. It's the culmination of a long search for a lot of characters, a very painful one, in which people might die, and I think no matter what, the audience can see there's a reconciliation, the search is over, and people can move on.
>
> One thing Tim was so good about was that he wanted to chart that journey and have us play the text. A danger in theatre is that you can get a lot of clever ideas without a link through the whole, so you wind

up watching a bunch of clever ideas rather than a journey, a story. And people *like* having stories told, simply and well.

Bowman, like his colleagues, enjoyed discussing his particular perceptions of performing in the different RSC theatres.

The RST is slightly easier to play in than the Barbican, but both acoustically aren't bad. They're easier to play than the Olivier at the National. Most theatres have parameters, and they focus your performance for you, but there's a size required in these bigger spaces, so when you play in The Other Place or The Pit, it's such a relief. The look of an eye or small movements read just as well there as large ones, whereas they don't in the larger houses. Acting feels more luxurious in the smaller spaces. The Other Place, where we did *Comedy,* is quite exciting, and it was great to do a Shakespeare there. I think Peter Brook said, the biggest problem with theatre is that the more you have to project, the less you sound organic and real. And that's the biggest problem for actors, making themselves heard in the big spaces, getting as many nuances as they can with their voices, and sounding as real as possible. But I don't think they're impossible spaces to work in.

As for the Swan, it's less intimate from the stage than it would appear from the audience. You've got the height; it's kind of nice that it wraps around, but I think we all found in the plays we did there that you feel as if you're on a kind of podium, and it took some getting used to. I thought I'd enjoy the Swan much more than I did. It took me a while to get comfortable there, and I think part of the problem is not feeling grounded on that stage.

To work in the Pit and the Barbican is more about working in that building. There's no natural light that gets to you, and that's a big thing. But at the RST, you've got the Avon, and there's a greenroom, so you can get a bit of fresh air and things like that.

The tour of *The Comedy of Errors* returned to London in the late summer of 1997, where it played a limited engagement at the Young Vic. When asked how he would script the next scene in his career, Bowman responded without hesitation. "Ideally, I'd like to carry on doing theatre, working with Tim at the Young Vic, doing some work at the Royal Court with Steven Pimlott, doing the odd film. That would be perfect for me. I really do like Shakespeare, so I'd be quite happy to do a number of different plays of his. I'd like to do some Arthur Miller and Tennessee Williams. I think I just like working with a good director and company and a good script. I think I still have a goal of a kind of performance, a style, that I'd like to achieve, where I know I've done the best I could do. I don't know if it ever really exists, but I'd like it so the audience isn't aware of the acting while they're watching it. Only at the end should they say, 'He was a good actor.'"

Conclusion

'Tis true that a good play needs no epilogue . . .
—Rosalind, *As You Like It*

The RSC has experienced a sea change in the last decade; and by the time this book appears in print, the company will have undergone further evolution. That is the way of the world with institutional theatres. Presently, the focus of the company is on the actor, language, education, and increased national touring. The inclination towards elaborate production values has waned, and the emphasis on Shakespeare's plays once again provides the rich nourishment the company lacked just a few years ago. The administration has learned to respond wisely to shifting theatrical tastes and financial exigencies. The company will continue to evolve; that much is certain.

The decades since Peter Hall invented the RSC and resolutely changed its course—by producing new and experimental work and by expanding the company's bailiwick to include London—have been a time of substantial growth and change for the company. No longer only a star-studded regional theatre excelling at Shakespeare, the RSC became associated with a volume of vital new work that created a sizable impact on international theatre. In just twelve years, four new theatres were established in Stratford and London. Successful productions enjoyed commercial transfers to the West End and Broadway, and some were filmed and televised. A new generation of actors gained international prominence as the result of their work with the RSC. Tours circled the globe and played throughout the British isles. The company received its first government subsidies. Its education and outreach programs made a significant impact on thousands of students and helped develop future audiences. The RSC enjoyed a period of unbridled growth and creative energy as well as a rise in domestic and international stature.

An examination of the RSC over the last decade provides a sharply defined example of the inevitable struggles, experienced by many not-for-profit theatres, to survive. Governments have grown less inclined to subsidize artistic endeavors, and the assault of sound bites and quick hits has seriously damaged audiences' ability to focus on the nuances of text in a dark room for three hours. Additionally, the RSC has suffered its own, idiosyncratic problems. Although the company's administration has usually balanced the idealistic with the pragmatic to great advantage when formulating company policy, the 1990s was a period in which the RSC rediscovered that it was not invulnerable to the vagaries of the theatrical marketplace and national politics. Government funding was frozen, seriously compromising the company's ability to sustain its record of excellence. The business of performing evolved to a point where the commitment to the idea of "company" was less attractive than in the past, especially in the regions, where actors were distanced from family as well as from increasing offers of work in radio, television, and film in London. The company experienced low audience attendance, a drop in box office revenue, and not infrequently, criticism in the press. This state of affairs could not continue indefinitely, and as the artistic and fiscal ground continued to erode, Adrian Noble and his colleagues found themselves in the unenviable position of appearing in the press like apologists for a company policy that was no longer practicable. Eventually, new methodologies had to be adopted if the company was to regain its viability and prominence.

It is difficult to effect change, no matter how necessary—especially in so large an institution—without roiling the waters. Some of the decisions taken in recent years did precisely that, most notably the curtailment of the London season. As wrenching as that proved to be, both in lost prestige as well as lost jobs, it marked a necessary turning point in the RSC's fortunes. The consensus now among the senior artistic and administrative staff is that the RSC was indeed burdened by the strain of attempting too much by running two simultaneous year-long seasons in Stratford and London. The shuffling of the seasonal repertoire allowed the workshops to produce at a more realistic pace, reduced the budgetary strain, and most critically, encouraged actors to commit for shorter periods of time, which resulted in the RSC's ability to attract a stronger ensemble and mount finer productions.

Change is doubly difficult to effect while avoiding media salvos, and the RSC found itself squarely in the cross hairs of journalists and critics in 1997–1998. But as Michael Attenborough observed in July 2000, that visibility is an accepted component of the RSC's national prominence.

> I think that the two big national theatres, if they hit anything like a wobbly period, will always get belted beyond what it warrants. As it happens, in certain areas the National Theatre is getting it now. I could have predicted that two years ago; as we got stronger, inevitably [the media] turned their gaze elsewhere. This has always been the case. It's open season, really, on the big companies, because understandably we swallow up a hell of a large amount of subsidy, and we're big and powerful, and you're in a sense the big fleshy target that they can fire shots at.
>
> But I don't think one can afford to sit back and say, "Oh, they're just hitting us because we're big." The truth of the matter is that I think our track record *was* inconsistent. I think some of the criticism that came our way was fair. . . . But I think in a way it was quite a watershed, and it forced us to close ranks and reassess our own priorities.[1]

The result was a renewed focus on Shakespeare, which some members feared was becoming obscured. Adrian Noble and his team of associates—Michael Attenborough, Michael Boyd, Gregory Doran, and Steven Pimlott—selected a slate of four Shakespeare plays in the RST for the 1999 Summer Festival—*Othello, A Midsummer Night's*

Dream, Timon of Athens, and *Antony and Cleopatra*—each directed by one of the associates. This season, however, would be different, both aesthetically and physically. The directors decided to extend the thrust stage farther into the audience to engender greater immediacy between performer and spectator as well as to reduce the distance from the acting area to the farthest reaches of the balcony. The removal of the seats necessary to accomplish this resulted in a loss of revenue. The directors collectively responded by trimming their production budgets, a decision that likely would have been unthinkable a few years earlier. But the excesses of the past had proved untenable in the present, and a new approach was necessitated. The associate directors, by virtue of their position within the administration, had a stronger commitment to the continued health of the RSC than would a typical free-lance director and were better able to balance the needs of their productions with those of the company. They chose to concentrate on the actor and the text rather than on extravagance of production. They also agreed to share certain scenic elements common to all four productions—a stripped back, bare-brick proscenium; a wood-planked, oval thrust; and a white, curved wall—something that had not been attempted since the 1971 season of the Roman plays. Here, the set designers worked with sufficient ingenuity that the audience experienced what appeared to be four discrete scenic designs. These productions garnered strong critical response and put much-needed wind in the company's sails.

Critics have assailed the decrease in the production of new plays since the change in the London season in 1996. Prior to that, once the Stratford transfers—which often included a new play or two—had opened at the Barbican, new productions were introduced as longer-running shows were phased out of the rep. Many of these new productions were premieres, and writers such as Howard Barker, Peter Barnes, David Edgar, Christopher Hampton, Richard Nelson, and Stephen Poliakoff saw their works debut at the Pit or the Barbican. This powerful new writing had been a critical factor in the rise of the RSC's star in the 1960s and 1970s. Now, with six months' less time in London, the directorate made the decision to decrease the number of new plays rather than truncate the runs of its classics. New writing is critical to the continued development of theatre as well as to the strength and dynamism of a company of artists, but the RSC had to make the pragmatic choice of balancing what it ideally would like to produce with what it realistically could accomplish in a season. Although the loss of this level of new play activity was a sad casualty of the financial pressures that confronted the RSC, the commitment to new playwriting is still alive. There have been new plays in one form or another every year since the first shortened London season, and in one Stratford season, five new works were produced. The RSC still commissions new plays and new translations of foreign works. It is too early to assess how the diminution of new play production will affect the RSC, but the company's artistic mission has always placed the production of Shakespeare's works at center stage. Audiences of the RSC expect and demand the classics as the centerpiece of production, and they will continue to be satisfied. This is one tenet of the RSC's mission that will not change; the company's royal charter ensures its preservation.

Within the company today, evolution is accepted, even embraced, with enthusiasm. There seems to be an absence of any artistic condescension that occupying a lofty position in the world of theatre might engender, which in turn could breed the arrogance of complacency. There is, rather, an optimism that stems from a reversal of fortune. Strong reviews, especially for the Shakespearean productions, and the increased box office revenues over the last two years have helped to bolster the company's spirits. The reviews, to some degree, reflect the wisdom implicit in the implementation of key changes in artistic policy. The company, too, senses that the productions are sturdier, and there is a greater enthusiasm for the work and a renewed sense of purpose. Recent changes in artistic and production policy, such as the formulation of two Stratford seasons and the increase in touring, have been greeted with enthusiasm by the media.

The press, perhaps unwittingly, played a key role in the RSC's self-examination and search for artistic renewal. The newspapers had trumpeted Trevor Nunn's decision to create an acting company at the National Theatre, which for years had assembled discrete casts for each production. Some senior RSC members, while pleased that the National had adopted the company formula, scoffed at the accolades bestowed on it by the press that, as one staffer put it, "had the National reinventing the wheel." But the change in the National's policy also impelled the RSC to examine its own. As Michael Attenborough described it, this introspection eventually proved beneficial to the RSC.

> I think it's given us the impetus, instead of resting on our laurels, to say, "Okay, let's shake it all up again," rather than say, "Oh, I see, this is the way you do it," and just keep doing it. That's deadly. I think it was out of that impetus that we all decided we wanted to do our eight-history play cycle. That obviously, again, is a very ambitious and expensive project. I would say it's been born out of confidence. It's interesting—we've only opened three out of eight so far—but so far, those three have all been received extremely well. And also, interestingly, we've broken a mold in that we've said, unlike *The Wars of the Roses* or *The Plantagenets*, we don't want to hammer these plays into one particular shape that conforms to a directorial or design concept. Our feeling is that they're all very different, that we should be looking at them as different texts, responding to them as individual artists, and assuming that the audience is grown up enough to be able to watch how Shakespeare was developing, how history was being explored, in different auditoria, with different directors and designers.[2]

The cycle's first three plays were well received. In his review of *Richard II,* Benedict Nightingale, of the *Times,* noted, "I have seldom heard Gaunt's famous speech about England delivered with more love and pain than by a wheelchair-bound Alfred Burke or Bolingbroke's voracious energy and passing self-doubts better embodied than by David Troughton. Samuel West's Richard is a success, too. . . . He is less effete and spoilt, shrewder and sharper than most Richards."[3] Charles Spencer, of the *Daily Telegraph,* was impressed with *Henry IV, Part 1.* "In Michael Attenborough, the RSC has chosen the right man to direct *Henry IV.* He has always been the most sane and humane of directors, with a particular talent for suggesting that mankind is both fallible and redeemable."[4] Robert Hewison, writing in the *Sunday Times,* called Attenborough's *Henry IV, Part 2,* "a fine production, which uses the intimacy of the Swan Theatre to bring you close to the hearts and minds of men who are leaders, but also suffering beings. [David] Troughton's Henry IV has tremendous presence, even as his ailing body gives place to [William] Houston's attractively maturing Hal."[5]

The self-assessment that led to the ambitious production of the history cycle fortuitously coincided with a loosening of the purse strings of subsidy. In recent years, a number of British institutional theatres have ceased operations, and all not-for-profit theatres have had to cut back their levels of production to some extent. The Arts Council drama panel concluded that this was no longer tolerable, and Gerry Robinson, chair of the Arts Council, requested a substantial increase in government funding for theatres. At this writing, the amount of money that will be earmarked for this increase is unknown, but as noted earlier, the RSC has finally seen its crucial Arts Council subsidy modestly increased. The company was greatly encouraged by this decision, which signals an important shift in government policy at a time when the RSC continues to redefine itself.

Should the Arts Council–funded feasibility study generate felicitous results and the RSC receive the full sum of £100 million envisioned for redevelopment of the Stratford theatres—half to come from the National Lottery and half to be raised by the RSC—change will be rampant. As discussed previously, the most frequently cited scheme calls for the redesign of the interior of the RST auditorium as well as expansion of its front-of-house services, the conversion of The Other Place into an education center, and the erection of a new theatre somewhere on the RSC's grounds. One senior administrator imagined this new building to be "like an airport hangar or a shed, a really big space which you could shutter off, curtain off; very flexible, with movable seating units. You could do something promenade, in the round, big space, small space, that allows with ease a director or designer to go in and completely redefine it. You dictate the space, rather than the other way around."

Institutional theatres in both the United Kingdom and the United States have evinced great interest in this sort of malleable space, which offers increased flexibility in configuring the actor-audience relationship and addresses the current needs of directors and designers as they continue to define the aesthetics of theatre architecture. Many existing black box theatres were built to house new and experimental work and were intended to accommodate relatively small audiences and playing spaces. The RSC envisions a new theatre of greater size and scope that, given the appropriate configuration, could respond to the demands of a variety of styles and genres. It is unknown, at this time, whether such a building's exterior would be integrated into the red brick motif of the three existing theatres in Stratford or whether the architect would break new visual ground. It is too soon to determine what this new building will be—but the company relishes speculating on the host of possibilities.

The RSC is now a tauter, more efficient producing organization. Although this metamorphosis occasioned the loss of its yearlong presence in London and the production of fewer new works, the RSC has in return discovered a renewed vigor and an artistic focus. The consensus, from within and without, is that it was a necessary adjustment. Now, with the return to the fold of more top-rank actors, a sharp upturn in attendance, and a string of artistically vibrant seasons, the RSC is better able to provide a more nurturing and stable artistic environment for the company, which in turn enhances the quality of production and the experience of the audience. As Michael Attenborough put it, "Where else can you rehearse for seven weeks with an excellent company on a Shakespearean text? Where else do you get the support of a four-person voice department? Where else do you have people who hand-make all the costumes and boots and armory? These are facilities the like of which people dream of, and we treasure them."[6]

As well they should. In the future, it is possible that a new artistic director will take the reins of the RSC and will articulate a new artistic policy, that the redevelopment of the Stratford facilities will radically alter the experience of attending theatre, that a different tenancy agreement with the Barbican will be implemented, that the contents and balance of the seasonal repertoire will shift, and that economic fluctuations will make another crucial impact upon the company's fortunes. Such events are cyclical and seemingly inevitable—and will continue to challenge the company. The RSC's ability to sustain its record of innovation and excellence throughout the past decades is a fair indicator that it will be likely to do so in the future and serves as a testament to the perseverance, wisdom, and talents of its company members.

Notes
Bibliography
Index

Notes

1. Introduction

1. Sally Beauman, *The Royal Shakespeare Company: A History of Ten Decades* (Oxford: Oxford University Press, 1982), 252–62.

2. Royal Charter of Incorporation, Oct. 31, 1925, issued by King George V and amended by Queen Elizabeth II, June 28, 1979.

3. Beauman, 301.

4. A new Other Place opened next to the site of the old building in 1991. The old theatre, beloved though it was, had become too dilapidated to continue to use.

5. Adrian Noble, telephone conversation with author, Apr. 8, 1997.

6. Brian Glover, interview by author, Stratford-upon-Avon, Dec. 12, 1995.

7. It is no longer true that the National casts every play with a discrete cast. In 1998, Trevor Nunn instituted a company system there.

8. Michael Attenborough, interview by author, London, Dec. 20, 1995.

9. Sir Geoffrey Cass, introduction to *Report: 117th Report of the Council, 1992/93*, annual report of the RSC Council to the Board of Governors, Oct. 27, 1993, 2.

10. Arts Council of Great Britain, "Royal Shakespeare Company, 1990," appraisal report, Nov. 1990, 24. In a move towards decentralization, this government funding agency recently changed its name to the Arts Council of England.

2. Stratford-upon-Avon

1. Although the RSC regularly performs much of its repertoire annually in Newcastle and Plymouth, the theatres there will not be included for discussion, because they were built for other purposes and most often house other events.

2. Arts Council of Great Britain, 21.

3. Brian Glover, interview by author, Stratford-upon-Avon, Dec. 12, 1995.

4. Beauman, 12.

5. Ronnie Mulryne and Margaret Shewring, *This Golden Round: The Royal Shakespeare Company at the Swan* (Stratford-upon-Avon: Mulryne and Shewring, 1989), 9.

6. Beauman, 111.

7. David Addenbrooke, *The Royal Shakespeare Company: The Peter Hall Years* (London: Kimber, 1974), 14.

8. Addenbrooke, 44.

9. Marian J. Pringle, *The Theatres of Stratford-upon-Avon, 1875–1992: An Architectural History,* Stratford-upon-Avon Papers, no. 5 (Stratford-upon-Avon: Stratford-upon-Avon Society, 1993), 53.

10. Clemence Dane, née Winifred Ashton, who was awarded the honorary title Commander of the Order of the British Empire, was also an author, a playwright *(A Bill of Divorcement),* and the model for the character of Madame Arcati in Noel Coward's *Blithe Spirit.*

11. Simon Bowler, interview by author, Stratford-upon-Avon, Dec. 14, 1995.

12. Geoff Locker, interview by author, Stratford-upon-Avon, June 27, 1992.

13. Geoff Locker, telephone conversation with author, Nov. 20, 1998.

14. Michael Attenborough, telephone conversation with author, July 7, 2000.

15. Locker, telephone conversation, Nov. 20, 1998.

16. Pringle, 61.

17. Mulryne and Shewring, 10.

18. The Swan opened for business in April 1986 with Barry Kyle's production of Shakespeare and Fletcher's *Two Noble Kinsmen.*

19. Glover, interview, Dec. 12, 1995.

20. Pringle, 97.

21. Mulryne and Shewring, 14.

22. Stuart Gibbons, interview by author, Stratford-upon-Avon, June 8, 1993.

23. Mulryne and Shewring, 100.

24. Adrian Noble, telephone conversation with author, Apr. 8, 1997.

25. Colin Chambers, *Other Spaces: New Theatre and the RSC* (London: Eyre Methuen, 1980), 32.

26. Chambers, 34.

27. Chambers, 35.

28. Chambers, 36.

29. Chris Parry, interview by author, San Diego, Apr. 17, 1995.

30. Tony Hill, interview by author, Stratford-upon-Avon, Dec. 15, 1995.

31. Bronwyn Robertson, interview by author, Stratford-upon-Avon, June 9, 1993.

32. Hill, interview, Dec. 15, 1995.

33. Katie Mitchell, interview by author, London, Nov. 4, 1998.

34. Graham Sawyer, interview by author, Stratford-upon-Avon, June 9, 1993.

3. London

1. Beauman, 241–42.

2. Addenbrooke, 246.

3. Stephen Fay, *Power Play: The Life and Times of Peter Hall* (London: Hodder and Stoughton, 1995), 112.

4. Maggie Roy, interview by author, London, June 15, 1993.

5. Addenbrooke, 280.

6. Addenbrooke, 234.

7. Beauman, 299–300.

8. Chambers, 48.

9. Roy, interview, June 15, 1993.

10. The Guildhall School occupied their facility in 1977. The rest of the complex opened in 1982.

11. In 1998, apartments for sale at the Barbican ranged in price from £132,000 for a one-bedroom to £205,000 for a three-bedroom unit.

12. Graham Sykes, interview by author, London, June 16, 1993.

13. Peter Cadley, interview by author, London, Nov. 6, 1998.

14. The constant struggle by the RSC to establish more of a visible identity inside and outside the Barbican Centre has historically been met with resistance by the Centre's administration. The 1995 decision to curtail the season in London reinforced the RSC's status as only a semipermanent tenant in the facility, according to many RSC staffers.

15. Graham Sykes, interview by author, London, Dec. 18, 1995.

16. Cadley, interview, Nov. 6, 1998.

17. Sykes, interview, Dec. 18, 1995.

18. Suzanne Cassidy, "Royal Shakespeare Tries to Move Ahead," *New York Times,* Jan. 31, 1990, sec. B, p. 4.

19. Cadley, interview, Nov. 6, 1998.

20. Victor Glasstone, "Tradition—Triumphantly Rethought," *The Royal Shakespeare Company, 1982/83* (Stratford-upon-Avon: RSC Publications, 1983), 49.

21. Chris Parry, interview by author, San Diego, Mar. 22, 1997.

22. Nigel Love, interview by author, London, June 14 and 17, 1993.

23. Sally Barling, interview by author, London, Dec. 23, 1995.

24. Because of the cross casting frequently utilized at the RSC, there are rarely rehearsals of plays during performances of the repertoire, since most of the actors are performing at that time.

25. Chris de Wilde, interview by author, London, Dec. 18, 1995.

26. Sykes, interview, June 16, 1993.

4. The Season

1. Beauman, 68.

2. David Brierley, letter to author, Aug. 7, 1992.

3. Adrian Noble, telephone conversation with author, Apr. 8, 1997.

4. Brierley letter, Aug. 7, 1992.

5. Simon Callow, "Theatre: Thrift, Horatio, Thrift! And Stuff the Quality," *Independent* (London), Nov. 14, 1998, 12.

6. Noble, telephone conversation, Apr. 8, 1997.

7. Michael Coveney, "The RSC Is Suffering from Commercial Failure and Waning Artistic Credibility. It Is Time to Scrap the Marketing Department and Make a Fresh Start." *New Statesman* (London), Apr. 10, 1998, 40.

8. Michael Attenborough, interview by author, London, Dec. 20, 1995.

9. David Brierley, interview by author, Stratford-upon-Avon, Dec. 15, 1995.

10. Geoff Locker, interview by author, Stratford-upon-Avon, June 7, 1993.

11. David Brierley, interview by author, Stratford-upon-Avon, June 3, 1993.

12. Brierley, interview, Dec. 15, 1995.

13. Noble, telephone conversation, Apr. 8, 1997.

14. Brierley, interview, Dec. 15, 1995.

15. Attenborough, interview, Dec. 20, 1995.

16. Vincent Canby, "Does Shakespeare Really Need B-12 Shots?" *New York Times,* June 14, 1998, Arts and Leisure sec., p. 4.

17. Ben Brantley, "Vintage Soap Opera (as in Castile Soap)," *New York Times,* May 18, 2000, sec. B, p. 1.

18. The Plymouth residency had previously followed directly on the heels of Newcastle, but the company felt it placed too great a strain on the actors and technicians who had to open a full slate of plays twice within two months.

19. David Lister, "End of Winter of Discontent? Spring for the Royal Shakespeare Company after Years of Damning Criticism . . ." *Independent* (London), Mar. 31, 1999, 11.

20. Coveney, 41.

21. Quoted from "Wot—No More Shakespeare?" *RSC Magazine,* summer 1998, 8–9.

22. Katie Mitchell, interview by author, London, Nov. 4, 1998.

23. Sarah Hemming, "Once More unto the Breach: Sarah Hemming Talks to the RSC Directors Who Have Taken on Shakespeare's History Plays under the Title 'This England—The Histories,'" *Financial Times* (London), Mar. 25, 2000, 8.

24. Nigel Love, interview by author, London, June 14 and 17, 1993.

5. Touring

1. Sir Ian McKellen, "Small Scale Tour," The Royal Shakespeare Company, 1978 (Stratford-upon-Avon: RSC Publications, 1978), 103.

2. Moira Hunter, "Get In, Get Out, Get On," *The Royal Shakespeare Company, 1979/80* (Stratford-upon-Avon: RSC Publications, 1980), 95.

3. Addenbrooke, 283.

4. Antonin Artaud (1896–1948) was a French playwright and actor who experimented with hallucinogenic drugs and was institutionalized frequently for insanity. He developed the Theatre of Cruelty—partly in response to his fascination with the effects of the Plague on medieval Europe—in which the spectators' bourgeois complacency was attacked and ruthlessly stripped away by an assault of graphic, violent, often perverse actions portrayed on stage. This would generate a catharsis of the audience's subconscious fears and terrors. His theories, articulated in his book *The Theatre and Its Double,* were of critical importance to writers such as Jean Genet and Fernando Arrabal and directors Jean-Louis Barrault, Julian Beck, and Peter Brook.

5. Lynda Farran, interview by author, London, Dec. 20, 1995.

6. Jasper Gilbert, interview by author, Cerritos, Calif., Nov. 5, 1994.

7. Martyn Sergent, interview by author, San Francisco, May 16, 1997.

6. Administration

1. Sally Barling, interview by author, London, Dec. 23, 1995.

2. David Brierley, letter to author, Oct. 27, 1994.

3. Nunn selected Hands to serve with him as joint artistic director (JAD), because of the growth of the RSC and because of Nunn's own burgeoning independent directorial career. There had been precedent for this: in 1951, Anthony Quayle had invited Glen Byam Shaw to join him as JAD.

4. The RSC member who offered these opinions in 1993 did so only with the qualification that they not be attributed to their source.

5. Arts Council of Great Britain, 7.

6. Cassidy, 4.

7. Arts Council of Great Britain, 40.

8. Graham Sykes, interview by author, London, June 16, 1993.

9. David Brierley, interview by author, Stratford-upon-Avon, June 24, 1992.

10. Arts Council of Great Britain, 40.

11. David Brierley, interview by author, Stratford-upon-Avon, June 7, 1993.

12. Geoff Locker, interview by author, Stratford-upon-Avon, June 7, 1993.

13. Tony Hill, interview by author, Stratford-upon-Avon, Dec. 15, 1995.

14. Kathy Elgin, "What Does an Executive Producer Do?" *RSC Magazine,* autumn 1992, 7.

15. Michael Attenborough, interview by author, London, Dec. 20, 1995.

16. Lynda Farran, interview by author, London, Dec. 20, 1995.

17. Hill, interview, Dec. 15, 1995.

18. Kevin Sivyer, interview by author, Stratford-upon-Avon, June 23, 1992.

19. Kevin Sivyer, interview by author, Stratford-upon-Avon, Dec. 13, 1995.

7. Finances

1. Clive Priestley, "The Financial Affairs and Financial Prospects of the Royal Opera House, Covent Garden Ltd., and the Royal Shakespeare Company," report commissioned by the Cabinet Office, Management and Personnel Office, Sept. 1983, 49, 46.

2. Priestly, 36.

3. Priestly, 47.

4. Nick Paladina, telephone conversation with author, June 12, 2000.

5. Arts Council of Great Britain, 2–3.

6. Arts Council of Great Britain, 3.

7. David Brierley, interview by author, Stratford-upon-Avon, Dec. 15, 1995.

8. John Rockwell, "A New Challenge for Thatcher's 'Best Brain,'" *New York Times,* Aug. 22, 1994, sec. B, p. 1.

9. Warren Hoge, "Pop Grants Unsettle British Arts," *New York Times,* June 25, 1998, sec. B, pp. 1, 7.

10. Antony Thorncroft, "Robinson to Shift Arts Cash Decision to Regions," *Financial Times* (London), Oct. 15, 1998, 1.

11. Royal Shakespeare Company, *Annual Report and Accounts: 123rd Report of the Council, 1998/99,* annual report of the RSC Council to the Board of Governors, Nov. 8, 1999, 5.

12. David Lister, "RSC Goes to War Against National," *Independent* (London), Jan. 7, 1999, News sec., p. 5.

13. Paladina, telephone conversation, June 12, 2000.

14. Tony Thorncroft, "Survey—Business and the Arts: Model Alliance of Opposites. Case Study: Allied Domecq/RSC," *Financial Times* (London), Feb. 17, 2000, 2.

15. Paladina, telephone conversation, June 12, 2000.

8. Education and Marketing

1. Wendy Greenhill, interview by author, Stratford-upon-Avon, Dec. 11, 1995.

2. Lister, "End of Winter," 11.

3. Membership in the RSC offers aficionados, for a nominal fee, advance notice of RSC performances, appealing perks such as priority booking, and invitations to a variety of events. Included, too, is the less tangible but equally important sense of supporting the company.

4. Stephen Browning, interview by author, London, Dec. 20, 1995.

5. Peter Cadley, interview by author, London, Nov. 6, 1998.

6. Browning, interview, Dec. 20, 1995.

7. Cadley, interview, Nov. 6, 1998.

8. Andrew Canham, fax to author, Sept. 5, 1994.

9. Browning, interview, Dec. 20, 1995.

10. Katie Mitchell, interview by author, London, Nov. 4, 1998.

9. The Production Process

1. Lynda Farran, interview by author, London, Dec. 20, 1995.

2. Alison Chard, interview by author, London, June 14, 1993.

3. Cassidy, 4.

4. Chard, interview, June 14, 1993.

5. Katie Mitchell, interview by author, Stratford-upon-Avon, June 8, 1993.

6. Farran, interview, Dec. 20, 1995.

7. Farran, interview, Dec. 20, 1995.

8. Tony Hill, interview by author, Stratford-upon-Avon, Dec. 15, 1995.

9. Robert Jones, interview by author, London, Nov. 3, 1998.

10. RSC design guidelines, distributed to company designers, 1992.

11. Jones, interview, Nov. 3, 1998.

12. Simon Ash, interview by author, London, June 14, 1993.

13. RSC design guidelines.

14. Jones, interview, Nov. 3, 1998.

15. William Lockwood, interview by author, Stratford-upon-Avon, Dec. 14, 1995.

16. Frank McGuire, interview by author, Stratford-upon-Avon, Dec. 14, 1995.

17. Jones, interview, Nov. 3, 1998.

18. Sonja Dosanjh, interview by author, Stratford-upon-Avon, June 22, 1992.

19. Michael Dembowicz, interview by author, Stratford-upon-Avon, Dec. 13, 1995.

20. Farran, interview, Dec. 20, 1995.

21. Chris Parry, interview by author, San Diego, Mar. 22, 1997.

22. Jones, interview, Nov. 3, 1998.

23. Parry, interview, Mar. 22, 1997.

24. Chris Parry, interview by author, San Diego, June 7, 2000.

25. Wayne Dowdeswell, letter to author, Sept. 24, 1994.

26. Chris Parry, interview by author, San Diego, Apr. 17, 1995.

27. Andrew Wade, interview by author, London, Nov. 5, 1998.

28. Andrew Wade, "Voice Work—Keeping It Practical," n.p., n.d., 8. Paper presented at various college training sessions.

29. Wade, interview, Nov. 5, 1998.

30. Mitchell, interview, June 8, 1993.

31. Mel Gussow, "Notes from Abroad: Tangible Ghosts," *American Theatre* 10 (Dec. 1993): 66.

32. Katie Mitchell, interview by author, London, Nov. 4, 1998.

10. Acting at the RSC

1. At present, there are more than thirty actors whom the RSC has honored by naming them associate actors. Among them are Derek Jacobi, Sinead Cusack, Harriet Walter, Penny Downie, Antony Sher, Joanne Pearce, Juliet Stevenson, David Suchet, Roger Rees, David Troughton, and Brian Cox.

2. Mel Gussow, "A New Spirit on the Old Bard," *American Theatre* 11 (Nov. 1994): 70.

3. Simon Russell Beale, interview by author, Stratford-upon-Avon, June 9, 1993.

4. Kate Duchêne, interview by author, Stratford-upon-Avon, Dec. 10 and 11, 1995.

5. David Troughton, interview by author, Stratford-upon-Avon, Dec. 15, 1995.

6. Quoted in a 1996 RSC spring/summer season brochure.

7. Robert Hurwitt, "Royal Company's Drama-dy of Errors," *San Francisco Examiner,* May 15, 1997, sec. C, pp. 1–2.

8. Robert Bowman, interview by author, San Francisco, May 17, 1997.

11. Conclusion

1. Michael Attenborough, telephone conversation with author, July 7, 2000.

2. Attenborough, telephone conversation, July 7, 2000.

3. Benedict Nightingale, "This Sceptic Isle," *Times* (London), Mar. 31, 2000, Features sec.

4. Charles Spencer, "Delicate Debauchery," *Daily Telegraph* (London), Apr. 21, 2000, 27.

5. Robert Hewison, "Infectious Disease," *Sunday Times* (London), July 9, 2000, Features sec.

6. Attenborough, telephone conversation, July 7, 2000.

Bibliography

Addenbrooke, David. *The Royal Shakespeare Company: The Peter Hall Years.* London: Kimber, 1974.

Arts Council of Great Britain. "Royal Shakespeare Company, 1990." Appraisal report. November 1990.

Beauman, Sally. *The Royal Shakespeare Company: A History of Ten Decades.* Oxford: Oxford University Press, 1982.

Behr, Edward. *The Complete Book of "Les Misérables."* New York: Arcade, 1989.

Brantley, Ben. "Vintage Soap Opera (as in Castile Soap)." *New York Times,* May 18, 2000, section B.

Callow, Simon. *The National: The Theatre and Its Work, 1963–1997.* London: Nick Hern, 1997.

———. "Theatre: Thrift, Horatio, Thrift! And Stuff the Quality." *Independent* (London), November 14, 1998.

Canby, Vincent. "Does Shakespeare Really Need B-12 Shots?" *New York Times,* June 14, 1998, Arts and Leisure section.

Cass, Sir Geoffrey. Introduction to *Report: 117th Report of the Council, 1992/93.* Annual report of the RSC Council to the Board of Governors. October 27, 1993.

Cassidy, Suzanne. "Royal Shakespeare Tries to Move Ahead." *New York Times,* January 31, 1990, section B.

Chambers, Colin. *Other Spaces: New Theatre and the RSC.* London: Eyre Methuen, 1980.

Coveney, Michael. "The RSC Is Suffering from Commercial Failure and Waning Artistic Credibility. It Is Time to Scrap the Marketing Department and Make a Fresh Start." *New Statesman* (London), April 10, 1998.

Elgin, Kathy. "What *Does* an Executive Producer Do?" *RSC Magazine,* autumn 1992.

Engle, Ron, Felicia Hardison Londré, and Daniel J. Watermeier, eds. *Shakespeare Companies and Festivals: An International Guide.* Westport, Conn.: Greenwood, 1995.

Fay, Stephen. *Power Play: The Life and Times of Peter Hall.* London: Hodder and Stoughton, 1995.

Glasstone, Victor. "Tradition—Triumphantly Rethought." *The Royal Shakespeare Company, 1982/83.* Stratford-upon-Avon: RSC Publications, 1983.

Gussow, Mel. "A New Spirit on the Old Bard." *American Theatre* 11 (November
   1994).
———. "Notes from Abroad: Tangible *Ghosts.*" *American Theatre* 10 (December
   1993).
Hall, Peter. *Making an Exhibition of Myself.* London: Sinclair-Stevenson, 1993.
———. *Peter Hall's Diaries: The Story of a Dramatic Battle.* Edited by John
   Goodwin. New York: Harper & Row, 1984.
Hemming, Sarah. "Once More unto the Breach: Sarah Hemming Talks to the RSC
   Directors Who Have Taken on Shakespeare's History Plays under the Title 'This
   England—The Histories.'" *Financial Times* (London), March 25, 2000.
Hewison, Robert. "Infectious Disease." *Sunday Times* (London), July 9, 2000, Fea-
   tures section.
Hoge, Warren. "Pop Grants Unsettle British Arts." *New York Times,* June 25, 1998,
   section B.
Hunter, Moira. "Get In, Get Out, Get On." *The Royal Shakespeare Company, 1979/
   80.* Stratford-upon-Avon: RSC Publications, 1980.
Hurwitt, Robert. "Royal Company's Drama-dy of Errors." *San Francisco Exam-
   iner,* May 15, 1997, section C.
Lister, David. "End of Winter of Discontent? Spring for the Royal Shakespeare
   Company after Years of Damning Criticism . . ." *Independent* (London), March
   31, 1999.
———. "RSC Goes to War Against National." *Independent* (London), January 7,
   1999, News section.
McKellen, Ian. "Small Scale Tour." *The Royal Shakespeare Company, 1978.* Stratford-
   upon-Avon: RSC Publications, 1978.
Mullin, Michael. *Theatre at Stratford-upon-Avon, First Supplement: A Catalogue-
   Index to Productions of the Royal Shakespeare Company, 1979–1993.* Westport,
   Conn.: Greenwood, 1994.
Mulryne, Ronnie, and Margaret Shewring. *This Golden Round: The Royal Shakespeare Company at the Swan.* Stratford-upon-Avon: Mulryne and Shewring,
   1989.
Nightingale, Benedict. "This Sceptic Isle." *Times* (London), March 31, 2000, Fea-
   tures section.
Parsons, Keith, and Pamela Mason, eds. *Shakespeare in Performance.* London: Sala-
   mander, 1995.
Priestley, Clive. "The Financial Affairs and Financial Prospects of the Royal Op-
   era House, Covent Garden Ltd., and the Royal Shakespeare Company." Report commissioned by the Cabinet Office, Management and Personnel Office.
   September 1983.
Pringle, Marian J. *The Theatres of Stratford-upon-Avon, 1875–1992: An Architectural
   History.* Stratford-upon-Avon Papers, no. 5. Stratford-upon-Avon: Stratford-
   upon-Avon Society, 1993.

Rockwell, John. "A New Challenge for Thatcher's 'Best Brain.'" *New York Times,* August 22, 1994, section B.

Royal Shakespeare Company. *Annual Report and Accounts: 123rd Report of the Council, 1998/99.* Annual report of the RSC Council to the Board of Governors. November 8, 1999.

———. *RSC Annual Review, 1998/99.*

Rubin, Leon. *The Nicholas Nickleby Story: The Making of the Historic Royal Shakespeare Company Production.* London: Heinemann, 1981.

Sher, Antony. *Year of the King: An Actor's Diary and Sketchbook.* New York: Limelight, 1987.

Spencer, Charles. "Delicate Debauchery." *Daily Telegraph* (London), April 21, 2000.

Thorncroft, Antony. "Robinson to Shift Arts Cash Decision to Regions." *Financial Times* (London), October 15, 1998.

———. "Survey—Business and the Arts: Model Alliance of Opposites. Case Study: Allied Domecq/RSC." *Financial Times* (London), February 17, 2000.

Wade, Andrew. "Voice Work—Keeping It Practical." N.p., n.d. Paper presented at various college training sessions.

Wells, Stanley, ed. *Summerfolk: Essays Celebrating Shakespeare and the Stratford Theatres.* Ebrington, Eng.: Long Barn, 1997.

Wolf, Matt. "Notes from Abroad: The Other RSC." *American Theatre* 13 (April 1996).

"Wot—No More Shakespeare?" *RSC Magazine,* summer 1998.

Index

Steven Adler, a native of Brooklyn, New York, heads the graduate program in stage management at the University of California, San Diego, where he is also Vice Chair and Director of Theatre in the Department of Theatre and Dance. He holds a B.A. in theatre from State University of New York at Buffalo and an M.F.A. in directing from Pennsylvania State University. As a professional stage manager, he has worked on numerous productions on Broadway, off Broadway, on national tours, in regional theatre, and in television.